Import Propensities of Industrialized Countries

Import Propensities of Industrialized Countries

Protectionism Revealed

James M. Lutz

palgrave

IMPORT PROPENSITIES OF INDUSTRIALIZED COUNTRIES

First published 2000 by
PALGRAVE™
175 Fifth Avenue, New York, N.Y. 10010 and
Houndmills, Basingstoke, Hampshire, England RG21 6XS.
Companies and representatives throughout the world.

PALGRAVE™ is the new global publishing imprint of St. Martin's Press
LLC Scholarly and Reference Division and Palgrave Publishers Ltd
(formerly Macmillan Press Ltd).

ISBN 0-312-22229-7 (hardback)

Library of Congress Cataloging-in-Publishing Data
Lutz, James M.
   Import propensities of industrialized countries : protectionism revealed
/ James M. Lutz.
      p.   cm.
   Includes bibliographical references and index.
   ISBN 0-312-22229-7
   1. Imports.   2. Protectionism.   I. Title.
HF1419.L88   2000
382'.5—dc21

                                        00–038240

A catalogue record for this book is available from the British Library.

Design by Letra Libre, Inc.

First edition: November, 2000
10 9 8 7 6 5 4 3 2 1

Printed in the United States of America.

*To the lights of my life
Brenda, Carol, and Tessa*

Contents

List of Tables

Figures

Foreword

The research in this book is a culmination of earlier explorations into the relationship between actual levels of imports and levels that would be predicted barring any barriers to trade. Public discussions and concerns about the unfair trade practices of particular countries suggested that an empirical approach to determine the extent to which these complaints were justified would be fruitful. In the process of comparing actual levels with expected ones, it became clear that at least some of the concerns that had been expressed were actually justified, notwithstanding my initial perception that most of the complaints would actually prove to be unfounded and would reflect the efforts of domestic groups in the United States or elsewhere to avoid the rigors of competing with imports. As it turns out, some countries do seem to have had restrictive import practices. The United States, on the other hand, has not been one of the countries that stands out as a nation that has increasingly relied on protection, even though there have been legitimate concerns that the United States has abandoned free trade. In at least a practical sense it has not; it remains very open to imports. The results in this volume are not just of academic interest. They have applicability to the real world and to real problems. They address a problem that has been widely discussed and frequently debated. While the problem has been understood reasonably well, the extent of protection and its effects have been less clear. At one level this book is an attempt to let facts get in the way of a good argument—and maybe to start a few new arguments as well.

There was in a way a long genesis for this book. Much of my previous work has been important in contributing to the research that went into this book. The book mirrors my own views in that it is interdisciplinary in its approach. Even though I am a political scientist, the book is as much economic as political and, therefore, clearly within the political economy tradition. I have learned to value interdisciplinary approaches, and they have been rewarding for me. This interdisciplinary approach would also explain my tendency toward the unorthodox or unconventional (at least in terms of particular disciplines). My work on international political economy issues began in graduate school but really began to blossom, as it were, once I started teaching. Work with Robert Green started the process, and it was furthered by my joint efforts with Young Kihl in following years on related trade issues. Teaching classes on international political economy has also been helpful. Teaching and research are indeed related. Research invariably improves teaching, and may even inspire it. Teaching also facilitates research. Teaching a class on a topic forces one to review the basic issues, provides a context for the specialized questions that researchers ask, and sometimes generates the questions that lead to more research. I do not know how often my students saw the light bulb go on over my head when I was teaching as some new insight came to me, but there have been times when that has happened in front of a class. Talking about the issues will sometimes engender new ideas or thoughts for new approaches. My students deserve thanks for helping me to focus and formulate ideas, both by preparing for the class and by answering their questions—or at least some of their questions.

My interest in protectionism in various countries eventually led me to consider questions about measuring the effects of protection in various countries, particularly when it became clear that some countries were much better at effectively restricting imports than others, even when they used some of the same methods. As critics of trade policy in the United States have noted at times, there have been limits placed on imports of automobiles, steel, textiles, clothing, and other products, yet sales continued to be lost to imports and trade imbalances with countries such as Japan persisted. Some preliminary explorations for some of the empirical work that appears in the following chapters were done in papers prepared for the various conferences of the International Trade and Finance Association. The settings for the conferences proved to be ideal for testing ideas and getting feedback. Papers related to the topic were prepared for the meetings in Laredo in 1992, Miami in 1993, Porto in 1997, and Atlantic City in 1998. Feedback and professional interaction with colleagues in these conferences were helpful and provided a stimulus to proceed. In the case of the trip to Porto, I am indebted to the Overseas Conference Fund at Indiana University for support for the travel to this conference, as well as support from departmental travel funds for the domestic conferences. I would also be remiss if I did not acknowledge the library staff here at Indiana University-Purdue University at Fort Wayne for their consistently prompt processing of my countless requests for materials via interlibrary loan. This work could not have been done without the material I obtained in this fashion. My volume of requests has probably meant that they know my name all too well, even if they would not recognize my face.

Everyone at the Scholarly and Reference Division of St. Martin's Press was very helpful. Karen Wolny and other editors accepted the original concept when I suggested it. Ella Pearce managed the submission process, making sure everything was where it was supposed to be. Enid Stubin did an excellent job copyediting and improving the manuscript. Without their assistance the book would never have been started, to say nothing of completed.

In addition, I need to especially acknowledge the special lights of my life commemorated on the dedication page. Brenda, my wife, encouraged me in the project and spent countless hours proofing the various versions of this work, finding errors, and making suggestions for improvements. She eased the load considerably and was an ongoing inspiration and a constant support as well. My two little girls (Carol, now six, and Tessa, now four) were also inspiring in their very special ways. Playing with them was often a good way to relax and unwind, and it made it easier to refocus my thoughts. Their presence and laughter was always a reason to proceed with the work so I could dedicate it to them. All three of these special ladies provided ongoing encouragement to finish the book—as well as the occasional, very necessary distractions to provide balance in life. When all is said and done, they are the ones who have made it all worthwhile.

There are two other persons who deserve acknowledgment, even if on a sadder note. While this book was being written there were two losses. My father passed away in 1999 while I was working on the book. He had constantly served as a source of quiet inspiration for me for virtually all my life. Much of what I have been able to do results from the example that he set for me. I can but hope that the example continues to serve me in the future. I would like to think that he would have been proud of the book. Just a few days before my father died, I learned of the death of Professor Alasdair A. Lonie of the University of Dundee, whom I had known for only a few years. Alasdair, too, was a source of inspiration for those who knew him, and similarly provided encouragement, often quite subtle, to those around him to reach for their potential. He was an example of all that an academic should be and was a delight to be around. I consider myself fortunate to have had the opportunity to know him. His passing has left a gap in my life. Ideally, I can provide similar examples and encouragement to those around me, most especially my girls.

The work in this book represents a stage along the way to understanding international trade processes as well as domestic political pressures that affect trade policy in the industrialized countries. Thus, there is more work to be done with this approach, and I sincerely hope that this book will inform and encourage others to utilize similar approaches and advance our collective understanding of trade and protection. Notwithstanding the help that I have had with this work, the positive examples of colleagues and friends and family, input and suggestions, I remain responsible for the material in the book and any of its shortcomings. May the shortcomings be few and the benefits for those interested in trade issues and protection more than enough to offset any of those shortcomings.

—*JML*
Fort Wayne
May 10, 2000

Chapter 1

Introduction: Imports and Protection

This book compares per capita levels of imports for the advanced developed countries; thus, it focuses on actual trade flows. But just as important as the imports that actually entered into the markets of the industrialized countries have been those imports that have not been allowed into those same markets because of the protectionist practices in place. International trade patterns, as a consequence, have been affected by imports that did not occur just as they have been by the actual imports that have been present. Thus, the emphasis in the chapters to follow will be both on the actual per capita imports in the aggregate and for selected product categories that were present and on the "missing" imports as well.

Governments and Trade Restrictions

Governments have been active participants in the international trading system for a very long time. Some ancient empires were predominantly free trade (Assyria) or statist (Hittites, Egyptians, Mycenean Greeks) in policy outlook.[1] The governments of Britain and the Netherlands were involved in the creation and support of the trading companies that colonized the Americas, India, and Indonesia. The mercantilist views of trade beginning in the sixteenth century argued for active government manipulation of trade to strengthen the state and to further the interests of the nation. State interventions in trade matters, including the provision of protection, have clearly had major implications for foreign relations and international politics. There have been trade wars as well as military conflicts that were designed to control economic resources or to weaken competing states.

Napoleon attempted to weaken Great Britain by attacking British commerce with Europe in his Continental system. Great Britain in turn blockaded France and its allies and attacked French commerce. The adoption of protectionist practices by states has had major effects on political events as well. The British Navigation Acts and other restrictions on trade fueled the fires that led to the successful rebellion of the American colonies. Arguably, the same Navigation Acts led to stunted economic growth in Ireland, which remained part of the British Empire for an additional century and a half. In the mid-nineteenth century, domestic interests fearing competition from imports were effective in leading Austria to refuse to join the German customs union (Zollverein) that was headed by Prussia.[2] The Zollverein eventually became one instrument for German unity under Prussian leadership sans the Hapsburg Empire. Austrian participation in the Zollverein might actually have changed the eventual patterns of nationalism and state-building in Central Europe. Within the German Empire that grew out of the Zollverein, Bismarck used tariff protection (as well as other economic and diplomatic policies) to unite farming and industrial interests in the "Marriage of Iron and Rye" in support of the new Germany. More recently, between World War I and World War II political antagonisms and economic conflict fed on each other, creating a relatively closed international trading system and a conflict-ridden international political system. Economic policies became extensions of politics in many cases. After World War II, the Soviet Union and its satellites chose autarkic development for a long period to "protect" themselves from potential manipulation and exploitation by the capitalist West.[3]

Actual Imports and Relative Openness

States have actively used economic policies to support other goals. They have also protected domestic economic sectors, either in response to domestic pressures, to support broader economic policies, to generate revenues, or for other reasons. In order to determine whether or not particular countries in today's world have been or continue to be protectionist in their actual practices, the starting point will be the actual per capita levels of imports entering countries in given years. Further, these actual levels of imports for the countries will be compared to each other rather than to any ideal import level presupposed by one model or another. It would be extremely difficult (i.e., impossible) to arrive at any figure that would represent what the true level of such imports should have been under conditions of pure free trade. Global trade has long been affected by state interventions (now known as strategic trade policy or managed trade). The resulting deviations from free trade in the past have obviously had effects on national economies and influenced the present import patterns as a consequence. Further, specifying current deviations from free trade for complex economies would be next to impossible. Changes in import levels and the prices for the imports or domestic substitutes would influence the decisions of firms that used these products as an input in their own production processes or the decision of any firm that purchased from suppliers that use the product. Thus, there could be ripple effects throughout the economy, which would be impossible to specify.[4] And ultimately, most goods have been inputs into production processes. Higher prices for computers increases overhead. More expensive trucks raise transport costs. Cheaper office equipment and furniture might make a product more price competitive domestically or internationally. Lower prices for food in a country could be associated with lower wages with a similar positive effect on price competitiveness.

The rather large deviations from free trade ideals in the recent international system have even led some analysts in favor of managed trade or government intervention to argue that intervention has actually counterbalanced distortions in the global economy induced by earlier trade interventions in other countries, thereby actually moving the global economic situation back toward a condition of freer trade rather than further away from it.[5] Mercantilistic policies by one state may have provided firms in that country with competitive advantages that would have necessitated compensatory actions by the governments of other countries.[6] While the validity of such arguments may be doubted, and even disproved in some circumstances, they cannot be totally discounted. It has even been possible that out-and-out neo-mercantile protectionists who would have felt no need to use these justifications or others might actually have introduced trade and economic policies that have moved countries closer to what the free trade situation would have been sans existing restrictions. The real difficulty in analyzing protection, thus, has been that it would be difficult to tell when or if such movements toward a free trade situation had happened or not.

Determining what a world of free trade would look like in reality has been complicated for other reasons. If free trade is regarded as a situation that is pure and without sin (clearly a controversial assumption), then the world has been full of sinners, and protection, as is the case for sin, has covered as vast a multitude of situations.[7] All the industrialized countries have practiced some form of protection with the differences being matters of degree, albeit quite large at times. The centrally planned Communist economies followed their own autarkic paths for decades and have only recently in most cases become full members of the international economic community. Industrialized countries have had to negotiate multiple rounds of tariff reductions and other changes in trade activities in order to deal with problems resulting from protection. While developing countries may have lacked the multitude of trade barriers available to the richer countries, whether Communist or free market, they too have implemented barriers to imports or used export subsidies to influence trade patterns. Of the world economies that have been of any size, only Hong Kong practiced near perfect free trade (i.e., the sins were few, and they were small ones). But Hong Kong was not simply a smaller version of other economies. It was a territory that had a special position as an entrepot for goods originating in China or destined for that country. That special position has now been changed, although not especially *because* Hong Kong was such a practitioner of free trade. In fact, Hong Kong's prosperity as a free trade city was essentially responsible for the special position that the city has come to have as an autonomous region in China. In any event, the global trading system has been one in which trade interventions have abounded, making calculations of revealed free trade levels impossible.

The types of protectionist measures used in the world have been many and varied. Tariffs have been a long-standing border barrier, but there have been variations on even the use of this relatively straightforward import tax. Tariff schedules of great complexity raise costs for importers and have given administrators discretion by providing opportunities for interpretation or reclassification of goods entering the country. Tariff schedules have been manipulated to favor some foreign producers and to handicap others. A classic example of how tariff schedules can be used to favor particular countries can be found in a 1904 trade agreement between Germany and Switzerland. German tariffs only on "large dapple mountain cattle reared at a spot at least 300 meters above sea level and having at least one month grazing each year at a spot at least 800 meters above sea level" were eligible for lower rates.[8] In theory, of course, these tariffs applied to all cattle imported into Germany from other states that had most-favored-nation status with Germany and that met this description. Needless to say, in practice only Swiss cattle met the description.

In addition to tariffs, many non-tariff barriers have been used. Quotas, including "voluntary" export restraints (VERs), have been common. The VERs on imports of Japanese automobiles into the United States and quotas on textiles and apparel in most of the developed world have been prominent examples. Antidumping regulations and provisions to counter the "advantages" provided to foreign producers by subsidies have become more frequently used. Such national regulations have been used not only to offset inappropriate foreign practices, they have also been used to discourage imports. Although health and safety regulations and standards are essential in some cases, they too have been used to restrict imports. Other administrative rules have hindered imports. The French decision in December 1987 to require Japanese VCRs to clear customs at the inland post of Poiters still stands out as an example of creative administrative flexibility designed to reduce imports. Since the inland post had a small staff, this requirement effectively prevented the Japanese products from reaching retailers in time for the Christmas season.[9] Overall, the effects of these nontariff barriers have been significant but difficult to measure in any meaningful way. For example, how many sales of Japanese VCRs would have occurred in 1987 if the Poiters restriction had not been put into place? How many Frenchmen waited until the VCRs cleared the post at Poiters before purchasing them, thereby delaying but not eliminating the sales? Were Japanese VCRs diverted elsewhere as a consequence of the slowdown in sales in France?

As a consequence of the difficulties involved in determining what free trade levels would have been, much of the analysis in this volume will focus on comparisons of actual per capita import levels among the industrialized countries with due consideration of basic exogenous factors that could have influenced these import levels. This comparison, of course, cannot provide any information about how far a country has deviated from free trade in an absolute sense, only how much it has deviated relative to other countries used in the analyses. In effect, this method will have provided a means of identifying the most open and least open nations. While not a traditional approach to the analysis of trade and protectionism, it does have the advantage of beginning with what is and then providing an indication of the level of revealed protection that has been present among countries. In this sense it is much like comparative advantage concepts. Countries have comparative advantages *relative* to other countries rather than in relation to an ideal prototype. The nations that are the best at producing cars, computers, or cameras have not been those states that meet an ideal of efficiency in producing these items. They have simply been better at producing these items than others, or these are the items they produce best (or least worst) compared to all other goods. In the same fashion, revealed protection simply identifies the most protectionist states, but does not measure how far they have strayed from a free trade ideal. As a consequence, it should also be noted that the level of revealed protection present will continue to be a relative one. Even in a world economy in which trade has been becoming freer and in which significant trade liberalization has occurred, some states will remain relatively more protectionist than others, even if they have reduced the actual levels of protection that existed in the past. The least open state of today may be more open than many of the relatively open nations of the 1960s or (with less doubt) many of the most open industrialized economies of past eras such as the situation that existed between the Great Depression and the outbreak of World War II.

Organization of the Volume

The chapters to follow deal with various elements of imports and barriers to imports, principally in the industrialized countries. The focus is on the developed countries with their size and wealth not simply because they have been the largest traders but more relevantly for the topic of this volume because they have been the most important markets in the world. Their willingness or disinclination to import thus has been crucial to the trade of each other and many other states.

Chapter 2 discusses many of the key determinants of trade and imports. All other things being equal, larger countries would be expected to import less since they would be likely to be capable of greater self-sufficiency than other states. It would be anticipated that richer countries, on the other hand, would import relatively more simply because they would have the wherewithal to do so. With greater wealth comes increased demand. Membership in free trade areas or customs unions like the European Community/European Union (EC/EU) or the European Free Trade Area (EFTA), while having potentially distorting effects on trade patterns, would be expected to lead to increases in overall trade activity. Factor endowment theories have also been proposed as important influences on levels and types of trade, although such theories have been less relevant for the intra-industry trade that has been so important to the advanced developed countries. Finally, government policies, including tariffs, quotas, subsidies, countersubsidy measures, and other programs and protectionist actions have all had major impacts on the levels and types of imports present for the individual industrialized nations.

Chapter 3 considers the overall trade patterns of 23 industrialized states for a number of years since 1960. With controls for wealth, it is obvious that population size is indeed an important determinant of total per capita imports and per capita imports of manufactured goods. In Chapter four multiple regression analyses are used to control for the separate effects that population size, relative wealth, and years of membership in the EC/EU and EFTA have had on per capita imports. Residual values from these regressions are then analyzed to determine which of these countries were active importers and which of them were relatively poor markets for imported goods. Relatively poor market countries would be those with natural disadvantages for involvement in trade (a rather unlikely situation) or those countries that have actively discouraged imports in general or in specific areas, either intentionally or inadvertently. Governmental actions of the intentional or inadvertent kind are, of course, more likely to be the cause for lower import levels.

Chapters 5, 6, and 7 deal with imports of specific product categories. Chapter 5 focuses on per capita imports of manufactured goods with the same controls used in chapter 4. Manufactured goods are singled out for special attention because they have been the most important class of goods traded internationally since World War II. As exports, they have been very important for the industrial base of both developed and developing countries—especially the Asian Newly Industrialized Countries (NICs). Some attention was also paid to imports of raw materials (i.e., imports of nonmanufactured goods). Chapter 6 concentrates on particular manufactured goods such as textiles, clothing, and toys that have been especially important for producers in the developing world. Exports of these products have been crucial in many cases for the industrialization and export led growth that have been characteristic of the Asian NICs and other developing countries. Differential levels of openness among the industrialized countries to these kinds of products could have special consequences for the developing world in its collective efforts to create industrial bases and to foster growth by exporting to markets in the more advanced nations of the world. Chapter 7 continues the analysis of particular categories by dealing with imports of selected types of manufactured products and introducing an additional control in the form of the level of domestic production present in industrialized nations. These analyses are an effort to assess more clearly the presence of protection and its extent in particular areas while taking into account that the fact that some countries might be quite open to imports due to a lack of any domestic industry in the product area. Countries without any domestic industry to be protected would be much less likely to erect barriers to imports since trade would be the only way to satisfy demand. The presence of such domestic industries, on the other hand, could be a spur to either intra-industry trade or protection depending upon circumstances.

Chapter 8 deals with overall per capita imports and per capita imports of manufactured goods for a group of developing countries, including most of the NICs and near-NICs of the world. The derivation of relative openness measures for these developing countries provides a base for comparisons of general patterns between them and the industrialized countries, which are used as the data set in the earlier chapters. The analyses also provide an indication as to whether relative openness to imports have been associated with NIC status, whether development was more likely with such openness, whether regional patterns existed, and what had been the effects of wealth and size on imports and trade policies in these countries.

Chapter 9 attempts to sum up the results from the analyses in the preceding chapters with particular reference to the industrialized countries. What have been the patterns of protectionism that have been revealed? Which countries have been relatively open and which countries have not? What have been the changes over time? What are the implications for the international trade regime that is now centered within the new World Trade Organization (WTO)?

Chapter 2

Variables Influencing International Trade

In the chapters to follow, the actual levels of imports moving into various countries were measured, while controlling for some of the other important factors that may have influenced these import levels. The analyses that were undertaken were based on the actual import levels among countries as a means of identifying those states that have imported relatively large amounts of goods and those countries that have imported less than would have been expected. These comparisons provided some indication as to whether these states had encouraged or discouraged certain types of imports based on what their policies were relative to each other. Or the comparisons might have indicated which states had been most effective in limiting such imports in a relative sense if all countries had sought to discourage the same kinds of imports.

Imports and exports have been at the center of international exchange. Exports and imports have balanced, of course, on a global basis even if particular countries have had surpluses of exports or imports. Exports obviously have been one means of paying for imports, but they could also have been financed through investments, through the provision of services (financial services or merchant shipping revenues, for example), or through foreign aid and grants. Notwithstanding the source of income for payments for imports, a number of variables could have been important in terms of influencing import levels and the types of goods that were imported. A variety of actions by governments that sought to limit imports or to influence their makeup fall into this category, including membership in customs unions, size, and relative wealth. Traditionally, comparative advantage and factor endowments were deemed sufficient to explain the makeup of international trade under free market conditions. Only about one-quarter of total world trade, however, has occurred within the framework of regulations of the General Agreement on Tariffs and Trade (GATT), which comes closest to approximating this free market trade ideal, in which comparative advantage would be expected to be operative. The other three-quarters of world trade, however, has consisted, in roughly equal parts, of intra-company trade, barter trade, and trade that occurs within preferential areas such as customs unions and free trade areas.[1]

Preferential Trade Areas

Preferential trade areas have become increasingly prevalent in the international political system. The Zollverein was an early example of an effective customs area. Not only did it bring together states that could benefit from the union, it also pressured states such as Baden and Saxony to join in order to avoid the danger of losing access to important markets for their exports.[2] Trade within such preferential trades areas has especially increased with the expansion of the European Community/European Union (EC/EU) and the creation of the North American Free Trade Association (NAFTA) as well as other trading areas.[3] The formation of one free trade area has apparently led to the formation of competing trade areas.[4] There have been fears that a new regionalism has pervaded the international system, undercutting the international system. NAFTA could potentially be the core of a Western Hemisphere trading group designed to compete with the EU. There have also been discussions about closer economic cooperation and even free trade areas in the Asian-Pacific region of the world. There have also been many efforts to create or revitalize free trade arrangements among developing countries.

Such free trade areas and customs unions can lead to trade creation in which new exchanges occur among the members where no such activity had existed previously, while trade diversion refers to trade among the members of the trade area that increases at the expense of or replaces imports from countries that are not members of the trade area.[5] Free trade areas have led to increases in overall trade with non-members in at least some circumstances.[6] In other cases, however, significant trade diversion occurs. Non-member states can suffer losses when such areas are created.[7] For example, European countries have lost market shares in Canada with the creation of the Canada-United States free trade agreements in 1989.[8] Such free trade areas have been permissible under GATT rules, provided they did not discriminate against outside nations and were primarily trade creating. But many of the preferential arrangements have not met these high standards. The chances for diversion of trade from the most efficient channels can occur because those regional trade schemes that have been trade diverting have been likely to generate more political support than the ones that have created trade.[9] Governments have been also more willing to enter free trade areas when they can tailor the agreements to favor domestic industries or economic sectors, thereby appeasing domestic interest groups.[10] Thus, the arrangements most likely to avoid adverse trade consequences may be the ones less likely to receive the necessary domestic support for implementation. Trade areas such as the EC also have led to corresponding increases in intra-industry trade among the members,[11] compounding the deviations from factor endowment expectations that can occur with trade areas in general. It has been suggested that while free trade agreements may initially have negative effects, they also ultimately could lead to more efficient producers that will increase global welfare by providing lower cost items in the global marketplace.[12] Ultimately, of course, "regional trading blocs are discriminatory," even when the discrimination has been legal under existing international rules or even when they have been innocuous in their effects.[13]

Market Size: Population and Wealth

In addition to membership in customs unions, there were other influences on import levels. All other things being equal, countries with larger populations would normally have relatively less need for imports. Such countries would have had sufficiently diversified economic bases to provide many products that might have to be imported by smaller countries. Economies of scale would also have been more likely to occur with larger populations and larger economies.[14] Smaller countries would have been more likely to specialize, including specialization for export and correspondingly larger levels of imports. Smaller domestic markets would force firms to export in order to attain the minimum effectiveness from scale economies, much more so than would have been the case for companies that operate in larger markets.[15] Such export efforts in smaller economies would also ultimately facilitate higher import levels by increasing domestic welfare. The fact that the smaller European countries have generally been more supportive of trade liberalization has been one indication of the importance that size could have on trade relationships and trade policies.

For example, the trade of the Czech Republic and Slovakia increased after the separation of the two now-smaller countries from each other. Economic transactions that had formerly been internal now became part of foreign trade, which was likely to remain high since the two countries have maintained a customs union. Even higher increases in trade resulted when Singapore left the Malaysian Federation. Singapore's role as an entrepot meant that much of the trade of the federation flowed through the port, a situation that continued after the separation into Singapore and Malaysia. The trade levels of the two new countries were much higher as a consequence of including commerce between them as trade. Conversely, the union of Hong Kong and the Peoples Republic of China reduced the amount of foreign trade for China since a fairly large volume of Chinese products were exported to Hong Kong, and China received imports, directly or as pass through trade, from the city as well. With the increase in size, minor though it was in many respects, foreign trade totals declined.

A second factor that would normally have influenced the level of imports is the relative wealth of a nation. Market size was measured by purchasing power as well as by population.[16] Thus, all other things being equal, a richer country would import more than less wealthy countries. Obviously in countries in which the per capita income was higher, consumers would have had more discretionary income to purchase both domestically produced goods and imported products. Luxury items would be more likely to be imported in wealthier countries, and funds would be available for capital goods and more complex products that could not have been produced locally. Higher levels of income would also have permitted individuals to purchase specialty products from the firms producing for export in smaller economies.

Comparative Advantage and Factor Endowments

The basic idea underlying international trade, of course, has been that all of the countries involved in such exchanges will benefit. In essence, each state will produce more of some goods so that it can trade them for items that have not been produced locally. With trade each state efficiently produces some item and exchanges it for products that have been more cheaply produced elsewhere. Two states trading with each other will thus increase their efficiency and output, both individually and collectively, through the medium of mutually beneficial trade.

One explanation for the presence of international trade that has occurred and does occur in a mutually beneficial fashion has been the concept of comparative advantage. Countries produced those goods that they
can produce most efficiently *relative* to other states in the system. A country that was an inefficient producer of everything in an absolute sense
would still trade; it would simply produce goods for which it was relatively
the most efficient or the least inefficient (such as plasticware or cheap toys)
compared to other nations, even those that produced all the other goods
even more efficiently. The inefficient producer would focus on its best production possibilities, overproduce those items, and trade for the other items
that it produces less well. With such comparative advantage international
exchange can flourish, especially with the decline of transportation and
transactions costs that have come with increased modernization and tech-
nical improvements.

The idea of comparative advantage has been joined with the concept
of factor endowments. Naturally enough, countries have been endowed
with different characteristics and resources that have contributed to their
comparative advantages. The relative availability of land, labor, and capital
were the initial factor endowments that were considered important for explaining trade. A country with large expanses of fertile land would produce
agricultural products—both food and industrial raw materials. The relative
availability of capital and manpower in conjunction with the land would
influence the types of agricultural goods produced to some extent as well.
Countries with abundant capital and limited labor and land would focus
on high technology products that would require large infusions of capital
and small labor components. Other combinations of these three factors
would lead to other types of comparative advantages in production. Later
additions or refinements to the basic three-factor model have introduced
the presence or absence of natural resources and the skill levels of the work
force (or human capital). The relative levels of these additional endowments would clearly have affected the comparative advantages that particular states would have had. These advantages could even have carried
forward in time, providing what has been termed ownership advantages,
locational advantages, or competitive advantages, all of which have reflected and arisen from the effects of prior comparative advantages, becoming part of the new comparative advantages in turn.[17]

Although comparative advantage would suggest that factor endowments
would be important, they have not proven to be especially useful in explaining patterns of for many types of trade. These theories, such as the Sto-
pler-Samuelson version, have worked quite well in explaining the exchange

of raw materials for manufactured goods in the years before 1960 when capital had not yet become extremely mobile.[18] There have even been some cases in which factor endowments have been effective in explaining more complex forms of trade.[19] For the most part, however, such theories have not been effective in predicting or explaining trade in complex products. For example, there have been extensive changes in the trade patterns among areas of the world even when there have not been major changes in relative factor endowments.[20] Risk and uncertainty have introduced perverse effects for factor endowments as well.[21] Factor endowments have been able to explain only a portion of the trade that has occurred between Eastern and Western Europe.[22] They have also failed to explain very much about the trade between Canada and the United States[23] or among the Organization for Economic Cooperation and Development (OECD) countries.[24] Nor have factor endowments generally explained the success of the Asian NICs in their growth and expansion of exports.[25] Such theories have been largely ineffective for explaining trade in complex manufactured goods, the volume of such trade, or intra-company and intra-industry trade.[26] Intra-company trade, i.e., trade within multinational corporations, could have followed quite different patterns than would have been suggested by factor endowments.[27] Multinational corporations have purchased goods from their own subsidiaries to enhance overall corporate profitability or to maintain sufficient production to ensure economies of scale for particular plants. As a consequence, they may have been able to ignore production sources that actually have had greater comparative advantage. It was also possible that concerns over security of supply rather than lowest cost could also have been an important consideration in purchases from subsidiaries or with other firms where a company has had an established relationship.[28]

Barter trade and countertrade have also been on the increase, and such practices do not fit very well with theories of factor endowments. At one level they have corresponded since the two countries engaged in barter trade usually did so in terms of comparative advantages relative to each other (but largely exclusive of any other countries). The products traded between the two states have usually not included goods for which these countries would be the most efficient global producers. If the countries in question were among the most efficient producers of the goods, it was unlikely that there would have been any need for barter trade or countertrade. As a consequence, this type of trade would have followed patterns suggested by theories of factor endowments only to a limited degree. The formation of preferential trade areas has also modified the effects of factor endowments. Factor endowments should still have explained at least some of the trade within such an area, but to the extent that there has been trade diversion, factor endowments would have been less useful in explaining overall trade patterns.

The presence of protectionists practices, past and present, in various countries would also have modified the effects that factor endowments would have on trade. It was even possible for a country to affect factor endowments in order to "develop" comparative advantage in certain fields.[29] National neomercantilist policies have given domestic firms competitive advantages in many cases, leading to situations in which other countries could even be forced into taking compensatory actions on behalf of their domestic production facilities.[30] The whole infant industry argument that has frequently been presented as a rationale for protection against imports has presupposed that comparative advantage can be developed over time. While a dynamic theory of factor endowments could incorporate the development of infant industries in some nations in a global trading system, the creation and persistence of such industries would be contrary to theories of factor endowments as such. Such infant industry protection and other forms of government support, for example, would explain the rise of the German steel industry to a position of export competitiveness in the early 1900s.[31] The rise to positions of competitiveness of many Japanese industries,[32] or more recently of Korean manufacturing firms,[33] has also been contrary to what factor endowment concepts would have suggested. The factors of production or endowments in a particular country could even have been developed and improved through international trade, and governmental trade policies could even have encouraged such changes.[34]

One way in which it was possible that comparative advantages could have been affected would have been by governments following strategic trade policies, which have been designed in some cases to provide industries with the advantages that can come with economies of scale.[35] There have also been arguments that some industries are key sectors for an economy because they provide positive learning curves (or learning-by-doing) for other sectors and have positive spillovers into other segments of national economies,[36] suggesting again that comparative advantage and factor endowments can be manipulated. These suggestions ultimately have stressed the need to develop industries that create the human capital and skills that would provide a comparative advantage in the future, and they have also suggested that such factors can be directly enhanced by government economic and industrial policy. Thus it is not surprising that Gilpin has argued that comparative advantage has become "increasingly arbitrary" due to the policies and strategies of multinational firms and as a consequence of government economic and industrial policies, and that, in effect, comparative advantage has indeed been created.[37] Nor has it been particularly surprising, therefore, that theories of factor endowments have remained relevant for explaining only some types of trade or have served better for explaining trade patterns in earlier time periods. Intra-industry trade has also been more responsive to created comparative advantages rather than natural ones,[38] providing one explanation as to why factor endowments do not do a very good job of explaining this type of trade.

Protectionism in the Global Economy

Other circumstances that can influence trade, including even the trade that has been subject to market forces, have been the various restrictions and impediments that have appeared as a consequence of the protectionist practices of the nations engaged in trade. Given the overwhelming importance of the markets in the industrialized countries for most products from all over the world, protectionist practices in these countries would have been by far the most important for the international trading system. Since comparative advantage and factor endowments have become less useful for understanding the flow of trade (or the non-flow of trade), the effects of government interventions have become even more important.

One conspicuous role that governments have played has been to protect markets for domestic producers in an effort to enhance national interest and accomplish other economic goals. Of course, even the practice of free trade at times has represented the pursuance of governmental objectives. The theories advanced to explain the congruence of free trade with the presence of hegemons in the international system fall into this category. Hegemonic theories have suggested that one reason that the leading economic powers created free trade systems was because it was in their best interests to do so.[39] Similarly, countries that currently have advocated free trade frequently have done so because they anticipate gaining from such an arrangement. In a very real sense support for free trade became support for a very particular type of strategic trade policy that has advantages for the country in question.[40] Similarly, it has been argued that the Treaty of Methuen, which liberalized trade between Britain and Portugal, ultimately was in the interests of British commercial interests and actually proved to have quite negative impacts on Portuguese industry.[41] Thus, while protectionism has usually been seen as a reflection of conscious government policies designed to gain or maintain some economic advantage, it is worth noting that support for free trade policies *may* reflect similar purposes on the part of governments.

Protectionism can be a major factor influencing the level of imports in a particular country. If the barriers to imports have been effective ones, imports could be reduced or even eliminated. The overall extent of such barriers could either have reduced imports in the aggregate or influenced their composition by favoring some types of products over others. Virtually every industrialized country and most of the developing ones have utilized a variety of protectionist practices. Some states have relied on them to a greater extent, and some countries have utilized them more effectively, but they have been an ever-present fact of international economic life. Ultimately this protection has been designed to shield specified domestic economic sectors from import competition. GATT has recognized the potential need for at least temporary protection by providing provisions accepting temporary measures when a country faces import surges that threaten domestic sectors. The protective devices in use, however, have gone far beyond temporary measures and frequently have included measures put into place in the absence of any such import surges.

Tariffs used to be a major impediment to imports. Countries used them to discourage imports while raising revenues and, in the case of prohibitive tariffs, to eliminate imports altogether. GATT multilateral negotiations, however, led to major tariff reductions for the industrial products and manufactured goods that had been traded among the developed nations of the world. These tariff reductions had a somewhat perverse effect on the types of protection that have been used since countries increasingly have been forced to rely on non-tariff barriers to impede imports. While the tariffs as barriers to imports were normally transparent and non-discriminatory, the non-tariff barriers that replaced them have often been very opaque and even country specific. Voluntary export restraints, for example, have been negotiated with specific exporters rather than affecting all imports regardless of source. Allegations of dumping and subsidization have usually been directed towards particular sources. The application of health, safety, or labeling standards can also be less than clear in terms of the requirements, and they can be applied selectively. These non-tariff mechanisms can be difficult to comply with or avoid, and the actual costs of dealing with them are frequently difficult to calculate. As a consequence, these types of barriers raise the costs of trade more than tariffs given the uncertainty of their applications, and they have generally been considered less desirable in terms of global efficiency and overall costs when compared to tariffs.[42] The additional costs are borne by consumers in the importing countries (including sectors that would use the imports as part of their production processes), while domestic producers or foreign exporters can receive extra profits as a consequence of the protection that is present.[43]

United States

Even though the United States has been a great supporter of trade liberalization as well as the architect of the liberal trading system that was constructed after World War II, it has experienced protectionists pressures. Agriculture was excluded from the initial GATT system primarily at the insistence of the United States, which at that time desired to support its own farm sector.[44] More recently, the United States began to advocate inclusion of agricultural goods in GATT multilateral negotiations and in the new WTO,[45] but only when it was apparent that such inclusion was in the best interests of the agricultural sector in the United States to have freer trade. However useful U.S. support for agricultural liberalization may have been in the negotiations that did lead to the WTO, it is important to note that such support was based on calculations of national interest rather than philosophical adherence to liberal trade principles.

U.S. support for freer trade in manufactured goods after World War II was essential for reducing barriers to the exchange of these items. The resulting increases in trade provided markets for American exporters and enhanced the economic and political stability of U.S. allies in Europe and elsewhere. With European and Japanese recovery, as well as the appearance of the export-oriented NICs, domestic pressure in the United States in favor of greater protection has increased. The United States has participated in the Multi-Fibre Arrangements (MFAs) limiting imports of textiles and clothing. Imports of Japanese automobiles have been subjected to voluntary export restraints. A trigger price mechanism was created for steel imports, providing for what in effect has been a quota on such imports. Congress has applied significant pressure on various presidents, the Department of Commerce, and the International Trade Commission to apply import sanctions more rigorously. While some of this congressional pressure has been political posturing for constituent interests,[46] in other cases it has been more earnest in actually seeking to limit imports.[47] The United States has also used Section 301 of the 1988 Omnibus Trade Act to pressure foreign governments to open their markets to greater levels of imports or else face limited market access with the United States, with Congress pressuring the executive branch to use the provisions of this section against imports more frequently.[48]

Congress has clearly been adept in responding to constituency pressures in dealing with legislation that has been designed to limit imports. Votes on specific bills providing protection to domestic groups have been positively associated with employment in congressional districts, i.e., members of Congress vote to protect the jobs of their constituents.[49] There have been occasions on which the executive branch has pressed for VERs or advocated other protectionist activity to forestall the possibility of even more protectionist action by Congress.[50] Even efforts designed to increase imports have included limitations. The Caribbean Basin Initiative was designed to increase exports from this region to the United States, but the manufactured goods receiving a preference have still faced a variety of non-tariff barriers to entry that have reduced the incentives that were supposedly being provided.[51] President Clinton even had to rely on Republican support and special favors for Democratic Congressmen in order to get the NAFTA agreement through the House of Representatives.[52] Perhaps most importantly, increased U.S. protection has reverberated throughout the whole international system since other nations frequently have followed the lead of the United States in terms of reducing or increasing their levels of protection.[53]

Congress has also been successful in creating new standards for contingent protection in the form of antidumping and subsidy hearings so that countervailing duties are more likely to be applied.[54] In addition, while reviews of antidumping levies have been possible under the current regulations, they have generally not led to reductions of the higher duties that have been imposed on imports—exactly those duties that have been most limiting to imports.[55] While revocations of such countervailing duties have also been possible in theory, such reversals of duties have been likely to occur only when there has been no domestic opposition to the change.[56] These countervailing duties, and even the hearings to determine whether duties will be imposed, can become obstacles for imports to surmount. It can be costly for foreign producers or the firms importing the goods into the United States to contest the allegations of unfair trade practices, which have originated with domestic groups that seek the duties. The proceedings have been so time-consuming and costly that their existence was one factor that encouraged Canadian support for the free trade arrangement with the United States that preceded NAFTA. Canadian producers wanted to avoid even the threat of such proceedings.[57] Such hearings or the threat of such hearings have also often led to "appropriate" changes in the export behavior of foreign firms.[58]

Such contingent protection also has the advantage of being product- and country-specific. Only some exporting firms have been targeted, and they may well be the most serious competitors for domestic producers. The United States has become one of the leading users of such types of protection.[59] The negotiations creating the WTO have also increased the importance of such contingent legislation. Non-tariff barriers such as the MFA will be phased out, and other, like VERs have been prohibited. The WTO rules, however, have left judgments about dumping and use of sub- sidies largely to national interpretation.[60] As a consequence, such protec- tionist devices have become more important, both because they are flexible and because they do not violate the letter of new international norms of behavior.

Japan

Unlike the United States, which has often been seen as a paragon of free trade virtues even when it was not, Japan has frequently been accused of protecting its domestic economic sectors. In agriculture, protection has re- mained prevalent with either tariffs or other major barriers to imports in place.[61] As a consequence, Japanese food prices have been quite high. Ja- panese consumers, however, appear to have been willing to subsidize the farm population that remains through protected food prices,[62] and not even the breakup of the Liberal Democratic Party that governed Japan for half a century led to declines in protection. With the creation of the WTO, Japan has appeared to be more committed to reductions in the level of protection that has been offered but not the elimination of barriers.

Like some other countries, Japan has a statist tradition of government involvement in the economy, thus leading political leaders and institutions to be involved in dealing with economic issues of international impor- tance.[63] At the present time Japanese tariffs have been reduced to very low levels on most goods, but the reductions generally occurred only when the protected producers had become competitive (i.e., when there was no longer any need of protection).[64] Even so, the government has consistently reserved the right under GATT Article XIX to rescind the tariff reduc- tions if the domestic sectors in questions were to face significant damage from imports.[65] The most effective forms of protection used have been a variety of non-tariff barriers, many of them quite subtle in their operation and effects.[66] For example, the preservation of the unique Japanese wholesale and retail distribution system has facilitated sales by domestic producers while hindering access for foreign firms. The Ministry of International Trade and Industry (MITI) has been very effective in formulating and supporting industrial policies, including the subsidization of domestic producers in a variety of ways. Further, the government has utilized expensive and complex labeling requirements, has had biases toward domestic producers in government procurement policies, and has maintained a large customs force with significant local discretion in interpreting a complex tariff schedule.[67] Such protection has permitted many Japanese firms to develop the size and concomitant economies of scale eventually to become competitive in the global market.[68] MITI, for example, was quite successful in creating informal barriers to imports of computer chips while supporting domestic producers, greatly facilitating the rise of Japanese producers.[69] Japan has also borrowed from the example set by the United States and other industrialized countries by threatening to charge foreign producers with dumping and to seek the application of countervailing duties. Such threats have been used to persuade foreign producers to modify the practices that the Japanese government has deemed unacceptable or harmful.[70]

While Japan has not participated in the MFA quota system, it has used some of these subtle means in order to limit imports of textiles and clothing. Prior approval by MITI has been required for textile imports from developing countries.[71] The large trading companies, which have been necessary for the importation and distribution of foreign produced goods, also have played a role in favoring domestic producers. They have had very close ties with domestic industry groups and government agencies such as MITI, and they have proved to be quite adept at limiting overall imports by placing small orders with foreign producers or none at all.[72] Korea actually established its own general trading companies after the Japanese companies refused to handle Korean goods that might compete with Japanese products in foreign markets.[73] In a similar vein, the linkages among companies in Japanese industrial groups or families (*keiretsu*), which include the trading companies, have also had depressive effects on imports. These relationships in the *keiretsu* have meant that companies purchase from each other rather than from foreign suppliers (or even other Japanese firms). These effects have been important enough for those economic sectors that have a greater prevalence of these industrial families to have lower levels of imports.[74] The *keiretsu* have been associated with higher net exports and lower net imports.[75] Even the limited intra-industry trade that has involved Japanese companies has taken place within the *keiretsu*.[76]

Europe

European countries have also provided protection to their domestic industries. Agriculture has been heavily protected in a number of countries especially France. First, national regulations limited imports and then the Common Agricultural Policy (CAP) of the EC/EU provided large subsidies and protection.[77] The formation of the EC led to higher subsidies than would likely have been the case than if the individual member states had created and administered such a policy on their own.[78] In the area of manufacturing, countries that have had long traditions of state involvement and intervention in the economy, as Japan has, have been the states most likely (and most able) to protect those domestic sectors that have faced competition from imports.[79] Many of these countries, as well as Japan, were also the ones that Gerschenkron referred to as "late industrializers."[80] Since these countries had to catch up with the early centers of manufacturing, which, like the United Kingdom, had the advantage of being first, a strong state structure was necessary to aid in the industrialization. This structure was then available for use in other circumstances. Where labor was abundant and capital was also available, as was true for parts of Europe and Japan, conflicts between the two were inevitable.[81] The strong state machinery in these countries was better able to control these conflicts than was the case in other states, and thus industrialization was further facilitated. The governments were also able to aid (and mollify) those domestic groups that were adversely affected by foreign competition or unfavorable international economic circumstances.

France has been one of the European countries with a long tradition of state involvement in the economy, going back to the days of Colbert, and it has also been one of the countries noted for utilizing protectionist mechanisms.[82] The French statist tradition, in fact, has provided great autonomy at the implementation stage, at which point protection for interests threatened by imports has been provided.[83] Red tape has also been used to keep imports at lower levels.[84] Within the framework of the EC rules, however, there has generally been little autonomy at the implementation stage, disadvantaging French interest groups.[85] French policy toward the EC in its early years reflected this protectionist trend. The French policy was a combination of both protectionist and free market concerns. Governments sought market advantages where possible while seeking to avoid subjecting domestic sectors to overly severe import competition from elsewhere in the EC.[86] The French desire to continue to subsidize and protect French farmers clearly prolonged the negotiations in the

Uruguay Round and delayed the final agreement that led to the new WTO. Within the EC/EU, France, as well as Italy to a lesser extent, has generally been seen as a country favoring more restrictions on trade. The United Kingdom, Germany, the Netherlands, and Denmark have clearly favored fewer restrictions on imports.[87]

Both Germany and Italy also have traditions of state intervention. Italy's statism goes back to the period in which the state was critically important for unification under the House of Savoy. Then, during the Fascist period, the state was heavily involved in the economy. More recently, Italy has been more supportive of protectionism than most EC members. Germany also has had a statist tradition going back to industrialization under the Prussian administration. This trend continued after unification, and may have been best exemplified by the "Marriage of Iron and Rye" under Bismarck protecting both industry and farmers. Pressure from constituency interests on parliamentary deputies and class factors were partially responsible for the resulting political and economic alliance between farmers and the industrial sector.[88] Interestingly enough, this example of a union of political convenience was not one that would be consistent with factor endowment theories.[89] This strong state tradition continued under the Nazi regime, especially the use of trade policy as an integral part of domestic economic policy and foreign policy.[90] Under the Federal Republic there has been a continuing capacity for managing foreign trade that has drawn on this tradition.[91] Even though Germany has often been seen as supportive of freer trade, the country has had much to gain from trade liberalization (much like the situation of the United States after World War II or Great Britain in the nineteenth century).

The United Kingdom, unlike the other large European countries on the continent, has not had a tradition of state intervention in the economy. The United Kingdom was rather a supporter of free trade, in part because it benefited from such trade as the first industrialized nation. As the leading economic power in the nineteenth century, it even supported global liberalization, of course under British leadership.[92] Notwithstanding this tradition of supporting free trade, the United Kingdom, like the United States, has favored selective protection at times,[93] and there are domestic groups that have pressed for greater protection against imports in order to preserve what are seen to be important economic sectors.[94]

The smaller European countries have usually been less protectionist in their attitudes for a variety of reasons. Some, like the Netherlands, have had merchant traditions similar to the United Kingdom—traditions that have emphasized smaller rather than larger roles for government. These smaller states have also generally been more integrated into the global economy due to their size and, consequently, more dependent on international trade. They have also clearly benefited from the increased market access that came with liberalization of international exchange. Many of these countries also have corporatist styles of decision making for economic and social policies that have avoided protectionist policies. Coordination and cooperation among manufacturers, labor, and the government have permitted governments to rely on policies other than protection when faced with economic problems due to increasing competition or lessened demand.[95] Adjustment assistance or subsidies have been utilized to deal with the problems arising from trade rather than creating barriers to imports.[96]

The EC/EU as a supranational organization has also been a more recent actor in the international trade system. While the member states can and do implement restrictive policies on imports, they have also worked through the EC/EU to affect trade policy. The creation and successive enlargements of the organization have had the usual effects of trade diversion and trade creation, admittedly with the trade creation effects being greater than the ones occurring from diversion,[97] except in the area of agricultural trade. Even so, non-member countries have suffered in terms of lessened market access for some types of products. When the EC was created, the external tariff was the arithmetic mean for the member states, which actually meant higher tariffs in many cases since West Germany, the largest market, had previously had the lowest rates. With the common tariff the West German market was less accessible to non-member producers. East European producers, heavily dependent on the West German markets, in particular suffered declines in the competitiveness of their exports.[98] The early expansions of the EC had a negative effect on imports of products from developing countries,[99] while the accession of Spain and Portugal negatively affected exports of some manufactured good by producers in Asia.[100] The new members of the EC/EU have also contained some threatened domestic sectors, and these members preferred to limit competition to producers in the other EC states and to exclude producers in non-members from effective access to the common market. As a consequence, expansion can lead and has led to the creation of new barriers to firms outside the customs area in order to compensate firms of the existing members or new members for the increasing competition they had to face as a result of the enlargement.[101]

The EC/EU has also developed an extensive system of arrangements and preferences with other countries. There have been or are preferences for the European Free Trade Association (EFTA) states, the Africa-

Caribbean-Pacific (ACP) countries—which include most of the former colonies of the EC/EU members, the countries bordering the Mediterranean, and some of the former Communist countries. These preferential arrangements have been ultimately effective, of course, only if they discriminated against other producers.[102] In fact, there has been such an extensive group of arrangements that it has become much easier to identify those countries for which the EC/EU has not had or does not have special relationships.[103] The Common Agricultural Policy (CAP) of the EC has clearly protected European farmers from import competition and subsidized export sales to the rest of the world, at the expense of producers in other countries.[104] In 1990, the CAP cost European consumers over $50 billion.[105] Protection has also been supplied through EC/EU mechanisms for manufactured goods, and non-tariff barriers to imports have been used.[106] Antidumping measures in the EC have been used in the same way as in the United States. Procedures favor the complainant, and even when the foreign producer wins, there still have been periods of uncertainty and delays present in the development of a market for the goods in question.[107] EC antisubsidy practices would appear to be similar in that a protectionist bias has existed.[108] EC/EU commercial policy has often been of the lowest common denominator type, reflecting the minimum of liberalization that was acceptable to all the members or acceptable to those members most interested in protection of some domestic sector.[109] Given the presence of important statist countries such as France, Italy, and even Germany, in the EC, it has not been surprising that policies have been less liberal than they otherwise could have been. The EC has even managed to constrain Dutch tendencies toward liberalism in the 1960s and later.[110] The EC/EU has provided a useful facade for those of its members that wish to appear as supporters of freer trade rather than managed trade. While Germany may have avoided pushing its free trade views in order to avoid alienating its European partners,[111] it has been suggested that Germany actually used the EC/EU to strike protectionist deals with the other members while maintaining the illusion of being committed to freer trade.[112] In fact, the EC/EU has been seen as one example of how a trade area could be manipulated by protectionist interests into providing defensive barriers against import competition.[113]

Other Countries

Among the other larger industrialized countries, Canada and Australia both have protected their domestic markets in the past. Infant industries were created and protected in both countries by tariffs and distance from the major production centers in Europe.[114] Canada built up its manufacturing sector behind import barriers and has continued to provide protection in some areas, such as the clothing and textile sector where it has participated in the MFA.[115] Australia has had a long statist tradition.[116] Consequently, it is not surprising that Australia had especially high and costly protection for domestic production for a long time, even though it did lead to the creation of an indigenous industrial capacity.[117] The formation of the federation from among the separate Australian colonies actually increased protection in the continent since the federation largely adopted the tariff schedule of the more protectionist colonies rather than the lower barriers of the more open ones—[118] another example of a lowest-common-denominator compromise in the area of trade policy similar to the common external tariff in the EC. Political unification and economic unification thus led to increases in protection. Notwithstanding the physical proximity of Australia to the Asian NICs, Australia has not been a particularly good market for the manufactured goods that have been exported from those countries.[119] More recently, domestic Australian opinion has moved toward the view that protection has failed and support for greater openness has been apparent.[120] Still, Australia has been one of the major users of contingent protective devices such as antidumping hearings and subsidy allegations,[121] indicating that protective impulses may still persist, even if in a different form. Nearby New Zealand has also gone through a period of high protection that carried into the 1970s.[122] This protectionism in New Zealand, plus the agricultural protection in the EC that included the loss of the markets in the United Kingdom after its accession, combined to undercut New Zealand's prosperity in the 1970s.[123] New Zealand, however, has reversed this trend with liberalization that began in 1984.[124] By 1999 New Zealand had become one of the world's most open economies, with no subsidies and few tariffs.[125]

The protectionist practices of the developed countries have been copied by the developing countries. The Asian NICs industrialized through a combination of export promotion and the protection of infant industries.[126] In a broader sense they followed a statist pattern of trade policy similar in outline to that of some of the developed states. Other developing countries have followed import substitution industrialization for those product areas in which the domestic market was large enough.[127] While such policies have often been unsuccessful, they are another example of the presence of protection. Other developing states have applied protection, even if not part of a larger import substitution policy or as part of a statist pattern. The developing countries have even begun to adopt contingent protectionist practices patterned on the ones created in the industrialized countries.[128]

The prevalence of protection among developed and developing countries has also led to continuing debates over "fair trade" and level playing fields. The increasing use of contingent protection, especially by the EU, the United States, and Australia, has been justified on the basis of the necessity of counteracting the practices of other states. It has been extremely difficult to measure the effects of such contingent protection since oftentimes these barriers discourage imports that otherwise would have occurred, and it is difficult to determine what the actual level of imports would have been sans the protection. The Super 301 provision in the United States has had a similar rationale, designed to serve as a corrective to unfair, mercantilist trade practices of other states. It has been very clear that protection does breed protection, just as tariff increases in the past led to tariff increases elsewhere and ultimately to tariff wars. While unfair trade practices have indeed been used by other governments, the use of contingent protection and unfair trade counteractions have been utilized at least part of the time to provide protection for domestic industries. Dumping policies have generally been directed toward objectives other than the prevention of dumping,[129] such as protection of threatened domestic industries. The fact that dumping allegations often lead to VERs and other negotiated settlements between foreign and domestic producers indicates the real goal of such actions—i.e., to limit imports to a level "acceptable" to threatened domestic interests.

Summary

Ultimately the presence of protectionist practices in countries around the world affects the level of imports into those countries. Population size, wealth, customs union membership, and perhaps especially protection would appear to be much more important influences on imports than relative factor endowments and comparative advantage, at least in the area of complex manufactured goods. Countries that have not protected their domestic producers in at least some sectors have been extremely rare; in effect, virtually all countries have used protection in some form. The real question has been the extent of such protection and its effectiveness rather than its presence or absence. The key, therefore, becomes the relative level of protection (revealed protection, if you will) that has been present in individual countries—how protectionist a country is compared to similar countries. It could also be important to determine how effective countries have been in the application of similar protectionist policies. All other things being equal, the more effective administration of protectionist policies would have impeded imports more than inefficient or less effective applications of those devices.

Factor endowments, of course, explain some elements of trade and of imports. Similarly, country size has been a factor. Larger countries, all things being equal, would have imported less per capita. Relative wealth also would have come into play. All other things being equal, richer countries would have imported more per capita than not-so-rich nations. One final influence on import levels to be considered in the following chapters is membership in customs unions and free trade areas. While such trade groupings may have led to different levels of trade diversion or trade creation, they almost always have led to increases in trade. Even if these increases occurred solely among the members of the trade area, higher levels of imports would still have been present. Of course, to the extent that these trade areas led to trade diversion, increases in trade would have been correspondingly less. The greater the amount of trade creation among the members, the greater the effects of the free trade area or the customs union on import levels. Analyses of the actual levels of imports with controls for wealth, size, and membership in important customs unions permit a better determination of the actual effects that protective practices have had on trade, or at least a determination of the effectiveness of the protection that was being provided.

Chapter 3

Imports of the Industrialized Countries: Influences of Wealth and Size

The previous chapter discussed some of the factors that might have been important influences on the import levels of the industrialized countries. The present chapter provides a broad survey of the overall import levels for twenty-three industrialized nations. The general effects that size and wealth could have had on the propensities to import are determined. Isolating the effects of wealth and size on per capita import levels is important in order to have some indication of the influences that overall government policies could have had on import levels. Such controls are essential for determining levels of revealed protection present in different countries. Failure to control for such variables would make it extremely difficult to have any idea of the effects of such government action.

Countries Included

The industrialized countries chosen for the analyses in this and the following chapters included virtually all the free market industrialized countries of any size in the world. The United States and Canada from North America, Japan, and Australia and New Zealand from Oceania were the major non-European industrialized countries included. They ranged in size from the small to the two most populous countries of the world. European countries that were included were the United Kingdom, France, West Germany (and then the reunified Germany after 1990), Italy, Belgium/Luxembourg,[1] the Netherlands, Denmark, Norway, Sweden, Finland, Switzerland, Ireland, and Austria. These eighteen countries have been considered developed nations for at least most of the years since World War II, and they have constituted important markets for imports in the aggregate and in some cases individually. These nations have been important markets because of their wealth if not necessarily because of their size in all cases. Even though some of them are not large, their wealth makes them at least modestly important markets due to the purchasing capacity that their smaller populations have. In addition, Spain, Portugal, Israel, Greece, and Yugoslavia (Slovenia instead of Yugoslavia for the most recent years) were included as examples of European states at lesser stages of development.[2] These countries at a different level of industrialization could have had different import patterns, either in the aggregate or for some particular kinds of imports. As a consequence, they constituted a useful addition to the countries chosen for analysis.

This set of 23 countries also included all the states considered to be developed free market economies by the United Nations for trade reporting purposes, with the exceptions of Iceland, the various mini-states in Europe that are not connected by custom union ties with their larger neighbors, and South Africa (sometimes considered developed, but it would have been a rather anomalous inclusion as an industrialized country with the others). The industrialized, centrally planned economies of Eastern Europe (the former East Germany and Czechoslovakia in particular) would have been potentially useful additions to any analysis of import markets, but comparable trade and economic statistics have not been consistently available for these countries. While trade of these nations with the free market economies was usually expressed in terms of dollars and thus import levels had a comparable meaning with other import figures, intra-bloc trade among the Communist countries themselves was usually expressed in local currencies. These currencies inevitably had arbitrary exchange rates with each other, making meaningful calculations of imports values for comparisons with imports of other industrialized countries difficult at best. Trade was often on a barter basis as well, and bilateral clearing arrangements were also frequently used. For all these reasons the trade figures for countries in this region for the most part were not comparable with import figures for other nations. There were also completely different methods for national accounting that made comparisons of other economic statistics between free market and centrally planned economies difficult, if not impossible. With the end of the Cold War and the demise of central planning in the region, these countries will be available for inclusion as subjects for analysis in the future with other countries. In some respects, they would perhaps be most similar to some of the NICs or near-NICs elsewhere in the world.

Data

A variety of types of import data were utilized in the chapters to follow. The specific trade data and other data utilized in the different analyses will be fully discussed at the points where they will be used. There were however, four key sets of data that were used in all the analyses in the different chapters. These four sets of data were population, wealth, the total value of imports, and values for imports of particular kinds of manufactured products.

Population estimates were taken from various World Bank sources.[3] These figures were generally mid-year estimates of total population for the countries that were included in the analyses. The measure of wealth was taken from the same sources. Wealth was measured with per capita GNP figures for each of the countries for particular years. There have always been some difficulties with GNP per capita figures as totally accurate measures of wealth. Such figures do not include subsistence activities or take into account the cost of living in different societies.[4] As a consequence, GNP per capita figures can be most misleading when comparing developed and developing states, but they have been reasonably good indicators of the *relative* wealth of different industrialized countries and can usefully be used for comparison purposes among these countries.

Trade figures were taken from the *Yearbook of International Trade Statistics*,[5] which had comprehensive import data both by country and product category. The compiled data with reasonably comprehensive coverage has usually become available for use three to four years after the calendar year in which the trade occurred (i.e., data for 1995 would be available for analysis by 1998 or 1999). The developing countries have usually been consistently less current in collecting or reporting such data than has been the case for the industrialized states.

The definition of manufactures established by the United Nations in its products and commodity codes was used with one exception. For trade reporting the United Nations had utilized the Standard Industrial Trade Classification (SITC) system for defining products.[6] Four of these categories, which are one-digit SITC codes in the UN classification, have been considered to consist of manufactured goods. SITC 5 has encompassed a variety of chemical goods, including chemical compounds, perfumes, and soaps. SITC 6 has consisted of primary manufactured goods. Two- and three-digit levels of this category have been organized by the basic materials (wood, rubber, cloth, minerals, etc), much of which has gone into the production of other manufactured goods. Such semimanufactures involve the partial processing of basic materials. Wood is transformed into plywood; iron ore becomes pig iron; cloth is material for apparel. Some of the products in this one-digit SITC group have been finished goods, such as specialty steel alloys, cork board, or carpets. SITC 7 has included transport equipment, electrical machinery, and non-electrical machinery. It has been the most important category of manufactures in terms of the overall value of global imports as well as for most of the countries of the world. This SITC group also has contained most of the more sophisticated or complex manufactured products, including the capital machinery that has been necessary for the production of other manufactured goods. SITC 8 consisted of those miscellaneous manufactured goods not readily subsumed within the other categories. The products in question have not had a principal material base. In some cases the items included have been more complex ones, such as medical instruments and some electronic products. Many of these items, such as clothing, footwear, and toys, have had important export potential for the nations of the developing world. These goods have also frequently been labor-intensive products that have not usually required high-technology inputs. As noted, there was one exclusion from the UN definition of manufactured goods that was made for the analyses to follow. SITC 68, which included semi-processed mineral ores that have been transformed into bars or ingots or similar forms before being exported, was excluded. The World Bank in its publications[7] has excluded these products from the category of manufactured products, a practice that was followed for the analyses in this volume. The processing involved in transforming such mineral ores would not necessarily have been indicative of an underlying industrialized sector or the presence of significant manufacturing skills. Such imports inevitably undergo more processing in the importing country before they are used in manufacturing processes that lead to final products.[8] While some definitions of manufactures include SITC 68 and processed food, beverages, cigarettes, and petroleum products,[9] these categories were not included in part because of their rather basic processing and also because data was not always available in these categories.

Preliminary Analyses

In order to have some idea of the relative import propensities of industrialized countries, an index for import levels was constructed for the overall import levels of the twenty-three countries as well as for their im-

ports of manufactured goods as defined above. The indices were derived
for 1960, 1970, 1980, and 1990 to provide an indication of trends and
broad changes that were occurring over time—changes that might reflect
both changing policies within individual countries or changing conditions in the global economy. The index that was constructed took into account the effects of relative wealth (GNP per capita) on the level of
imports per capita or imports of manufactured products per capita. The
per capita levels of imports were then multiplied by \$10,000/GNP per
capita. The use of the standard figure of \$10,000 provided a control for
the greater import potential of richer countries. It also facilitated comparisons across the different time periods. Dividing by the \$10,000 figure
"inflated" the import figures for less wealthy nations while "deflating" the

Table 3-1
Import Indices, 1960

Country	Population (mil)	GNP/ Capita	GNP (bil)	Import/ Capita (000)	% Manu- factures	Index Imports	Index Manufac- tures
Japan	94.1	\$ 458	\$ 43.1	.05	.18	1.07	.19
United States	180.7	2830	511.4	.08	.37	.30	.11
Canada	17.9	2195	39.3	.31	.67	1.43	.96
Australia	10.3	1446	14.9	.20	.68	1.39	.94
New Zealand	2.4	1530	3.7	.33	.62	2.15	1.32
W Germany	55.4	1303	72.2	.18	.33	1.41	.46
France	45.7	1337	61.1	.14	.27	1.03	.28
Italy	50.2	696	34.9	.09	.29	1.35	.39
Netherlands	11.5	978	11.2	.39	.48	4.00	1.92
Belgium/ Luxembourg	9.2	1242	11.4	.43	.47	3.50	1.63
United Kingdom	52.4	1347	72.0	.25	.25	1.80	.45
Ireland	2.8	659	1.8	.23	.57	3.44	1.95
Switzerland	5.4	1597	8.6	.41	.53	2.55	1.35
Austria	7.0	897	6.3	.20	.57	2.17	1.24
Denmark	4.6	1295	6.0	.39	.52	3.04	1.57
Norway	3.6	1258	4.5	.41	.76	3.23	2.46
Sweden	7.5	1836	13.8	.39	.53	2.11	1.12
Finland	4.4	1123	4.9	.24	.57	2.15	1.23
Spain	30.3	341	10.3	.03	.37	.80	.30
Portugal	8.9	288	2.6	.06	.42	2.25	.94
Greece	8.3	427	3.5	.08	.61	1.98	1.21
Yugoslavia	18.4	137	2.5	.02	.59	1.72	1.02
Israel	2.1	1192	2.5	.23	.55	1.98	1.09

Index = \$10,000/GNP per capita x imports or manufactured imports per capita (000) figures for the richer ones. It inflated figures for earlier time periods (when dollars bought much more) and deflated the figures for later years.

A number of basic facts were clear if the figures for 1960 are looked at. The larger countries had in fact imported relatively less than the smaller nations when wealth was factored in through the form of the index (see Table 3–1). The United States was the overall smallest per capita importer. Japan was a less active importer as well. Australia imported less than New Zealand. Of the original EC members, France, Italy, and West Germany obviously imported less than Belgium and the Netherlands. Among the five less industrialized countries of the Mediterranean, the index for Spain was far below the indices for the other four. Size, however, was still not a perfect predictor of import levels. For example, less populous France had a lower index than West Germany, Italy, or the United Kingdom. Even for a year when the Common Market had just been formed, France would appear to have had a smaller propensity to import than West Germany or Italy or even the United Kingdom, which was not yet a member. The indices for manufactured imports were similar to those of overall imports for the most part. It was obvious that Japan was a smaller importer of manufactured goods than had been the case with overall imports. The larger European countries also imported at relatively lower per capita levels of manufactured goods than their smaller counterparts. Ireland, Norway, and the Netherlands had the largest indices for overall imports of goods and imports of manufactures, confirming to at least some extent that there was a tendency for the smaller European states to be active traders.

The same general patterns that were present in 1960 also held for 1970 (see Table 3–2). Larger countries continued to import at relatively lower levels than smaller ones. Japan and the United States had the lowest index numbers, and the larger European countries continued to have relatively low numbers for overall import propensities. While the index number for Spain remained lower than the figures for many of the other countries, the 1970 figure did represent a significant increase over the figures for 1960. Portugal also increased in terms of its relative level of imports by a substantial amount. A number of countries had experienced declines in their overall import indices, suggesting that income growth had outpaced the growth in total imports. Index levels for manufactured goods, however, increased for every country but Norway, and even Norway had a high level compared to many other countries. These indices clearly indicated that trade in manufactured goods had become increasingly important. The smaller European countries, especially Belgium, the

Netherlands, and Ireland, again had the highest indices for these goods. Japan and the United States had the same index number for manufactured imports despite their differences in population, suggesting that Japanese imports of manufactured goods were declining relative to the other industrialized countries, that U.S. imports were exceptionally high with a large population, or that a combination of the two influences was in effect.

Between 1970 and 1980 the import indices for all the countries increased at least marginally, and sometimes substantially, while the manufactured import indices increased in 22 cases with a marginal decline for Portugal being the only exception (see Table 3–3). Clearly, the expansion of trade had affected the import levels for all the developed world in

Table 3-2
Import Indices, 1970

Country	Population (mil)	GNP/ Capita	GNP (bil)	Import/ Capita (000)	% Manu- factures	Index Imports	Index Manufac- tures
Japan	104.3	$ 1890	$ 197.2	.18	.24	.96	.23
United States	204.9	4901	1004.1	.20	.59	.39	.23
Canada	21.3	3651	77.8	.62	.76	1.70	1.30
Australia	12.5	2627	32.8	.36	.79	1.36	1.08
New Zealand	2.8	2179	6.1	.44	.68	2.04	1.38
W Germany	61.6	3043	187.4	.48	.49	1.59	.78
France	50.8	2870	145.7	.37	.51	1.30	.67
Italy	53.6	1740	93.2	.28	.40	1.61	.64
Netherlands	13.0	2456	32.0	1.03	.59	3.69	2.47
Belgium/ Luxembourg	9.7	2678	26.0	1.18	.55	4.39	2.43
United Kingdom	55.4	2201	122.0	.39	.43	1.78	.76
Ireland	2.9	1354	4.0	.54	.67	3.99	2.66
Switzerland	6.2	3343	20.7	1.05	.66	3.13	2.07
Austria	7.4	1932	14.3	.48	.66	2.48	1.63
Denmark	4.9	3182	15.7	.89	.63	2.81	1.76
Norway	3.9	2926	11.4	.95	.65	3.25	2.10
Sweden	8.0	4087	32.9	.88	.62	2.14	1.33
Finland	4.6	2231	10.3	.57	.62	3.46	1.59
Spain	33.6	960	32.8	.14	.47	1.46	.68
Portugal	8.6	786	6.8	.29	.59	3.62	2.14
Greece	8.8	1114	9.8	.22	.68	2.00	1.36
Yugoslavia	20.4	702	14.3	.16	.62	2.27	1.40
Israel	2.9	1906	5.5	.50	.64	2.62	1.69

Index = $10,000/GNP per capita x imports or manufactured imports per capita (000)

these ten years. The indices for the United States were noticeably higher, and U.S. imports of manufactured goods were now higher than those for Japan. The larger European countries continued to import at lower per capita levels than the smaller ones, and New Zealand continued to be a more active importer than Australia. The United Kingdom was relatively more open to imports than France, West Germany, or Italy among the larger states. These differences were present even though the three continental countries were established members of the EC while the United Kingdom was a former member of EFTA and a new EC member. The EC, as a complete customs union, should have stimulated trade more than a free trade area. Further, established membership would have meant that these trade-creating and trade-diverting influences would have been

Table 3-3
Import Indices, 1980

Country	Population (mil)	GNP/ Capita	GNP (bil)	Import/ Capita (000)	% Manu- factures	Index Imports	Index Manufac- tures
Japan	116.8	$ 9890	$ 1155.2	1.20	.23	1.22	.28
United States	227.7	11360	2586.7	1.12	.54	.98	.53
Canada	23.9	10130	242.1	2.45	.65	2.42	1.57
Australia	14.5	9820	142.4	1.40	.79	1.43	1.13
New Zealand	3.3	7090	23.4	1.66	.72	2.25	1.69
W Germany	60.9	13590	827.6	3.09	.57	2.28	1.30
France	53.5	11730	627.6	2.52	.57	2.14	1.22
Italy	56.9	6480	368.7	1.74	.45	2.69	1.21
Netherlands	14.1	11470	119.4	5.45	.58	4.76	2.76
Belgium/ Luxembourg	9.8	12180	161.7	7.26	.64	5.95	3.81
United Kingdom	55.9	7920	442.7	2.15	.63	2.68	1.69
Ireland	3.3	4880	16.1	3.38	.71	6.93	4.92
Switzerland	6.5	16440	106.9	5.59	.73	3.41	2.49
Austria	7.5	10230	76.7	3.27	.72	3.19	2.30
Denmark	5.1	12950	66.0	3.80	.61	2.93	1.79
Norway	4.1	12650	51.9	4.14	.70	3.27	2.29
Sweden	8.3	13520	112.2	4.03	.63	2.98	1.88
Finland	4.9	9720	47.6	3.18	.58	3.28	1.90
Spain	37.4	5400	202.0	.91	.42	1.69	.71
Portugal	9.8	2370	23.2	.96	.52	4.06	2.11
Greece	9.6	4380	42.0	1.10	.62	2.00	1.56
Yugoslavia	22.3	2620	58.4	.63	.66	2.39	1.58
Israel	3.9	4500	17.6	2.03	.64	4.52	2.89

Index = $10,000/GNP per capita x imports or manufactured imports per capita (000)

operative over a longer period of time. The differences in the indices would indicate that the British free trade tradition may still have been having an influence on government policies in terms of leading the United Kingdom to establish fewer barriers against imports. Among the smaller countries, Belgium and Ireland continued to have especially high index numbers. The index numbers for Spain, the largest industrializing economy in the Mediterranean area, indicated that it still was importing at lower per capita levels than the other countries with similar industrial structures. Israel appeared for the first time to be a very active importer in the Mediterranean region.

Table 3-4
Import Indices, 1990

Country	Population (mil)	GNP/ Capita	GNP (bil)	Import/ Capita (000)	% Manu- factures	Index Imports	Index Manufac- tures
Japan	123.5	$25430	$ 3140.6	1.87	.43	.74	.31
United States	250.0	21790	5447.5	2.06	.73	.95	.68
Canada	26.5	20470	542.5	4.37	.80	2.13	1.70
Australia	17.1	17000	290.7	2.32	.79	1.36	1.08
New Zealand	3.4	12680	43.1	2.78	.80	2.19	1.75
W Germany	62.0	22720	1408.6	5.50	.72	2.42	1.73
France	56.4	19490	1099.2	4.12	.74	2.11	1.56
Italy	57.7	16830	971.1	3.05	.63	1.81	1.14
Netherlands	14.9	17320	258.1	8.45	.71	4.88	3.44
Belgium/ Luxembourg	10.0	15540	155.0	9.82	.82	7.70	6.32
United Kingdom	57.4	16100	924.1	3.92	.75	2.43	1.84
Ireland	3.5	9550	33.4	5.92	.76	6.20	4.71
Switzerland	6.7	32680	219.0	10.36	.83	3.17	2.63
Austria	7.7	19060	146.8	6.49	.81	3.40	2.77
Denmark	5.1	22080	112.6	6.19	.73	2.80	2.05
Norway	4.2	23120	97.1	6.40	.80	2.77	2.20
Sweden	8.6	23660	203.5	6.34	.78	2.68	2.10
Finland	5.0	26040	130.2	5.42	.76	2.08	1.58
Spain	39.0	11020	429.8	2.24	.70	2.03	1.43
Portugal	10.4	4900	51.0	2.44	.71	4.98	3.55
Greece	10.1	5990	60.5	1.95	.71	3.26	2.32
Yugoslavia	23.8	3060	72.8	.80	.62	2.61	1.62
Israel	4.7	10920	51.3	3.23	.76	2.96	2.25

Index = $10,000/GNP per capita x imports or manufactured imports per capita (000)

In 1990 the patterns were similar in some respects. Larger countries had lower indices, but size now appeared to be less of a determining factor. Compared to Japan, the United States now had higher index levels, not only for manufactured goods but for overall import levels as well (see Table 3–4). After Japan, Australia had relatively low indices given the population size of the country. Spanish index numbers were still lower than those of the other Mediterranean economies as expected. The smaller countries generally continued to have high propensities to import, with Belgium and Ireland again leading the way. GNP per capita had generally doubled between 1980 and 1990, which would have accounted for some of the declines in the indices for some countries—they were importing much more, but deflating for wealth meant they were importing less in a relative sense. Among the countries included, Israel's import indices had clearly declined, probably more so than would be explained solely by the increase in wealth levels. Of course, this time period was one in which the trouble in

Table 3-5
Longitudinal Comparison of Import Indices

Country	All Imports				Manufactured Imports			
	1960	1970	1980	1990	1960	1970	1980	1990
Japan	1.06	.96	1.22	.74	.19	.23	.28	.31
United States	.30	.39	.98	.95	.11	.23	.53	.68
Canada	1.43	1.70	2.42	2.13	.96	1.30	1.57	1.70
Australia	1.39	1.36	1.43	1.36	.94	1.08	1.13	1.08
New Zealand	2.15	2.04	2.25	2.19	1.32	1.38	1.69	1.75
W Germany	1.41	1.59	2.28	2.42	.46	.78	1.30	1.73
France	1.03	1.30	2.14	2.11	.28	.67	1.22	1.56
Italy	1.35	1.61	2.69	1.81	.39	.64	1.21	1.14
Netherlands	4.00	3.69	4.76	4.88	1.92	2.47	2.76	3.44
Belgium/Luxembourg	3.50	4.39	5.95	7.70	1.63	2.43	3.81	6.32
United Kingdom	1.80	1.78	2.68	2.43	.45	.76	1.69	1.84
Ireland	3.44	3.99	6.93	6.20	1.95	2.66	4.92	4.71
Switzerland	2.55	3.13	3.41	3.17	1.35	2.07	2.49	2.63
Austria	2.17	2.48	3.19	3.40	1.24	1.63	2.30	2.77
Denmark	3.04	2.81	2.93	2.80	1.57	1.76	1.79	2.05
Norway	3.23	3.25	3.27	2.77	2.46	2.10	2.29	2.20
Sweden	2.11	2.14	2.98	2.68	1.12	1.33	1.88	2.10
Finland	2.15	3.46	3.28	2.08	1.23	1.59	1.90	1.58
Spain	.80	1.46	1.69	2.03	.30	.68	.71	1.43
Portugal	2.25	3.62	4.06	4.98	.94	2.14	2.11	3.55
Greece	1.98	2.00	2.52	3.26	1.21	1.36	1.56	2.32
Yugoslavia	1.72	2.27	2.39	2.61	1.02	1.40	1.58	1.62
Israel	1.98	2.62	4.52	2.96	1.09	1.69	2.89	2.25

the occupied territories populated by Palestinians began to peak, a situation bound to have had major implications for economic conditions, including trade policy.

A comparison of the indices over time for the twenty-three countries revealed some other trends and patterns. Between 1960 and 1980 overall imports per capita increased, even when the level of increasing wealth was factored into account (see Table 3–5). Between 1980 and 1990, however, there were clear declines in the relative import levels for many countries and marginal declines for a few others such as the United States and France. A number of countries, however, did become more active importers over this time period, contrary to the trend. The indices for manufactured imports, on the other hand, increased for most of the countries, though not all of them. Thus, for many countries overall imports had not kept pace with increases in per capita income over this 20-year period, but imports of manufactured goods had. Such results would be in keeping with the general view that in developed nations the income elasticity for raw materials (including food) has been much less than it has been for manufactured goods.

The patterns over time also indicated that population size was indeed a relevant factor for import levels. All other things being equal (wealth, region of the world), a smaller country imported more than a larger one. The size effects were not perfect. By 1990, smaller Japan was importing at relatively lower levels than was the case for the much larger United States. The smaller Scandinavian countries had not been keeping pace with Belgium or the Netherlands, which had larger populations. Further, even among the Scandinavian countries themselves, differences were not totally related to size. Norway and Denmark had index numbers that were similar to Sweden, which had twice the population. Obviously, other factors were influencing import levels, and government policies towards imports would be one important additional variable that would help to explain relative import levels.

Summary

Clearly, the initial analyses undertaken above indicated that market size as measured by population was important for import levels. In addition, market size as measured by relative wealth also appeared to be important. The effects of EC/EU membership were less clear, but Belgium and the Netherlands were among the original members of the EC, while Ireland was one of the later additions, and these three countries had been extremely active as importers. The other smaller European countries were relatively less active. Further, while the index numbers for Germany, France, and Italy were not especially high, they were larger than some of the indices for a few of the smaller non-European nations that were used. The figures in Table 3–5 also indicated that imports of manufactures increased quite rapidly for the large EC countries, Belgium, Ireland, and the United Kingdom. From 1960 to 1990 there was an increase in the indices. Per capita incomes were increasing, but since the indices took into account greater wealth, it was clear that trade was expanding even faster than the standards of living were rising. Even in those instances in which the indices had declined over a ten year period, it was a relative decline rather than an absolute one, and the general trend was still one of increasing imports.

It was also clear that patterns for some of the countries changed over time. Some nations became relatively more active as importers while other nations became less active compared to the others. There were also differences between the indices for overall imports and those for imports of manufactured goods. Some of differences would have been related to different elasticities for raw materials versus manufactured products. In addition, the value of manufactured goods and raw materials in the import mix would have been sensitive to the price of petroleum and the amount of petroleum products in the import mix of the countries in different years,[10] and differential uses of domestic energy sources (including the development of the North Sea oil fields). Still, there was a clear overall temporal trend in which manufactures were of increasing importance in the imports of the industrialized countries.

Given these findings, the next chapter will consider overall import levels for the 23 industrialized countries, controlling for the potential effects of wealth, population size, and membership in free trade areas. While there were clearly differences between overall trade and trade in manufactures as represented by imports (and by implication trade in raw materials), an analysis of overall trade patterns will provide a basis for comparisons with the analyses for particular types of imports that were being conducted in subsequent chapters.

Chapter 4

Overall Import Levels of the Industrialized Countries

The preliminary analyses in chapter 3 indicated that population size and wealth indeed had a clear influence on overall levels of imports as expected, but additionally there were other factors present since the relationships were only partial ones. In order to determine the relative openness of the industrialized countries to imports, the actual levels of imported goods per capita were used, controlling for population size, wealth, membership in the EC/EU, and membership in EFTA. Analyses of actual per capita import levels with these controls provided some indications of what the effects of government policies in different countries had been. There were also changes over time as well.

Methodology

The 23 industrialized countries continued to be the data set for analysis. The set of years used was more comprehensive than the set used in the preceding chapter. The analyses relied on data points for 1960, 1965, 1970, 1973, 1976, 1980, 1982, 1984, 1986, 1988, 1990, 1992, and 1994—13 years in all. Since the unified Yugoslavia had disintegrated by 1990, there was no data available after that year. Nor were trade data available for rump Yugoslavia in subsequent years; therefore, Slovenia was substituted for 1992 and 1994. Slovenia is in the far north of old Yugoslavia, so it has been distant from the problems that have plagued Croatia, Bosnia, Serbia, and Kosovo. In addition, the necessary trade data and other data became available for Slovenia beginning in 1992. Compared to the old Yugoslavia,

Slovenia was a country that was more industrialized. It included some of the richest, most developed, and industrialized areas of the old Yugoslavia. For 1992 and 1994 it was the smallest country in terms of population that was included in the analyses.

Since it was necessary to control for the trade-enhancing effects of smaller size, wealth, and membership in trade areas, multiple regression was chosen as the analytic technique that would be most appropriate. Imports per capita served as the dependent variable in the regression equations, while there were four independent variables—population, wealth, number of years of EC/EU membership, and number of years of EFTA membership. Any part of a year in which a country was a member of either trade area was counted as one year for the purposes of measurement. Finland joined EFTA in 1961 as an associate member, preferring not to seek full membership to avoid antagonizing the Soviet Union. Given its generally full participation within EFTA, it was coded as a full member in that year and all subsequent ones. Ireland never became a member of EFTA, but it signed a free trade agreement with the United Kingdom in 1965. Irish trade was very heavily concentrated with the United Kingdom (then and now); thus, this arrangement linked the Irish economy more closely with its dominant trade partner, which was a member of EFTA, and increased Irish contacts with EFTA. (The fact that Ireland joined the EC at the same time as the United Kingdom is another indication of the close economic links between the two countries.) As a consequence, Ireland effectively became part of the EFTA grouping with the free trade agreement, and it was considered a de facto member of EFTA from 1965 on.

Multiple regression was also able to control to some extent the interactive effects of population and per capita GNP combining to create a relatively larger or smaller market for domestic and foreign producers. Other analyses of trade and imports have also taken size into account, but they have generally utilized measures such as total GNP or total GDP or even population.[1] Controlling for size in this fashion would have been counterproductive since it would have equated a country of 10 million people having a GNP per capita of $10,000 with a country of 100 million having a GNP per capita of $1,000. The types of imports and the amount of imports per capita would be very dissimilar for these two countries. All other things being equal, the larger and poorer country would import less in total and per capita than the smaller, richer one.[2] There would also obviously be significant differences in the types of goods that would be imported by richer and poorer countries. As a consequence, population size and per capita wealth were entered into the regression equations separately.[3]

Multiple regression was an ideal analytic tool, not only because it fa-cilitated the use of controls but also because it generated residual values. The residual values for each country indicated how distant the individual nation's per capita import levels were from the predicted import levels—the predicted import levels that had already controlled for the influences of size, wealth, and trade area membership. The residuals for each country indicated how active each had been in terms of import levels. Countries with high residual values were those nations that had a greater propensity to import than would have been expected. Countries with negative resid-ual values were the ones that had imported less per capita than antici-pated. Countries importing above expected levels thus would be those that had been much more open, whereas those exporting less would have been less open. It would seem evident that the less open economies would have been more likely to have been availing themselves of direct, indirect, or subtle forms of protection in the years indicated. A related possibility would be that the less open economies were the ones that had found more effective mechanisms for providing or applying protection that favored domestic producers. Countries with highly competitive sec-tors in the global marketplace would still have been open since other states would have comparative advantages elsewhere in manufacturing or raw material sectors.

Since the residuals permitted a determination of which countries devi-ated from expectations in terms of their relative propensity to import, there was no necessity to try to attempt to calculate the actual levels of protection that were present, whether it would have been from tariffs or tariff equivalents. If tariff schedule complexity, fears of dumping or subsidy allegation, or quotas negotiated under the MFA were the real barriers to imports, then imports would have been below the anticipated levels. If an economy was very open relative to the other countries, imports would have been higher than anticipated, notwithstanding any notational or cal-culated measure of protection. Similarly, if there were import barriers that were present but they were highly porous or ineffective, imports might be higher than expected or close to predicted levels. Since residuals were used, none of the analyses in this and following chapters had to attempt to determine what the levels of per capita imports would have been or should have been for the industrialized countries had protection been totally ab-sent. The emphasis in the analyses rather was on *relative* levels of protection (revealed protection, if you will). All 23 industrialized countries have been protecting domestic producers in at least some sectors of their economies, some just more so or more effectively than others.

Results

Regression Analyses

The results of the regression analyses for each of the years are contained in Table 4–1. It was clear that wealth, population, and EC membership all had the anticipated effects on imports. Wealthier countries had indeed imported more per capita, while those countries with larger populations imported at lower per capita levels as indicated by the negative sign for this variable in all 14 equations. The use of purchasing power parity (PPP) figures, which were available for 1994, did not generate dramatically differ-

Table 4-1
Multiple Regression Equations Results for Import Levels

Year	GNP per capita	Population	EC	EFTA	Adjusted R^2	F-Ratio
	Independent Variables					
1960	.706***	-.686***	.261*	.252+	.704	14.073***
1965	.605***	-.669***	.277*	.269+	.691	13.292***
1970	.658***	-.653***	.328*	.236	.693	13.415***
1973	.619***	-.541***	.338*	.188	.671	12.217***
1976	.667***	-.484***	.313*	.051	.679	12.653***
1980	.602***	-.403**	.340*	.127	.667	12.010***
1982	.606***	-.423**	.478**	.149	.682	12.786***
1984	.673***	-.512**	.430**	.093	.619	9.927***
1986	.651***	-.538**	.414**	.153	.643	10.887***
1988	.615**	-.469*	.349*	.137	.607	9.508***
1990	.386+	-.339+	.501**	.333	.546	7.617***
1992	.424+	-.425*	.455*	.173	.478	6.039**
1994a	.480*	-.479*	.356*	.169	.434	5.220**
1994b	.570*	-.604*	.331+	.179	.484	6.165**

+ $p = .90$ * $p = .95$ ** $p = .99$ *** $p = .999$ for inclusion of variable in equation or for the F-ratio value for the equation.

The 1994b equation replaces GNP per capita with purchasing power parity per capita figures.

ent results for that year compared to the explanatory power available with GNP per capita. EC/EU membership was also positively associated with overall higher imports. EFTA membership, on the other hand, had only marginal effects on import levels and only in the 1960s. Of course, it was not particularly surprising that a free trade area had less of an impact than the more complete customs union with a common external tariff, but it had been expected that the free trade area would have had some positive effect on per capita import levels. Given these results, it was possible that the formation of EFTA had primarily led to trade diversion rather than trade creation for the members of the organization.

One trend was readily apparent in Table 4–1. While the adjusted R^2 values indicated that the equations with the independent variables explained an important amount of variation for all years, the trend has been toward declining explanatory value over time. This decline was particularly noticeable between 1988 and 1990. As a consequence, it would appear that population, wealth, and EC membership have come to explain progressively less about overall levels of per capita imports than had been the case in earlier years. It was not surprising that the effects of EC membership might decline somewhat over time, since the largest increases in trade would be in the initial years of membership and increases in imports in later years would be likely to be relatively smaller.[4] Population and wealth, however, should have continued to explain similar amounts of variation in imports per capita or even larger amounts of variation in the equations. Since trade was being successively liberalized with GATT reductions in tariffs and even the beginnings of reductions in non-tariff barriers, these basic factors could have actually explained even more about per capita imports rather than less. Obviously, with the passage of time additional factors were becoming important in determining imports levels, which presumably would have included the effects of government trade policies or other economic policies that adversely affected imports. The CAP in place in the EC/EU, for example, changed import levels over time, especially from producers outside the area, and until the completion of the Uruguay Round agreements, the CAP continued to limit imports even further by encouraging even more production with the EU. Given increasing global liberalization, or at least superficial liberalization, government policies restricting imports could have been becoming more subtle, and, perhaps more importantly, they may have been becoming more effective in at least some cases. Since the analyses have been dealing with relative import propensities, it was also possible that there was in fact increasing liberalization, but that some countries were liberalizing their trade and commercial policies more rapidly or effectively than some of the other countries included in the analyses.

Country Results

The residuals derived from the equations were used to indicate which of the industrialized nations imported relatively freely and which of them were relatively poor markets for imports at the per capita level. With residuals available for so many years, it was also possible to observe changes in the propensity to import that occurred over time. The 23 countries were ranked on the basis of their relative openness. The countries that imported much more than anticipated based on their positive residuals were ranked highest (with 1, 2, and 3 being considered the highest ranks), while the

Table 4-2
Rankings for Total Imports for Industrialized Countries

Country	1960	1965	1970	1973	1976	1980	1982	1984	1986	1988	1990	1992	1994a	1994b
Japan	1	3	3	8	8	11	10	11	18	20	17	20	21	14
United States	11	8	7	6	5	3	3	3	2	2	3	2	2	4
Canada	18	12.5	17	14	18	14	11	10	13	7	6	8	6	10
Australia	21	19	22	21	22	21	21	23	21	19	19	19	19	21
New Zealand	8	10	14	16	16	19	13	13	17	16	11	13	10	19
Germany	17	17	21	22	21	22	22	20	20	21	20	18	20	16
France	23	23	23	23	23	23	23	22	22	22	22	22	22	22
Italy	19	22	20	19	20	20	8	21	23	23	23	23	23	23
Netherlands	2	2	2	2	3	4	5	4	5	3	5	3	4	5
Belgium/ Luxembourg	3	1	1	1	1	1	1	1	1	1	1	1	1	1
United Kingdom	9	15	12	11	7	10	20	16	14	10	16	16	14	18
Ireland	5	5	6	4	4	2	2	2	4	4	4	4.5	3	3
Switzerland	7	6	4	5	11	6	6	6	3	5	2	4.5	6	6
Austria	20	21	18	18	14	12	14	7.5	9	9	8	6	9	7
Denmark	6	7	9	10	6	18	9	12	7	15	10	12	15	11
Norway	4	4	5	3	2	7	7	17	11	14	12	11	12	13
Sweden	12.5	16	19	20	17	15	15	7.5	15.5	11	15	15	11	9
Finland	10	20	16	17	19	9	12	19	19	18	21	21	16.5	17
Spain	14	14	11	12	12	16.5	17	14	12	13	13	14	16.5	15
Portugal	22	9	15	15	15	16.5	19	15	8	8	9	9.5	13	12
Greece	16	18	13	13	13	13	18	18	15.5	17	18	17	18	20
Yugoslavia/ Slovenia	15	12.5	10	9	10	8	16	9	10	12	14	-- / 7	-- / 6	-- / 2
Israel	12.5	11	8	7	9	5	4	5	6	6	7	9.5	8	8

1994b has purchasing power parity figures substituted for GNP per capita.

countries importing much less than predicted were given the lowest ranks (21, 22, or 23). Note that a country with a rank such as 1 or 2 imported more per capita than expected compared to the other countries in the analyses, but if it was a small country the total value of the extra imports was not necessarily the highest in an absolute sense. A larger country with a lower rank would have imported more than expected in terms of total value than other smaller countries with higher ranks. Similarly, a large country that imported very much less than predicted would have represented a more significant reduction in market opportunities for exporters elsewhere in the world than would be the case for a small country that imported below expected levels.

Table 4–2 contains the ranks from the residuals for the various years that were used in the regression analyses. Some countries were consistent in terms of their ranks while others varied rather significantly over time. Japan started out as the most active per capita importer in the group. Over time, however, Japan became less and less open until the 1990s, when it was among the least active per capita importers. The United States followed the opposite path. It was an average importer in 1960 but by the 1980s had become one of the most active importers in the group. Canada started out as a poor market compared to the others but had improved to an average position by the later years. Australia was a consistently below-average per capita importer throughout the period, while nearby New Zealand was a somewhat better importer but never was an especially active one.

Among the European nations, Belgium, the Netherlands, and Ireland were especially strong per capita importers. While all three were initial or later members of the EC, such membership would not seem to have been a strong factor in explaining their import levels, since the three larger initial EC members—France, Italy, and Germany—were consistently below average in terms of their propensity to import. In fact, these three countries usually had the largest negative residuals. The reunification of Germany had no particular effect on the rankings for Germany. With a larger population and a reduced per capita income, per capita imports would have been predicted to be lower, but the residuals were still quite negative, indicating that actual per capita import levels had decreased in a relative sense. Size was not a sufficient explanation for the negative residuals for these three EC/EU countries. Japan at times and the United States imported actively despite being larger, and the United Kingdom, whose population base was similar to the three large EC/EU initial members, had better rankings both before and after EC membership than France,

Germany, and Italy had. Among the other countries in northern and western Europe, Switzerland was almost always an above-average importer, while Austria went from being one of the lowest ranked importers to being one that was generally better than average. The Scandinavian countries presented a mixed picture. Sweden and Finland were pretty consistently below-average importers, whereas Norway and Denmark were active importers in the early years but had inconsistent rankings in the later ones. In later years they were often average importers, but they never recovered their early positions as some of the most active per capita importers among the industrialized countries.

Of the five smaller Mediterranean countries included in the analyses, there was no pattern or congruence. Greece was invariably below anticipated levels. Notwithstanding the fact that Spain had a large number of import restrictions before 1960 and liberalized slowly,[5] Spain usually had a level of imports close to what had been predicted, while Portugal's ranks were rather inconsistent. Israel and Yugoslavia/Slovenia had ranks that indicated they were among the more active importers, especially in the later years of the analyses. Israeli policies after 1969 focused on reductions in protection and eliminating the biases against exports,[6] and the results in Table 4–2 would suggest that these efforts have been successful.

A number of other pertinent observations can be derived from Table 4–2. Ranks based on purchasing power parity in 1994 were not dramatically different from those for GNP per capita. Perhaps the most important difference was that the United States had greater purchasing power for each dollar compared to most other nations; thus its import propensity was somewhat lower with this measure. High-cost Japan was less obviously a below-average importer with purchasing power parity figures than it had been with GNP per capita. Of course, it should be noted that the high costs that resulted in less purchasing power have been due at least in part to protectionist policies and subsidies for local firms that are present in many countries. High food prices in Japan, for example, reduced purchasing power, but these prices have been a direct result of limitations that have been placed on imports. Similar effects on food prices and prices in other areas, such as limits on auto imports or steel, would have raised costs. Purchasing power parity figures, moreover, have been based on nontraded items, but most items have been traded internationally, and internationally traded items have had much the same price everywhere.[7] The distorting effects of protection on PPP figures would be likely to have been the greatest with intermediate goods where the presence of protection would have raised costs and thus lowered purchasing power parity.

Restrictions or prohibitions on intermediate goods can dramatically change prices. It was found, for example, that if U.S. barriers to imports of textiles and steel were eliminated, employment in the U.S. auto industry would actually have increased, since textile and steel inputs for auto production would have been cheaper![8] The same effects were present in other countries that had divergences between purchasing power parity and GNP per capita.

Another fact that was apparent in Table 4–2 was that the effects of the global recession of 1979 and 1980 could be seen in the ranks. Probably the greatest volatility in the ranks appeared for 1980, 1982, and 1984 for at least some of the countries. For example, Italy had the eighth position in 1982, an unusually active importing rank for that country compared to any other year. Norway fell to the seventeenth rank in 1984, an unusual rank given its ranks in the other years. Some of the unusual ranks were aberrations reflecting the relatively unsettled economic conditions of this particular period. In most cases the countries reverted to ranks similar to the years before the recession. In other cases, however, this period may have represented a change from earlier patterns. Norway was consistently a less active importer in the years following this period compared to the earlier years. The United Kingdom also appeared to have begun to import relatively less after the global recession than before.

The rankings in Table 4–2 were indications as to where countries were located on a continuum from most open to least open, and ranks were relevant for comparisons, since economic openness has been very much a relative concept. The residuals for individual years were also sensitive to the amount of trade that was present in the international economic system. Residuals were much larger in 1990 than in 1960 or 1965 as a consequence of the greater volume of trade in later decades. It was possible to standardize the residual values for each of the nations by dividing them by the standard deviations for the residuals for each of the years. Relative openness could thus be compared across time. These standardized residuals for each of the years for the twenty-three nations are contained in Table 4–3.

One thing that was obvious from Table 4–3 was that the most open importers were so active that there were fewer countries that were above-average importers when compared to those that imported less than predicted. Belgium, for example, was so much above average in terms of per capita imports that from 1965 on it was at least two standard deviations above the anticipated level and almost three standard deviations in some years. By comparison, France, usually the least-open industrialized country, was not quite so far below expectations as Belgium was above. Thus, on a per capita basis, France was actually closer to the predicted levels than Belgium. There was no other country that was consistently above predicted levels that matched the performance of Belgium. The United States, Ireland, Switzerland, and the Netherlands usually occupied the next ranks in terms of relative openness, but they never came close to the Belgian levels. In effect, Belgium was clearly an outlier on the positive end. The other countries open to imports were actually noticeably a bit less open, even if they were more open than the other states.

Of the states that were less open to imports based on the standardized residuals, France and Italy were usually more closed than Germany among the large European countries. Australia was much more variable in its relative disinclination to import. At times its negative values approached those

Table 4-3
Standardized Scores for Total Imports for Industrialized Countries

Country	1960	1965	1970	1973	1976	1980	1982	1984	1986	1988	1990	1992	1994a	1994b
Japan	1.878	1.379	1.190	.510	.405	-.102	.085	-.025	-.414	-1.043	-.544	-.788	-1.220	-.366
United States	-.066	.397	.441	.690	.749	1.072	1.040	1.011	1.141	1.323	1.156	1.312	1.455	1.117
Canada	-.804	-.328	-.568	-.206	-.538	-.194	-.104	-.003	-.150	.354	.350	.249	.580	.020
Australia	-.995	-.799	-1.189	-1.497	-1.694	-1.412	-1.148	-1.713	-1.154	-.929	-.633	-.712	-.695	-1.127
New Zealand	-.458	.183	-.405	-.542	-.312	-.475	-.144	-.078	-.331	-.399	-.133	-.286	-.116	-.555
Germany	-.687	-.597	-1.110	-1.557	-1.644	-1.530	-1.682	-1.162	-.982	-1.063	-.828	-.689	-.809	-.505
France	-1.682	-1.962	-1.895	-.753	-1.778	-1.722	-2.146	-1.698	-1.560	-1.422	-1.406	-1.404	-1.316	-1.356
Italy	-.822	-1.218	-.984	-.757	-.674	-.963	.176	-1.277	-1.571	-1.533	-1.783	-1.754	-1.517	-1.714
Netherlands	1.636	1.750	1.706	1.456	1.250	1.019	.691	1.006	.846	.980	.868	.947	.833	.807
Belgium/Lux.	1.553	2.026	2.282	2.545	2.446	2.754	2.816	2.862	2.839	2.809	3.009	2.940	2.923	2.755
United Kingdom	.025	-.410	-.244	-.124	.450	-.095	-.693	-.281	-.163	.040	-.280	-.446	-.374	-.543
Ireland	.960	.903	.710	.762	.934	1.575	1.110	1.100	.934	1.043	.897	.905	1.174	1.328
Switzerland	.499	.688	1.107	.724	-.402	.600	.649	.732	1.009	.899	1.263	.906	.563	.585
Austria	-.960	-1.132	-.703	-.583	-.008	-.105	-.165	-.097	.075	.140	.205	.605	.304	.185
Denmark	.857	.620	.261	.261	.609	-.347	.037	-.033	.251	-.292	-.013	-.259	-.381	-.203
Norway	1.200	1.064	.928	.793	1.415	.086	.338	-.293	.023	-.143	-.232	-.191	-.213	-.333
Sweden	-.262	-.509	-.834	-.919	-.137	-.233	-.199	.102	-.284	-.021	-.269	-.434	-.165	.078
Finland	.118	.990	-.497	-.557	-.671	-.066	-.132	-.480	-.854	-.907	-1.000	-.913	-.503	-.530
Spain	-.327	-.335	.086	.103	-.127	-.286	.339	-.106	-.001	-.112	-.237	-.351	-.501	-.391
Portugal	-1.583	.354	-.449	-.374	-.237	-.286	-.497	-.178	.219	.170	.116	.216	-.285	-.294
Greece	-.537	-.676	-.304	-.174	.086	-.191	-.377	-.356	-.281	-.545	-.558	.477	-.670	-.627
Yugoslavia/ Slovenia	-.422	-.322	.157	.277	.015	.006	-.215	.014	.036	-.062	-.246	.413	.571	1.492
Israel	-.263	-.088	.314	.675	.062	.721	.899	.796	.733	.784	.292	.211	.362	.176

1994b has purchasing power parity figures substituted for GNP per capita.

of the larger European countries, and at other times it was not quite so closed. While Japan had indeed become more closed to imports over time, it never approached the high standardized negative residuals of France or Italy. The other countries in the data set had lower standardized residual values, whether they were negative or positive. Some of them, such as the United Kingdom, clearly fluctuated around the predicted levels, sometimes importing a little more per capita than anticipated, sometimes a little less.

Neither the rankings nor the standardized residuals indicated that there was much in the way of additional effects or changes resulting from EC membership. The initial regression equations captured the influences of trade areas quite well. Of the original members, two (Belgium/Luxembourg and the Netherlands) were the most open, and three (France, Italy, and Germany) were among the most closed. The United Kingdom's relative openness changed little with admission to the EC, at least with the control for the length of membership. Ireland did appear to have been somewhat more open in a relative sense after EC membership, but Denmark became less open in a relative sense after membership. It was possible, of course, that Denmark was becoming more open in an absolute sense in this period, but other countries could have been removing restrictions to imports even more quickly than the Danes were. Spain and Greece were little affected by EC membership in terms of relative openness, while the Portuguese trend toward greater openness that was present before membership continued after accession.

Summary

Overall levels of imports were positively influenced by wealth and EC membership and negatively affected by larger population size as anticipated. While the length of EC membership helped to explain the variation in per capita levels of imports, the effects of EFTA membership were marginal at best. When all was said and done, the question of fair trade and import levels was indeed a relative one. Overall trade was on the increase between 1960 and 1994, and every nation came to import larger quantities on a per capita basis, even when differential levels of wealth were controlled for; therefore, changes in ranks and openness were relative ones among the countries included in the analyses. All of the industrialized countries were important markets, and all of them interfered with trade. It was the extent of openness or restrictions that was variable. Per capita import propensities did change over time for some countries, while other nations were consistent in their relative propensities to import. Some of the smaller European countries were consistently above-average importers, including Belgium and the Netherlands, even when size and EC membership were controlled for. The United States started as an average importer and progressively became more open to imports, while Japan was initially an excellent importer and then declined relative to many of the other industrialized countries. France, Italy, Germany, Australia, and Finland consistently were below-average importers compared to other industrialized nations. There was no apparent effect from German reunification in terms of changed import propensities for the country. Overall, before reunification and afterward, it would appear that the EC/EU did serve as a brake on Germany's free trade attitudes, or at least Germany was willing to let the more statist and protectionist members win the trade policy debates about the relative openness of the EC/EU.

Chapter 5

Imports of Manufactured Goods
(and Raw Materials too)

Chapter 4 dealt with per capita levels for the total imports of the 23 industrialized countries. The current chapter focused on per capita manufactured imports for these same countries, in part because of the great importance that such products have had in international trade. The import levels of non-manufactured goods (raw materials) are also briefly analyzed in order to provide a basis for comparisons between the two types of products. Were countries active importers for both kinds of products, for one but not the other, or for neither? The chapters that follow will focus on more detailed analyses of particular kinds of manufactured goods in an effort to understand the role of the industrialized countries as markets in even greater depth.

The Importance of Manufactured Goods

For many observers, trade is normally considered to have consisted of the relatively simple exchange of raw materials for manufactured goods, and, in fact, in some periods of the history of the international economy such trade was indeed the normal type of exchange that took place. Colonial America, later the independent United States, supplied raw materials to European markets in exchange for manufactured items. While infant industries were being created and prospering in many cases in the United States, the market for the products of these industries was largely domestic rather than global. (In effect, the early United States was practicing a policy of import substitution industrialization.) Agricultural produce, such as tobacco, cotton, and indigo, and other raw materials such as furs, timber, and naval stores, were exported to Europe and manufactured goods were in turn imported. Even in these early years, however, there were at least some exports of manufactured goods. The infamous triangular trade with Africa required that New England would process sugar from the West Indies into rum and other liquors to be used for the process of acquiring more slaves in Africa to be transported to the West Indies to produce, among other things, more sugar. Colonial America also imported agricultural goods as well, of which tea was one prominent example. Tea had great symbolic economic and political significance for the colonies, and it was a bellwether of the trade conflicts going on between Great Britain and the colonies over the Navigation Acts.

More recently, however, the exchange of raw materials for manufactured goods has been displaced to a large extent by trade of one kind of manufactured good for another kind. In fact, the largest amount of trade in the world today has consisted of trade of manufactured goods between the industrialized countries. Well over half of global trade has been of this variety, building upon earlier trade in manufactured goods.[1] The processes by which countries came to export such manufactures to each other varied in time and circumstance, but their increasing importance has never been doubted.

One type of trade in manufactures developed because of products that were based upon particular raw materials, such as steel. Products such as iron or steel, which were dependent upon local deposits of iron ore and coal, provided locational advantages for particular regions or countries. In such cases of comparative advantage, specialization could and did occur, and trade in manufactured goods between countries became possible and profitable. Minor locational advantages or historical accidents frequently determined where a good was initially produced, producing an advantage that was later built upon.[2] In other cases, firms in particular countries developed expertise in particular product lines, perhaps due to some initial raw material advantage or to the presence of a skilled work force knowledgeable about the production of an item.[3] This initial edge in the production of a particular good then could have formed the basis for profitable trade opportunities. Venetian glass, Irish linen, English woolens, porcelain from Limoges, and eventually German optical devices and chemicals, Swedish steel, French designer clothing, or Swiss watches became export specialties that provided the basis for mutually profitable trade and a source of foreign exchange for paying for imports of all kinds.

The possibilities inherent with specialization have left open the chance for firms in different countries to fill certain niches within broader markets. Producers in the different industrialized countries have abandoned some segments of the textile and apparel sectors while continuing to produce specialty items for textile or clothing niches.[4] These areas of continued production have been ones in which they have still had advantages—whether it be from brand-name recognition, locational advantages, the presence of an appropriate and skilled labor force, or marketing ties and expertise (or even from protection or subsidies). For example, France and Italy currently produce designer apparel and have largely left the low cost ready-to-wear segments of the market for producers in other countries. Similarly, U.S. automobile producers abandoned the subcompact car market to the Japanese and eventually to others. The Netherlands and Belgium produce specialty china products rather than attempting to cover the entire market.

Perhaps the largest amount of trade in manufactured goods among the developed countries has not resulted from the exchange of different manufactured goods (inter-industry trade) or from niche production but rather from intra-industry trade. Firms in the various industrialized states produce similar items (i.e., automobiles, electronics, some types of clothing, machinery, etc.), and trade them with each other. Such trade in related products has become increasingly important for world markets.[5] This trade has represented in some cases brand loyalty among consumers, but more frequently it has reflected the practice of firms in one country importing components or intermediate goods from plants in other countries as part of the production process for a final good. A portion of this trade has been not only intra-industry, but also intra-company in nature. Multinational firms have subsidiaries, branch locations, or joint ventures preparing parts or goods for a final product. Automobiles have frequently had such integrated production with materials shipped from one country to another.[6] Intra-industry trade has been more likely to occur within an oligopolistic or monopolistic setting and within firms.[7] While intra-industry trade has been likely to result in increases in global welfare, the results from intra-firm trade have been more ambiguous in terms of the distribution of benefits given the oligopolistic possibilities inherent in intra-firm trade.[8] Protection becomes costly for companies when there is intra-industry trade, but it would be less harmful, and therefore more likely, when there have been lower levels of such trade.[9] The creation of the EC increased the opportunities for this type of intra-industry specialization between countries within the common market.[10] Intra-industry trade and specialization within the EC and with the countries that have been linked to the EC by trade agreements have been associated with somewhat lower levels of protection.[11] In North America the Autopact between Canada and the United States provided in essence for free trade among plants in these two countries long before the Canada-U.S. free trade arrangement or NAFTA. Plants have been located in different countries to take advantage of wage scales or skilled labor forces or natural resources (factor endowments) or transportation linkages or management and marketing expertise (locational advantages). Productive facilities have been moved offshore to take advantage of lower costs or expertise elsewhere in the world, as has been the case with assembly plants in Mexico connected with U.S. firms or production facilities in Southeast Asia linked with parent firms in Japan. Plant locations can even simply reflect the utilization of production facilities established in the past that continue to be more cost effective to operate than new facilities that could be built from scratch in some other country with current comparative or locational advantages. In other cases, when trade has been between companies, the component units could be purchased more cheaply from foreign suppliers than from domestic sources, thus leading to an increase of intra-industry foreign trade. While intra-industry trade can involve both developed and developing states, such intra-industry trade has been much more likely among industrialized countries that have the capacity to take advantage of such opportunities. Such trade has also been greater with higher levels of wealth and market size,[12] factors that have also been associated with greater trade overall as demonstrated in the previous chapters.

Some countries actually facilitated such intra-industry trade by tariff schedules or rules of origin regulation. U.S. tariff rates have been lower on materials imported back into the country if they have a significant portion of U.S.-produced materials or components in them. For example, electronic products built with U.S. chips or other components have faced lower tariffs than similar products that have not utilized intermediate goods of U.S. origin. Such arrangements have led to increased trade between the United States and some countries, especially Singapore in the case of computer components.[13] The EC/EU has also established rules of origin procedures that favor member states or those countries that have had commercial treaty arrangements with the EC/EU. The ACP states, for example, have such favorable treatment when competing with other producers in the developing world. The EC/EU has also sought to make sure that foreign firms do not circumvent the rules of origin specification and other limits on imports that exist within the customs union by setting up simple assembly (screwdriver) plants inside the EC/EU or in some other state that has a special trade arrangement with the EC/EU.[14] Ultimately, this type of preferential treatment has been designed to encourage the use of locally produced items, thus increasing employment, exports, and the financial viability of domestic firms. As such it has been a form of subsidization of local firms, but one that has been limited since the subsidy only directly applies to re-imports. To the extent that such government support has facilitated economies of scale and minimum production runs, it has subsidized exports to the rest of the world as well.

Intra-industry trade has not been uniform across the industrialized countries. Effects of intra-industry trade on domestic lobbying for protection have been ambiguous in the limited number of analyses that have been undertaken. In the United States, firms more heavily involved in intra-industry trade have been more likely to seek protection,[15] whereas as in France greater intra-industry trade at a national level has been associated with greater liberalization.[16] Japan has been a country noticeably limited in terms of the amount of intra-industry trade that has been occurring. The United States has also been somewhat less active in this regard.[17] Of the industrialized countries, these two countries, especially the United States, have had the largest domestic markets (if the single European market, which is more or less in place today, is ignored). In addition, they have lacked the facilitative mechanisms of a customs union such as the EC/EU to increase intra-industry trade, although there has been intra-industry trade between the United States and Canada over the decades, especially in the automotive sector. The Canada-U.S. Free Trade Agreement and NAFTA have now begun to encourage more of this kind of trade in manufactured goods, but these agreements have been much more recent than the treaties creating the EC/EU. The smaller countries of the developed world have been prime candidates for such trade since their domestic economies have been too small to provide the means for the total production in complex goods, leaving intra-industry trade as a logical alternative.

Trade in manufactures has, of course, been important for the industrialized nations of the world. They have been the primary exporters of such goods, whether they are being exchanged for other manufactured goods or for raw materials. As a group they have been central to the increasing intra-industry trade, although the involvement of individual nations has been variable as noted above. They have even been niche exporters or importers (Rolls Royce and Ferrari, for example) catering to their own specialized clienteles. Manufactured products as defined in this volume have also been quite important in the import mix of the industrialized countries as can be seen in Table 5–1. Most of the industrialized countries were active in terms of importing such products.

There have been some decreases in the percentage of imports accounted for by the imports of manufactured goods. Between 1973 and 1976 the lower figures reflected the increase in the price of petroleum (the large price increases for oil quite naturally changed the portions that raw materials accounted for in the import mixes of various countries). The early 1980s for many countries reflected the global recession that was going on. On the whole, however, the patterns through time have been ones of steady increases in the relative weight of manufactured goods, to the point that in many nations in the developed world manufactured

Table 5-1
Importantance of Manufactured Goods as Imports for
Industrialized Countries

Country	Percentage of Manufactured Goods												
	1960	1965	1970	1973	1976	1980	1982	1984	1986	1988	1990	1992	1994
Japan	18	18	24	26	21	23	20	24	35	43	43	44	49
United States	37	44	59	60	54	54	54	63	78	82	73	76	78
Canada	67	69	76	77	76	65	67	81	85	79	80	81	83
Australia	68	74	79	73	79	79	75	79	87	84	79	77	85
New Zealand	62	68	68	70	74	72	69	70	82	86	80	61	82
Germany	33	44	49	51	55	57	55	58	67	72	72	74	73
France	27	41	51	55	59	57	53	57	69	74	74	75	75
Italy	29	32	40	41	44	45	42	43	58	66	63	66	54
Netherlands	48	57	59	56	59	58	45	54	68	69	71	72	71
Belgium/ Luxembourg	47	54	55	60	65	64	58	61	69	72	82	69	70
United Kingdom	25	32	43	51	54	63	62	67	72	78	75	76	79
Ireland	57	61	67	69	66	71	68	69	74	78	76	77	74
Switzerland	53	61	66	73	72	73	73	74	81	84	83	84	84
Austria	55	61	79	75	71	72	65	71	77	80	81	83	83
Denmark	52	57	63	64	68	61	57	61	73	75	73	73	74
Norway	76	64	65	69	76	70	71	77	82	82	80	81	79
Sweden	53	60	62	65	70	63	62	64	75	79	78	78	78
Finland	57	62	62	65	65	58	55	60	72	77	76	71	72
Spain	37	47	47	48	46	42	36	37	58	68	70	72	70
Portugal	42	47	59	59	71	52	51	50	62	64	71	75	72
Greece	61	59	68	58	65	62	60	53	59	70	71	71	69
Yugoslavia/ Slovenia	59	50	62	58	72	66	56	54	59	63	--	--	--
Slovenia											--	68	72
Israel	55	60	64	69	65	64	55	68	78	79	76	79	82

goods accounted for four-fifths of total imports by the 1990s. The smaller countries were somewhat more likely to import higher percentages of manufactured goods since they could not possibly produce all such goods in an increasingly complex world. In 1960 the larger countries like the United States, the United Kingdom, Germany, France, and Italy were importing basic materials rather than manufactures, but by the 1970s, levels of manufactured imports had grown. Japan clearly was less likely to have imported manufactured goods than raw materials when compared to the other industrialized countries. By 1994, manufactured goods accounted for almost half of all Japanese imports, but that level was well below the figures for the other nations. Japanese imports of manufactured goods have been low even when raw materials or land availability have been taken into account or when capital or other factor endowments were considered.[18] Spain also had low percentage of manufactured imports well into the 1980s, while the other Mediterranean countries—Portugal, Greece, Yugoslavia, and Israel—were more dependent on manufactured imports than on raw materials. The smaller West European countries and New Zealand consistently had high levels of manufactured imports as did resource-rich Australia and Canada. By the 1990s, moreover, with the exception of Japan, all of the industrialized countries had import mixes that reflected a preponderant proportion of manufactured goods. All these increases, even those for Japan, resulted from greater complexity in the trade of goods, the growth of inter-industry trade, and the growth of intra-industry trade. Raw materials and primary goods were of declining importance on average, even though they never became unimportant in the import mix of these countries. The question that remained to be answered, however, was the relative openness of these countries in the area of imports as measured by regression equations and the analysis of the associated residuals.

Results

Regression Analyses

The regression equations were run with per capita imports of manufactured goods as the dependent variable, and the independent variables were population size, wealth, and length of membership in EFTA and the EC/EU. As was the case with total imports, the regression equations explained the most variation in the earlier years (see Table 5–2). The explanatory value was slightly better than was the case for overall imports for the years before 1990, and noticeably not as good for the years from 1990 on (compare Table 5–2 with Table 4–1). Overall, however, as was the case with total imports, the equations progressively explained less and less of the total variation through time.

No single variable was a significant addition to all the equations. Population was consistently the most important, with wealth usually being a significant factor as well. Membership in trade areas was much less important than had been the case for overall per capita imports. The EC/EU years of membership variable was important less than half the time. Oddly enough, membership in EFTA was important only in 1992 and 1994 (with

Table 5-2
Multiple Regression Equations Results for Import Levels
of Manufactured Products

Year	Independent Variables				Equation Results	
	GNP per capita	Population	EC	EFTA	Adjusted R^2	F-Ratio
1960	.700***	-.762***	.047	.118	.671	12.234***
1965	.695***	-.790***	.099	.095	.728	15.733***
1970	.740***	-.768***	.150	.136	.748	17.349***
1973	.687***	-.611***	.159	.149	.704	14.082***
1976	.696***	-.543***	.182	.065	.691	13.302***
1980	.622***	-.461**	.226	.113	.639	10.720***
1982	.649***	-.476**	.307*	.154	.672	12.283***
1984	.756***	-.590***	.250+	.051	.648	11.136***
1986	.725***	-.592**	.291+	.116	.663	11.839***
1988	.631**	-.488*	.264*	.155	.614	9.756***
1990	.357	-.343+	.449*	.356	.499	6.474**
1992	1.034	-1.275	.563**	.543*	.406	4.754**
1994a	1.148	-1.362+	.533*	.526*	.357	4.051**
1994b	.638**	-.656**	.228	.180	.529	7.188***

+ $p = .90$ * $p = .95$ ** $p = .99$ *** $p = .999$ for inclusion of variable in equation or for the F-ratio value for the equation.

The 1994b equation replaces GNP per capita with purchasing power parity per capita figures.

GNP capita as the measure of wealth), when the organization was about to lose three members. EC/EU membership was also important for these two years, suggesting that the agreements between the EU and EFTA for closer trade (creating in effect a European free trade area, or at least a West European free trade area) may have prompted increases in imports of manufactures for the countries involved. Of course, in 1992 and 1994, when these memberships were important, the explanatory values of the equations were the lowest values achieved. When purchasing power parity was used as the wealth measure in 1994, wealth and size explained per capita import levels, and trade area memberships faded in importance. The explanatory value of equation 1994b was much higher, however, than was the case for equation 1994a.

A discontinuity in the results did appear between 1988 and 1990 in terms of the variation explained. Two possibilities for this discontinuity

Table 5-3
Rankings for Total Imports of Manufactured Products

Country	1960	1965	1970	1973	1976	1980	1982	1984	1986	1988	1990	1992	1994a	1994b
Japan	2	4	6	11	14	19	19	18	19	23	19	20	23	20
United States	9	7	7	5	4	3	4	3	2	2	3	3	4	4
Canada	12	12	12	9	15	12	20	6	12	7	6	4	3	9
Australia	17	14	20	22	21	21	20	23	22.5	18	17	15	11.5	21
New Zealand	7	10	16	18	12	13	8	13	15	15	10	12.5	10	17
Germany	18.5	19	21	23	23	22	22	20	18	19	20	18	19	14
France	23	23	23	21	22	23	23	22	21	21	22	21	20	22
Italy	11	21	19	17	19	20	7	21	22.5	22	23	23	17.5	23
Netherlands	3	1	2	2.5	5	6	15	7	6	6	5	5	7	6
Belgium/Luxembourg	4	2	1	1	1	1	1	1	1	1	1	1	1	1
United Kingdom	22	22	18	13	7	8	14	11	13	8	12	10	11.5	11.5
Ireland	5	5	5	4	3	2	2	2	4	4	4	6	5	3
Switzerland	8	6	3	2.5	18	4	3	4	3	3	2	2	2	5
Austria	20	16	15	14	9	9	11	8	9	9	8	8	9	7
Denmark	6	8	9	12	6	18	13	17	11	16	11	7	8	11.5
Norway	1	3	4	6	2	7	5	10	7	12	13.5	14	14	15
Sweden	18.5	17	22	20	16.5	16	16	14	17	13	16	17	16	10
Finland	10	20	17	19	20	11	21	19	20	20	21	22	22	19
Spain	13.5	13	11	10	16.5	15	18	15	14	14	13.5	11	15	16
Portugal	21	9	13	15	13	14	17	12	8	10	9	12.5	17.5	13
Greece	15	18	14	16	10.5	11	12	16	16	17	18	19	21	18
Yugoslavia	13.5	11	8	8	8	10	10	9	10	11	15	--	--	--
/Slovenia												16	13	2
Israel	16	15	10	7	10.5	5	6	5	5	5	7	9	6	8

1994b has purchasing power parity figures substituted for GNP per capita.

are worth noting. First, German reunification (pending for 1990 and a reality for 1992 and 1994) could have had an effect on imports of manufactures in the EC/EU in general and Germany in particular.[19] Changes in the relationships for Germany and EC/EU members could then have led to lower adjusted R^2s. The second possibility was related to the PPP measure. The results with this measure of wealth were similar to those for 1988. It was possible that the effects of reduced or enhanced purchasing power were becoming quite important from 1990 on, whereas in the prior years divergences in purchasing power based on PPP or GNP were less. It thus becomes possible that GNP per capita has been becoming a measure that is of declining utility for future use. A third possibility for the decline in explanatory power was simply that as trade became increasingly complex, many more factors influenced the makeup and levels of imports (and exports).

Table 5-4
Standardized Scores for Total Imports of Manufactured Products

Country	1960	1965	1970	1973	1976	1980	1982	1984	1986	1988	1990	1992	1994a	1994b
Japan	1.650	1.375	.838	-.116	-.153	-.670	-.740	-.835	-.995	-1.544	-.779	-1.105	-1.446	-.902
United States	.185	.573	.662	.914	.987	1.240	1.187	1.204	1.324	1.459	1.186	1.138	1.219	1.243
Canada	-.314	-.374	-.189	.121	-.254	-.257	.033	.457	.008	.476	.436	.999	1.287	.120
Australia	-.559	-.467	-1.089	-1.518	-1.505	-1.067	-.752	-1.637	-1.466	-.837	-.491	-.263	-.077	-1.106
New Zealand	.315	.191	-.543	-.587	-.137	-.303	.088	-.083	-.235	-.232	-.039	-.219	.004	-.520
Germany	-.631	-.719	-1.138	-1.622	-1.656	-1.406	-1.328	-.991	-.959	-.977	-.795	-.562	-.827	-.333
France	-1.497	-1.948	-1.805	-1.489	-1.567	-1.477	-1.774	-1.386	-1.337	-1.199	-1.200	-1.117	-1.160	-1.174
Italy	-.201	-.823	-.827	-.475	-.476	-.882	.529	-1.095	-1.462	-1.440	-1.727	-1.680	-.714	-1.756
Netherlands	1.375	1.769	1.848	1.094	.861	.617	-.455	.367	.675	.696	.500	.834	.508	.685
Belgium/Lux.	.956	1.732	1.981	2.442	2.483	2.648	2.634	2.685	2.596	2.549	3.135	2.329	2.320	2.427
United Kingdom	-1.159	-1.313	-.666	-.158	.272	.227	-.351	.069	-.019	.229	-.186	-.103	-.077	-.316
Ireland	.615	.889	1.033	1.049	1.003	1.883	1.686	1.515	1.133	1.145	.806	.622	.631	1.443
Switzerland	.242	.746	1.361	.091	-.422	.983	1.253	.918	1.169	1.174	1.382	1.861	1.746	.848
Austria	-.668	.597	-.404	-.197	.043	.158	-.156	.268	.134	.104	.218	.367	.297	.364
Denmark	.408	.486	.163	-.044	.500	-.609	-.088	-.467	.066	-.345	-.113	.416	-.314	.327
Norway	2.901	1.579	1.057	.902	1.848	.236	.714	.079	.223	.345	.049	-.227	-.227	-.424
Sweden	-.633	-.642	-1.329	-1.301	-.345	-.511	-.493	-.270	-.444	-.123	-.326	-.534	-.461	.000
Finland	-.088	-.789	-.587	-.681	-1.039	-.526	-.767	-.976	-1.123	-1.094	-1.067	-1.524	-1.355	-.829
Spain	-.397	-.413	-.117	.316	-.347	-.505	-.652	-.360	-.079	-.195	-.242	-.140	-.410	-.433
Portugal	-1.092	.252	-.212	-.335	-.146	-.340	-.584	-.058	.216	.345	.049	-.220	-.736	-.326
Greece	-.479	-.679	-.298	-.327	-.076	-.200	-.258	-.404	-.345	-.512	-.518	-.981	-1.304	-.615
Yugoslavia/	-.392	-.284	.224	.344	.204	.131	-.101	.147	.116	-.080	-.252	--	--	--
Slovenia												-.303	-.129	1.573
Israel	-.539	-.533	.096	.775	-.078	.632	.564	.855	.804	.812	.265	.311	.583	.289

1994b has purchasing power parity figures substituted for GNP per capita.

Country Results

The results from the analyses of the residuals indicated that countries had some differences between overall per capita import levels and per capita imports of manufactured goods. The rankings of the countries for the various years are contained in Table 5–3, while the corresponding analysis of the standardized residuals are contained in Table 5–4. In some cases the rankings and residual values were similar to those for Tables 4–1 and 4–2, while in others the patterns were dissimilar.

Belgium was as active an importer of manufactured goods as had been the case for overall imports. Except in 1960, Belgium was a extremely active importer, being well above predicted per capita levels, and by 1973 was far more active than any of the other industrialized countries. Ireland and Switzerland were consistently above predicted levels of per capita imports of manufactured goods at high levels as well, although not at the Belgian level. Norway and the Netherlands were far above anticipated levels in per capita import levels in the earlier years, but they eventually became less open to imports of manufactured goods in the later years, although they avoided being among the least open economies.

The United States was a relatively good market for manufactured goods in 1960 and became progressively more open to such imports over time. The Japanese performance was just the opposite. In 1960, Japan was the second most active per capita importer in terms of its position of being well above predicted levels. The Japanese standardized residual for 1960 was well below that of the Norwegian case but was similar to that for the Netherlands. In 1965 and 1970, Japan was still an important market in terms of being above expected per capita import levels, although the figures were lower than in 1960. By the 1970s, however, Japanese imports had clearly dropped in a relative sense, and by 1980 Japan was consistently one of the countries importing manufactured goods well below those predicted levels. The standardized residuals were negative and larger; therefore, Japan was not just a marginally closed market relative to the other industrialized countries but was very much less open.

The three large initial members of the EU were relatively poor markets for the imports of manufactured goods for all the years. France, Italy, and Germany had low rankings and high negative residual values for the per capita imports. The United Kingdom was initially a very poor market as well. By the mid-1970s, however, it had become an average market compared to the other countries. The standardized residuals were either marginally negative or positive from 1973 on, indicating that the United Kingdom was importing manufactured goods pretty much as anticipated. Overall size did not explain the lower relative imports levels for France, Italy, and Germany since the United Kingdom had maintained levels of per capita imports close to anticipated levels from the time that it joined the EC. Interestingly enough, the improvement in per capita import levels for the United Kingdom occurred before that country joined the EC. After joining, it maintained its position as an average importer of manufactured goods, but there was no dramatic improvement in the per capita import levels. Of course, since membership did lead to higher predicted per capita import levels, the predicted overall imports would have been somewhat higher for the United Kingdom as a member than had been the case when it was not a member.

Except for Norway in the 1960s, the Scandinavian countries were not among the most open markets for manufactured goods. Denmark fluctuated greatly in terms of the rankings, but the standardized residuals indicated that Denmark, Norway, and Sweden in the 1980s and 1990s were fairly close to the predicted levels of per capita imports, even if somewhat lower than anticipated in most years. In the 1970s Sweden had been a particularly poor market, while Finland has been a poor importer of manufactured goods relative to the other countries in virtually all years. The standardized residuals for Finland, and for Sweden in the earlier years, indicated that these countries were indeed considerably below anticipated levels of imports.

Among the other countries included in the study, Australia and New Zealand were not particularly open to imports of manufactured goods. The residual values indicated that Australia was especially poor, with values similar to the larger European countries and by the 1990s, Japan. New Zealand was a somewhat more active importer of manufactured products, perhaps reflecting the advantages to Australian producers resulting from the greater access to the New Zealand market that came with the customs union between the two countries. Canada, on the other hand, proved to be a fairly good market for imports of manufactured goods. Some of this import activity undoubtedly reflected the intra-industry and intra-company trade between the United States and Canada that was occurring well before the agreement to form a free trade area. Relative to many other countries, Canada has been accessible and has improved over time in terms of its openness to per capita imports of manufactured goods.

The European NICs in the Mediterranean displayed a mixed pattern. Spain, Portugal, and Greece were not especially open to high levels of per capita imports of manufactures. Yugoslavia imported about as much per capita as expected, controlling for its size and its relatively low GNP per capita. Yugoslavia's per capita imports of manufactured goods were important even though the state favored domestic production with protection or subsidies.[20] Israel was a relatively closed market in 1960 but by the 1980s had become relatively open. Slovenia would appear to have had a misvalued currency in the 1990s since it was a relatively poor market based on

Table 5-5
Multiple Regression Equations Results for Import Levels
of Raw Materials

| Year | Independent Variables | | | | Equation Results | |
	GNP per capita	Population	EC	EFTA	Adjusted R^2	F-Ratio
1960	.566**	-.441*	.490**	.377*	.556	7.897***
1965	.585**	-.391*	.524**	.512**	.602	9.308***
1970	.455**	-.397*	.587***	.377*	.588	8.844***
1973	.410*	-.338*	.627***	.237	.587	8.831***
1976	.518**	-.294+	.552**	.016	.589	8.895***
1980	.501**	-.247+	.530**	.140	.642	10.868***
1982	.428*	-.262	.661***	.115	.554	7.838***
1984	.370*	-.255	.687***	.155	.481	6.097***
1986	.326	-.291	.707***	.236	.549	7.706***
1988	.468*	-.338+	.575**	.059	.518	9.756***
1990	.460*	-.280+	.659***	.190	.644	10.945***
1992	2.463+	-2.642+	.725***	.205	.427	5.105**
1994a	1.754*	-1.885*	.811***	.287	.473	5.938**
1994b	.297	-.369	.561*	.137	.338	3.810*

+ p = .90   * p = .95   ** p = .99   *** p = .999 for inclusion of variable in equation or for the F-ratio value for the equation.

The 1994b equation replaces GNP per capita with purchasing power parity per capita figures.

the GNP measures but an excellent one when the wealth measure used was based on PPP. The standardized residuals indicated, however, that for the most part these five countries were neither well above expected import levels nor well below expectations. While all five of these countries were relatively small markets individually, they combined to be important for firms in other countries seeking export outlets. As such, their import performance at anticipated levels was of some importance.

Imports of Raw Materials

While the focus of this chapter was on the per capita imports of manufactured goods given their weight in import mixes, a brief look at imports of raw materials was relevant for understanding overall import activities.

Table 5-6
Rankings for Imports of Raw Materials

Country	1960	1965	1970	1973	1976	1980	1982	1984	1986	1988	1990	1992	1994a	1994b
Japan	3	3	2	3	3	3	3	3	2.5	4	4	18	18	4
United States	14	12	11	8	11	7	6	7	5	3	5	2	2	6
Canada	18	14	19	18	20	11	13	17	19	12	12	8	4	15
Australia	19	19.5	22	22	22	22	21	22	21	20	21	17	19	21
New Zealand	8	11	14	17	18	19	18.5	12	18	19	17	19	17	17.5
Germany	16	17	18	21	21	21	22	20	20	21	20	21	22	19
France	21	23	23	23	23	23	23	23	23	23	23	23	23	23
Italy	20	21	21	19	19	20	16	21	22	22	22	22	10	22
Netherlands	4	2	3	2	2	2	2	2	2.5	2	1	3	3	3
Belgium/Luxembourg	2	1	1	1	1	1	1	1	1	1	2	1	1	1
United Kingdom	1	4	9	5	5	14	20	18	17	17	19	15	20	20
Ireland	6	5	10	10	7	6	10	11	8	8	3	13.5	6	5
Switzerland	7	7.5	4.5	13	15	17	17	10	6.5	14	9	5	7	11.5
Austria	17	22	20	20	14	18	11	15	13	9	11	13.5	15	15
Denmark	5	6	7	4	4	9	7	5	4	13	6	6	9	9
Norway	22	10	4.5	6	7	15	14	19	16	16	15	16	12	10
Sweden	10	15	13	14	10	8	8	4	11	7	10	9	14	8
Finland	9	19.5	16	15	12	4	5	8	15	15	16	10	13	7
Spain	12	13	8	9	9	10	9	9	9	10	13.5	4	8	15
Portugal	23	9	17	16	16	12	12	16	10	6	7	12	16	13
Greece	15	18	15	12	13	13	18.5	13	12	18	18	20	21	17.5
Yugoslavia/ Slovenia	13	16	12	11	17	16	15	14	14	11	13.5	--	--	--
												7	5	2
Israel	11	7.5	6	7	8	5	4	6	6.5	5	8	11	11	11.5

1994b has purchasing power parity figures substituted for GNP per capita.

The equation results for raw materials are contained in Table 5–5. Through 1988 the equations for raw materials explained much less than was the case for manufactured goods. After 1990, the equation results were low for raw materials but somewhat higher than had been the case for the corresponding manufactures equations. Another major difference was that EC membership was much more important in explaining imports of raw materials; size and wealth were less relevant. It would appear that EC membership had greater effects on agricultural and raw materials trade than for manufactures, and given the effects of the CAP on EC/EU food trade, some of the increases in imports for individual countries were a consequence of both trade diversion (French wheat substituting for U.S. or Canadian wheat; Danish or Dutch butter replacing that from New Zealand) and trade creation (greater trade of these foodstuffs among members).

A brief look at the rankings of the twenty-three nations for per capita imports of raw materials in Table 5–6 and the standardized residuals in Table 5–7 provides some examples of differences between raw materials and manufactured goods. Japan, while becoming a very poor market for manufactured products remained an excellent market for raw materials (at least until the 1990s). The Japanese market was never the most important one, and it did decline somewhat in the 1980s in terms of how much above expected levels it was as measured by the residuals. Even so, raw materials, including food products, remained quite important for the import mix of Japan. Belgium and the Netherlands were the most active importers in most years, well above the anticipated levels. It is worth noting that they tended to be active in importing both manufactured goods and raw materials, although the Netherlands declined somewhat over time as an importer of manufactured goods but not raw materials. The positions of these two countries indicated that high per capita import levels in both areas were not mutually exclusive. Obviously, a failure to import manufactured goods need not be due to the need to import raw materials.

The larger countries had a mixed pattern in terms of imports of raw materials. The United States began as a fairly poor market for raw materials but improved through time. The United Kingdom began as a well-above-average importer, but eventually it became a comparatively below-average importer of raw materials. These patterns indicated that it was not necessary for a resource-poor island country to focus on importing raw materials at the expense of manufactured goods (as Japan had apparently done). While Canada and Australia were not active importers of raw materials, their ranks and scores were similar to those for manufactured goods. Similarly, France, Italy and Germany were relatively poor markets for raw materials just as they had been for per capita imports of manufactured goods. The Scandinavian countries were generally better markets for raw materials than they were for manufactured products. The Mediterranean industrializing countries were rather less likely to import raw materials than they had been to import manufactured products, as might be expected with industrializing countries. Israel was an exception in this regard, being an excellent per capita importer of raw materials.

Summary

Clearly, the propensity to import manufactured goods by the industrialized countries was highly variable—variable over time for some countries and variable among nations in other cases. In addition, there were differences between overall imports, imports of manufactured products, and imports

Table 5-7
Standardized Scores for Imports of Raw Materials

Country	1960	1965	1970	1973	1976	1980	1982	1984	1986	1988	1990	1992	1994a	1994b
Japan	1.364	1.186	1.532	1.263	1.349	1.047	1.005	1.275	1.128	.632	.799	-.457	-.446	.936
United States	-.326	.109	.116	.238	.206	.455	.497	.442	.475	.654	.691	1.064	1.111	.661
Canada	-1.003	-.222	-1.002	-.696	-.967	-.030	-.255	-.736	-.522	-.073	-.180	.235	.558	-.234
Australia	-1.084	-1.120	-1.205	-1.253	-1.777	-1.796	-1.303	-1.393	-1.367	-1.005	-1.182	-.253	-.577	-1.025
New Zealand	.432	.146	-.190	-.394	-.579	-.716	-.411	-.049	-.517	-.803	-.576	-.626	-.390	-.567
Germany	-.466	-.350	-.969	-1.237	-1.370	-1.448	-1.606	-1.134	-.866	-1.096	-.776	-1.102	-1.514	-.829
France	-1.199	-1.697	-1.830	-1.926	-1.886	-1.841	-1.940	-1.758	-1.846	-1.776	-2.074	-1.732	-2.100	-1.612
Italy	-1.191	-1.550	-1.093	-1.098	-.928	-.916	-.360	-1.237	-1.568	-1.448	-1.585	-1.319	.098	-1.358
Netherlands	1.262	1.475	1.363	1.825	1.761	1.599	1.998	1.766	1.126	1.606	2.508	.784	.702	.972
Belgium/Lux.	1.596	2.122	2.530	2.349	2.008	2.376	2.131	2.408	4.794	2.986	1.555	3.530	2.223	3.100
United Kingdom	1.757	.837	.320	.553	.703	-.186	-.926	-.767	-.498	-.518	-.683	-.194	-.704	-.995
Ireland	.960	.791	.230	.203	.667	.628	-.035	.154	.264	.270	1.119	-.155	.448	.868
Switzerland	.586	.514	.678	.042	-.305	-.275	-.383	.248	.423	-.087	.317	.360	.314	-.106
Austria	-.898	-1.672	-1.024	-1.110	-.099	-.591	-.123	-.202	-.087	.216	.081	-.151	-.258	-.240
Denmark	1.017	.707	.363	.706	.712	.245	.464	.572	.675	-.078	.528	.288	.115	.074
Norway	-1.237	.231	.675	.509	.420	-.218	-.281	-.812	-.489	-.242	-.118	-.203	.013	-.050
Sweden	.271	-.261	-.120	-.185	.258	.381	.265	.671	.017	.281	.097	.007	-.025	.178
Finland	.304	-1.113	-.334	-.282	.096	.802	.771	.436	-.209	-.174	-.388	-.013	-.045	.218
Spain	-.115	-.185	.338	.229	.289	.212	.196	.328	.198	.152	-.147	.510	.215	-.234
Portugal	-1.494	.437	-.712	-.383	-.364	-.099	-.216	-.323	.188	.529	.426	-.100	-.341	-.174
Greece	-.382	-.572	-.282	.092	.090	-.132	-.412	-.187	-.068	-.529	-.610	-.622	-.962	-.560
Yugoslavia/	-.283	-.325	.056	.130	-.407	-.242	-.300	-.199	-.173	.004	-.148	--	--	--
Slovenia												.258	.472	1.093
Israel	.162	.511	.564	.436	.306	.744	1.056	.498	.421	.539	.348	-.067	.072	-.124

1994b has purchasing power parity figures substituted for GNP per capita.

of raw materials. Japan was the most obvious case of variation in many respects. It has been suggested that Japan had begun to favor freer trade and was less committed to strategic trade in the nineties than in the past.[21] Japan was an above-average importer of raw materials and a quite poor importer of manufactured goods in the 1980s and later. Early in the process of industrialization and growth in the 1960s, however, Japan was one of the best overall per capita importers, but this propensity to import very clearly changed. It would appear that as Japan grew, the domestic market received greater protection against imports. Interestingly enough, Saxonhouse found that Japanese import levels from 1959 to 1973 were pretty much at the levels predicted for most products and in keeping with Japanese factor endowments compared to nine other countries.[22] These results and others have led some to conclude that Japanese imports of manufactured goods have been at an appropriate level that would be expected when Japan was compared to other countries.[23] The analyses in this chapter and the preceding one would support that view that for these early years Japan was a relatively active importer, but it would seem unwise to judge later Japanese import behavior on data from the 1960s given the changes that were observed for the later years, resulting in a situation in which Japanese imports, especially of manufactured goods, were significantly below anticipated levels. In fact, a later study that took into account factor endowments discovered that Japanese imports were less than predicted,[24] conclusions perfectly in keeping with the present results. As time has gone by, Japan has become more closed with the advent of greater industrialization and wealth. Intra-industry trade has expanded elsewhere, but the low level of such trade for Japan might explain the lower levels of imports of manufactures and of goods overall. The fact that Japan is an island lacking in raw materials would explain higher imports of raw materials, but it would not explain such low levels for manufactured goods. Resource-poor Austria, Switzerland, the United Kingdom, and even Israel imported larger volumes of manufactured products in per capita terms. Overall, the suggestion that Japan has been protecting its own producers would seem to be supported by the results from the above analyses.

The United States followed a different pattern for total imports. It was never a poor importer any time, and it progressively became more open and more involved in importing. The United States was somewhat less active in regard to imports of raw materials, but there have been indigenous sources for many commodities, and the country has been a major surplus producer of food. Some of the raw materials sectors have even been provided with protection against import competition.[25] Given the strength of protectionist sentiment that has existed in recent years in the United States, it was possible that the relative openness in the country has reflected ineffective protection or leaky barriers to imports rather than a lack of barriers. Lacking any tradition of statist practices, in a relative sense the United States has been less capable of utilizing strategic trade policy.[26] Canada started out as a relatively poor importer but became more active in later years, both in terms of raw materials and manufactures. There were some preliminary indications that in the late 1980s there was an increase in Canadian import activity that could have resulted from the Canada–U.S. free trade arrangement.

Australia and New Zealand were never especially good markets for imports of any kind. The customs union between the two would explain why New Zealand was relatively more open. The size differential would mean that producers in New Zealand would not provide much new competition for Australian firms other than selectively. Australian firms, on the other hand, would press companies inside New Zealand and would be likely to displace a much larger portion of domestic production. While liberalization in New Zealand took time to develop and to become policy,[27] the liberalization that came with the customs union provided an excellent dose of competition, even if it was less liberalizing than overall openness would have been, or less liberalizing than if Australia had reduced its own barriers and the common external tariff.[28] Australia did show some indications of becoming more open with time, but reductions in protection in that country would seem to have been proportional to reductions elsewhere.

The large initial EC member countries, especially France, were not particularly good markets for manufactured goods or raw materials (which included foodstuffs and other agricultural products for which French farmers has received significant subsidies). The United Kingdom was a better market for manufactured goods, although it was not especially better than average for most years. The position of the United Kingdom was not noticeably affected by accession into the European Community for good or ill. The British tradition of free trade would appear to have influenced trade policy in that there were fewer impediments to imports than was the case for Germany, Italy, and France with their more statist traditions of economic policy. The Netherlands and Belgium, on the other hand, were among the most active importers in the industrialized countries. Belgium was frequently by far the best market per capita for all kinds of imports. While the Netherlands was usually a good market, it was not as open as Belgium. In fact, over time it became somewhat less open in a relative sense, suggesting that EC membership may have resulted in somewhat lower relative levels of trade than otherwise would have been the case, controlling for wealth, size, and EC membership. Interestingly enough, Belgium did not display the same pattern. Ireland was the other active importer among the earlier members, but Ireland was an active importer even before EC membership, a trend that continued after accession. Overall, membership in the EC in the early years did not facilitate greater trade once membership was controlled for in the regression equations. Of course, to the extent that the EC facilitated economic growth, there were other additional increases in relative trade due to membership, but the EC has not been totally conducive to greater trade in all cases.

The Scandinavian countries were again variable. Finland and Sweden were generally better as raw materials importers than they were importers of manufactured products. Switzerland and Austria, on the other hand, were less active in terms of importing raw materials compared to manufactured goods. Even though they were countries with limited resource bases, they were not raw materials importers; rather, they imported manufactured goods, most likely as part of intra-industry trading networks. It should be noted that some of the manufactured products could be semi-processed materials rather than high-technology final products. The Mediterranean NICs were not particularly active importers of either raw materials or manufactured goods, nor were they especially poor markets overall. Their import patterns for both types of goods were middle range. Israel was the most active importer in this group for both kinds of products, while Spain was more active in terms of imports of raw materials than for imports of manufactured goods.

Overall, there was some indication that countries that have had long statist traditions were indeed likely to import at lower levels once controls were introduced. Italy, France, Germany, and Japan were less active importers. Countries with free trade traditions such as the United States, the United Kingdom (and Ireland through association, if not choice), the Netherlands, and Belgium have had such backgrounds, and these countries were much more open to imports of all kinds. Canada and Australia had a mixed pattern, but while not countries with especially long statist traditions, they are countries with some practices such as marketing boards and protection for fledging industries in the early development of the country that have favored a statist approach. The Mediterranean NICs also have traditions of state involvement, ranging from the semi-corporatist practices of the authoritarian regimes in Spain and Portugal, the military regime in Greece, the active involvement in the economy of the semi-official Yishuv, the Jewish Agency, and the Histadrut that even predated the establishment of the state, and, of course, the large element of central planning in Yugoslavia. Overall, none of these countries were particularly active importers, yet they were not among the least active either. Israel was no doubt the most active of these five countries. Part of the Israeli ability to import might have been due to special factors such as foreign aid from the United States and the reparation payments from Germany that provided valuable foreign exchange for so many years.

The above patterns are broad ones, and the next two chapters will look at some detailed import categories to determine if the various countries imported differently in terms of certain types of manufactured goods. Are the industrializing Mediterranean countries competitive with the NICs elsewhere in the world? How have per capita import levels of other industrialized countries been modified by the presence of import competing domestic sectors? Are some countries more involved in products likely to be reflective of intra-industry trade while others are less involved?

Chapter 6

Manufactured Exports
from the Developing World

Trade in manufactured products has been extremely important for the industrialized countries, both as exporters and importers (although with significant variation for them as importers, as was demonstrated in chapter 5). At the same time, these industrialized countries have become particularly important as markets for the manufactured goods that have been produced in the developing world. The industrialized countries have been the key markets for the manufactured goods that have been essential for the economic and developmental advances of the Newly Industrializing Countries (NICs). Without access to prosperous markets in the developed world, it would have been extremely difficult for these countries to have grown through the expansion of export industries, and it would be extremely difficult for additional countries to follow the NIC path of export-led growth without such markets. The markets in the developing countries generally lack sufficient size or domestic demand to foster export-led growth elsewhere in the developing world. Further, many developing countries have similar rather than complementary economies, limiting even more export opportunities to each other. The opportunities for the developing world to utilize comparative advantage in manufactured goods consequently depends principally on access to the large markets in the industrialized countries, markets in which there also have been better chances of complementary economic activity rather than competitive activity.

The relative openness of the developed countries to imports of manufactures from the developing world thus has been of special importance for development that has been based on the exports of manufactured goods.

The relative openness to imports of all manufactured goods was considered in the previous chapter, but circumstances could be different for the types of goods that have been produced in the developing world as part of the initial stages of export led growth strategies and for efforts to develop indigenous industrial capacities. Europe and North America have protected domestic producers against imports of Japanese automobiles, and Japan has protected its domestic market, but to what extent do these countries guard against imports of inexpensive shoes, toys, clothing, or textiles?

Developing Countries as Targets of Protection

Unfortunately, there has been a variety of protectionist barriers designed to block exports that originate in the developing world. In fact, such exports have frequently suffered from special discriminatory import barriers, even from other developing countries.[1] It has been estimated that non-tariff barriers in the EC/EU have affected 30 percent of the exports of developing countries, while the figure for Japan was 26 percent and for the United States was 24 percent.[2] The EC/EU in the past has "abused" countervailing duties to limit imports from developing countries.[3] Such barriers have even affected products that have been eligible to receive special treatment under the Generalized System of Preferences (GSPs) in place for industrialized countries.[4] The developed countries frequently have limited the number of import barriers that apply to each other because they have a mutual need for each others' markets. Massive protection against products from one could have led to effective retaliation from other industrialized countries (or at least major diplomatic difficulties, as can be seen in disputes between Japan and the United States or between the United States and the EC/EU). Lower barriers could also have facilitated mutually advantageous intra-industry trade among developed countries. In the case of the developing countries, however, the roles have been more unequal.[5] The industrialized countries have not needed market access in the developing world nearly as much as the developing countries have needed access to industrialized markets.[6] These circumstances also explain in large measure why GATT negotiations on tariff reductions and the creation of the WTO largely had focused on products traded among the industrialized countries rather than on goods that have been important exports from the developing nations.[7] The creation of the WTO may eventually redress some of these imbalances since developing countries have been more involved in the WTO than they were in GATT. But it remains to be seen in the future to what extent the potential gains for developing countries from the new organization will actually be realized. In any event, past exports from the developing countries have clearly been affected by protection in the developing world.

In fact, it has been manufactured goods that can be competitively produced in the developing world that have frequently faced barriers. Many industrialized nations have so-called cascading tariffs that have higher percentage levies on imports as the degree of processing increases.[8] For example, basic ores might face a 15 percent *ad valorem* tariff; ore that is partially processed a 25 percent tariff; and ore that is processed and shaped into ingots or bars a 45 percent levy. Such tariff schedules serve not only to limit imports of semi-manufactured intermediate goods; they also can hinder the development of processing industries in the developing world, which have been exactly the initial industrial sectors that could be created in some developing states. The cascading tariffs, of course, also have preserved existing investment and jobs in mineral processing sectors that already were present in the developed countries (which, of course, has been the intent of these kinds of tariffs).

Just as cascading tariffs have been used to discourage the processing of raw materials in the developing countries, expensive versions of products face higher tariffs than the cheaper ones do. These tariffs again could have affected goods that were likely to be among the initial manufactured items that have been produced in developing countries.[9] These differential tariffs have provided a not-so-subtle encouragement for manufacturers in the developing world to concentrate only on those goods that are no longer being produced in the developed world. They also have indicated that developing world producers should avoid competing with the production that still occurs in the domestic sectors of these industrialized countries. This type of protection has not only limited the level or value of exports from the developing world, but it has limited further industrialization as well.

The developed countries have also protected declining manufacturing sectors from import competition in other ways.[10] Industries in decline have often been labor-intensive, low-technology manufacturing operations, exactly the type of industrial activity in which developing countries would have the best opportunities for creating their own indigenous capacities. With indigenous production these countries would then also be able to export to the industrialized markets of the world, displacing domestic production (and workers) in those nations. Countries such as Japan in the 1950s, and Hong Kong, South Korea, Taiwan, and Singapore in later years first began to manufacture these types of products and eventually to export them. Labor-intensive, low-technology products, which corresponded to the declining industries in the developed countries, however, have been protected precisely because the labor intensity has meant that increased imports would have led to larger numbers of workers who would have faced unemployment, workers who might find it difficult to find equivalent jobs elsewhere.[11] The various Multi-Fibre Arrangements (MFAs) that have been negotiated to limit developing world exports of textiles and apparel to the developed countries have been prime examples of protection being offered for labor-intensive manufacturing sectors.[12] The MFA framework was even used by West European countries to limit exports from the East European countries after they entered the international trading system with the passing of their Communist governments.[13] While some developing countries have benefited from restrictions placed on their competitors, it is clear that the elimination of the MFAs would have benefited the developing world as a whole to a significant extent and would have opened up important opportunities for industrial development in many developing countries.[14] One of the benefits for the developing world with the new WTO has been the specification of a ten-year transition period for the phasing out of the current MFA. It is very likely, however, that the developed countries will be able to find ways of extending the agreement or to come up with different ways of providing protection to these sectors.[15] Antidumping procedures or other types of contingent protection devices could easily take over the role that was previously played by the MFA agreements.[16]

The differential tariff, rates, the MFAs, and other import barriers all have provided obvious encouragements for producers in the developing world to concentrate only on those goods that are no longer being produced in the developed world. Further, it has been made clear to them that they should avoid competing with the domestic producers who still serve markets in these industrialized countries. The continuation of such protection would limit not only the level or value of exports from the developing world but the possibilities for further industrialization. The situation has helped the initial countries that were able to penetrate the markets in the developed countries and gain shares in those markets. The first NICs, especially those in Asia, captured existing markets with their own production, leading to protectionist demands in the developed states. It was then difficult for other developing countries to create export sectors based on manufacturing similar products in the face of new barriers like the MFA. As a consequence, to date there has been little evidence that production has shifted from the first NICs to other developing states in any major fashion.[17]

Overall, the opportunities for major increases of manufactured goods from the developing world to the 23 industrialized countries have been limited by import barriers. Both tariff schedules and the plethora of non-tariff barriers restrict such exports. As was the case with imports in the previous chapters, the relative openness of the countries would have been variable. As a consequence, the levels of imports of some of the manufactured goods that have been important to the developing world will be analyzed in terms of per capita imports of the industrialized countries to determine which nations have been better markets for the developing world, either because they have been less interested in protection or because the barriers that they have been using has been less effective in terms of limiting these particular imports.

SITC Categories Utilized

There were seven categories of manufactured goods chosen for detailed analysis. These products were either two- or three-digit subgroups of the UN SITC categories. All the products in questions were ones that have been important in the export mix of the developing world at some point in time. The product categories were textiles (SITC 65), clothing (SITC 84), footwear (SITC 851), travel goods or luggage (SITC 831), toys and sporting goods (SITC 894), clocks and watches including parts (SITC 864 and then 885 after the reorganization of the SITC categories in the 1970s), and selected stereo equipment—basically record players, recorders, cassette recorders, and components (SITC 891 and then 763). UN trade sources[18] contained both individual country data detailing imports as well as lists of major importers by two- and three-digit SITC categories and by even more detailed SITC levels. In most cases, beginning in 1970 the imports for the twenty-three industrialized countries for these seven categories could be found in the pages with the import data for individual countries. In other cases, levels of imports could be found where the largest importers and exporters for an SITC category were listed. In the rare cases in which no data were available from either of these places, it was still possible to specify an upper limit for imports since the levels for the smallest of the top forty importers were known. For example, if the goods in an SITC category imported by any state in the list totaled a minimum of $3 million, then any country missing from the list imported less than $3 million.

In cases such as these, countries were given a value for this lower level of possible imports (i.e., $3 million). The assignment of values such as these might have overstated the amount of imports to a small extent, but the values still placed these countries very low on per capita import levels compared to the other industrialized countries.

The developing countries have become increasingly important as exporters of all of these products. Totals for world exports in the seven categories and shares of the developing world for selected years are contained in Table 6–1. Textiles and clothing were the most important categories in terms of overall value. Electronic products have shown the greatest relative increase, and production in this area is likely to become more important in the future with increasing use of such products. The other product lines were important in the aggregate, and producers in the developing world have become increasingly important as exporters for them as well. Travel goods was the one area that was relatively small in volume but that has been increasingly dominated by developing country producers. In other cases, the products in questions have been especially important in the export mix of particular developing nations (toys or watches for Hong Kong, shoes for Brazil).

These products have been important exports for the developing world, and they have frequently been the target of protectionist barriers. It is obvious from Table 6–1 that much of the production for export has originated in the industrialized countries themselves, although at declining

Table 6-1
Global Imports of Selected Products and
Percentage Shipped by Developing Countries

Product Category	1970 Total (mil)	1970 Per Cent	1980 Total (mil)	1980 Per Cent	1990 Total (mil)	1990 Per Cent
Textiles	$12,391	15.5	$55,432	22.3	$109,928	39.0
Clothing	4,079	28.2	40,090	36.3	109,002	56.4
Footwear	1,641	9.7	9,542	20.9	26,182	43.0[*]
Luggage	274	17.0	2,025	38.6	7,576	55.0[*]
Toys and Sporting Goods	1,325	16.0	7,227	25.8	20,732	45.0[*]
Clocks & Watches	1,110	4.8	7,524	28.6	15,315	37.0[*]
Stereos	1,635	1.4	5,509	6.8	15,848	25.0[*]

[*]Low estimate of total of developing world, based on nearly complete data available in the source.

Source: United Nations, *Yearbook of International Trade Statistics* (New York: United Nations, various years).

levels over time. An industrialized country that was a poor market for footwear in general, however, was unlikely to have been an above-average market for such exports from the developing world. In fact, the various MFAs, restrictive tariff structures, and contingent protection have all been usually designed to limit developing world exports, not imports from other industrialized countries as already noted. The MFA arrangements have involved bilateral "voluntary" restrictions reached by negotiation between a developed and a developing state. Such arrangements have not involved agreements between two developed countries (although there are examples of voluntary export restraints involving two industrialized countries that do not deal with textiles or clothing). Also, in some cases it has clearly been developed countries that have gained from negotiations under the MFA. Italian producers gained not only from the protection provided for their domestic markets, but also because they were able to capture larger shares of the domestic markets of other members of the EC/EU. Italian production in effect displaced exports from other countries (trade diversion), including those in the developing world.[19] Portugal and Spain were also in a position to gain advantages in EU member markets at the expense of non-member countries. Spanish advantages were in intermediate goods while Portuguese gains were for some types of textiles and clothing upon Portugal's joining the EU.[20]

Overall, it was anticipated that countries that had been generally good markets for the manufactured goods analyzed would also be reasonably good markets for similar exports from the developing world. Countries that were poor markets in general were unlikely to be good markets for exporters in the developing countries, and they might even be worse markets for the developing countries than the industrialized ones, given the weak negotiating power of developing states compared to industrialized ones. To the extent that barriers affected countries differently, the exports for the developing countries were likely to face at least as many, if not more barriers, than exports from the other industrialized countries.

Results

In order to determine the relative openness of the markets of the various industrialized countries for these types of products, the per capita import levels were used as dependent variables in regression analyses. The wealth, population size, length of EU membership, and length of EFTA membership were again used as independent variables. The residuals derived from the regression analyses were then utilized to determine the relative openness of countries once the four variables had been used as controls. The ranks and standardized scores for the products for the 23 countries were then compared to determine which were above average per capita importers and which had been importing below anticipated levels. The ranks and scores were again relative ones. If every country protected its clothing producers, then the highest ranking nation would simply have been the country providing less protection to its domestic producers (or less effective protective measures) than the other developed nations.

Textiles and Apparel

Textiles and clothing have been important exports for the developing world. Restrictions on textiles have been especially limiting for development possibilities in developing countries since the textile sector has traditionally been an important area in which industrialization could initially begin.[21] Total global exports are higher than in other categories, and the developing countries in the aggregate have captured roughly half the world export market in recent years. These gains have occurred despite the many import barriers and restrictions present in the MFA. The MFA has indeed limited the export levels for many developing countries, although in a few cases the quotas imposed under the MFA framework have provided advantages for some states. As individual developing countries have approached the quotas negotiated with particular developed nations, producers have shifted their production to other developing countries that have not fully used their quotas or to countries that were not subject to such quotas.[22] Of course, once any country did become a significant exporter of either textiles or clothing to the markets of one or more industrialized countries, it was quickly brought into the MFA framework of restrictions. These new producers, however, were seldom in a position to capture important market shares from the already existing exporters in the developing world when the markets fell within the quotas of these established exporters. While European governments used adjustment assistance as well, protection in the clothing and textile industries was frequently the easiest type of policy to adopt.[23]

In the case of imports of textiles and apparel, it was possible to derive fairly complete import data for 1960 and 1965 as well as later years; therefore, the analysis began with these years instead of 1970. Textiles as a product category included both intermediate goods and final goods. Some textiles, such as thread, were intermediate goods designed for incorporation into other products, such as clothing, while items such as carpets and bedding were themselves final products. The regression analyses for the analyses of textile imports explained from one-third to two-thirds of the variation in per capita imports (see the bottom of Table 6–2). The explanatory power was the greatest between 1973 and 1986. Relative wealth

Table 6-2
Rankings for Total Imports of Textiles for Industrialized Countries

Country	1960	1965	1970	1973	1976	1980	1982	1984	1986	1988	1990	1992	1994a	1994b
Japan	6	4	18	8	8	12.5	14	14	14	13	14	15	16.5	13
United States	11	9.5	3	5	6	4	4.5	5	4	2	5	5	3	6
Canada	21	21	22	22	22	21	19	22.5	16	15	10	12.5	23	23
Australia	4	11	12.5	11	16	14	13	16	13	11	12	17	12	16
New Zealand	1	1	5	3	4.5	5	2	2	2	8	8	11	8	8
Germany	10	12	20	19.5	20.5	23	17	18	15	23	13	16	15	15
France	20	22	23	23	23	22	23	22.5	22	18	21	22	21	21
Italy	14	19	12.5	17	17.5	16	22	20	23	19	23	23	22	22
Netherlands	2	2	1	4	7	5	10	9	7	6	7	6	9	9
Belgium/ Luxembourg	12	8	4	1	1	1	1	1	1	1	1	1	1	1
United Kingdom	13	15	21	14	9	9	12	8	10	9.5	16	9	14	11
Ireland	7	7	2	2	2	2	3	4	6	3	6	7	10	10
Switzerland	23	23	11	12	15	8	6	6	3	5	2	4	5	5
Austria	8	6	7	6	3	3	4.5	3	5	4	3	3	2	2
Denmark	3	3	6	7	4.5	10	8	7	19	9.5	16	9	14	11
Norway	5	5	10	15	11	17	18	21	20	22	22	19	19.5	20
Sweden	9	9.5	19	21	13	17	21	17	21	17	19	18	16.5	17
Finland	16	17	8	9	10	7	7	10	12	16	17	21	18	18
Spain	18	16	14.5	13	17.5	19.5	20	19	18	21	18	20	19.5	19
Portugal	17	14	17	19.5	14	15	9	12	9	7	4	2	4	4
Greece	19	18	16	16	19	19.5	15	15	11	14	11	12.5	13	12
Yugoslavia/	15	13	9	10	12	12.5	11	13	17	20	20	--	--	--
Slovenia					.							10	6	3
Israel	22	20	14.5	18	20.5	11	16	11	8	12	9	8	7	7
Equation Results														
Adj. R^2	.383	.399	.450	.629	.641	.524	.565	.576	.585	.399	.494	.362	.334	.347
F-Ratio	4.41	4.65	5.51	10.32	10.81	7.05	8.15	8.48	8.75	4.65	6.38	4.12	3.58	3.92
p	.988	.991	.996	.999	.999	.999	.999	.999	.999	.991	.998	.985	.978	.982

Population significant addition to equation except in 1970 and 1980.
Wealth a significant addition to equation 1960-1986.
EC membership a signficant addition to equation 1976-1986 and 1990-1994.
EFTA a significant addition to equation in 1986 and 1990.

1994b has purchasing power parity figures substituted for GNP per capita.

levels were important independent variables until 1986, while population (larger size being associated with lower imports) was important for most years. EC/EU membership was relevant beginning in 1976 in terms of explaining import levels.

Tables 6–2 and 6–3 contain the rankings and standardized values for the twenty-three countries. Germany, and especially France and Italy, imported at per capita levels well below those that were predicted. The French tradition of protection was brought to bear on textiles when French domestic firms faced increasing competition from imports.[24] The Netherlands, and especially Belgium, however, were much better importers for these types of goods among the original EC members. Ireland, Austria, and Switzerland generally imported well above the levels predicted by wealth, size, and customs union membership, even though Switzerland was a relatively poor importer prior to 1980. The Scandinavian countries generally

Table 6-3
Standardized Scores for Imports of Textiles for Industrialized Countries

Country	1960	1965	1970	1973	1976	1980	1982	1984	1986	1988	1990	1992	1994a	1994b
Japan	.828	.777	-.744	.398	.163	-.245	-.271	-.319	-.404	-.401	-.198	-.432	-.664	-.280
United States	.081	.338	1.519	.803	.928	1.136	1.125	1.050	1.048	1.132	.870	1.056	1.124	.960
Canada	-1.289	-1.204	-1.558	-1.357	-1.444	-.789	-1.044	-1.280	-.530	-.443	-.054	-.363	-1.460	-.427
Australia	1.045	.213	-.210	-.041	-.492	-.318	-.191	-.499	-.331	-.113	-.164	-.477	-.250	-.427
New Zealand	2.397	1.890	1.161	1.386	1.049	.626	1.684	1.953	1.261	.330	.364	-.004	.380	.196
Germany	.199	.110	-.907	-.861	-1.035	-2.352	-.645	-.680	-.465	-2.540	-.183	-.489	-.469	-.326
France	-1.180	-1.661	-1.856	-1.612	-1.570	-.889	-1.239	-1.283	-1.181	-.646	-1.178	-1.184	-1.064	-1.064
Italy	-.629	-.686	-.205	-.732	-.688	-.427	-1.085	-.956	-1.543	-.720	-1.546	-1.520	-1.079	-1.142
Netherlands	1.202	1.559	1.743	1.106	.635	.612	.037	.002	.665	.707	.451	.305	.052	.023
Belgium/Lux.	.047	.503	1.225	2.056	2.028	2.406	2.414	2.379	2.532	2.509	2.615	2.882	2.969	2.863
United Kingdom	-.203	-.411	-1.173	-.396	.086	.145	-.149	.040	.059	.308	-.280	-.416	-.244	-.311
Ireland	.429	.596	1.639	1.950	2.011	1.793	1.421	1.144	1.006	.993	.495	.252	-.048	-.004
Switzerland	-1.926	-2.179	-.075	-.071	-.434	.310	.494	.665	1.237	.931	1.618	1.167	1.018	1.021
Austria	.405	.617	.655	.753	1.175	1.147	1.134	1.361	1.031	.984	1.206	1.311	1.141	1.095
Denmark	1.103	1.525	.789	.692	1.058	.014	.193	.213	-.952	.307	-.546	.034	-.326	-.248
Norway	.893	.733	-.060	-.584	-.160	-.532	-1.020	-1.190	-.994	-.843	-1.238	-.845	-.813	-.868
Sweden	.243	.332	-.812	-.921	-.245	-.628	-1.068	-.589	-1.003	-.555	-.876	-.688	-.664	-.561
Finland	-.413	-.484	.307	.147	.033	.377	.313	-.048	-.282	-.535	-.734	-.974	-.701	-.707
Spain	-.529	-.431	-.364	-.311	-.690	-.714	-1.058	-.827	-.823	-.755	-.801	-.859	-.815	-.763
Portugal	-.515	-.313	-.450	-.864	-.367	-.471	.160	-.252	.146	.654	1.056	1.354	1.035	1.049
Greece	-.706	-.617	-.384	-.700	-.775	-.708	-.584	-.431	-.190	-.419	-.072	-.361	-.291	-.259
Yugoslavia/ Slovenia	-.299	-.264	.175	.102	-.231	-.239	-.017	-.285	-.667	-.737	-.935		--	--
												.027	.679	1.075
Israel	-1.544	-1.117	-.369	-.855	-1.033	-.202	-.605	-.219	.379	-.149	.129	.122	.492	.408

1994b has purchasing power parity figures substituted for GNP per capita.

stabilized at levels at which they imported less than would be expected, notwithstanding the fact that Denmark and Norway had frequently been quite good importers relative to the other states in the earlier years of the analysis. Since there has been no indication that the Danish or Norwegian governments suddenly sought to create massive protection for domestic

Table 6-4
Rankings for Total Imports of Clothing for Industrialized Countries

Country	1960	1965	1970	1973	1976	1980	1982	1984	1986	1988	1990	1992	1994a	1994b
Japan	--	--	4	8	10	15	10	16	16	19	17	19	21	10
United States	4	6	11	10	9	4	5	6	4	5	5	5	2.5	7
Canada	7	16.5	21	18	20	19	19	19	19	17.5	10	16	16	19
Australia	10	13	18	17	19	20	20	20	20	17.5	20	18	18	20
New Zealand	11	15	17	21	18	18	21	17.5	18	16	11	12	13	15
Germany	9	9	12	11	15	14	16	10	9	6	6	8	8	8
France	14	20	23	23	23	23	22	21.5	21	20	21	21	22	21
Italy	--	18	20	20	21	21	15	21.5	22	23	23	23	23	23
Netherlands	1	1	1	2	1	2	3	4	3	5	4	4	6	5
Belgium/ Luxembourg	6	10	9	3	4	3	4	3	4	3	2	1	1	3
United Kingdom	13	16.5	19	14	7	9	18	12	14	21	17	17	15	17
Ireland	5	8	7	7	2	1	1	1	1	1	3	2	5	4
Switzerland	3	3	2	1	5.5	5	2	2	2	2	1	3	4	2
Austria	--	14	15	13	11	8	17	7	11	11	8	7	7	9
Denmark	12	11	13	19	13	17	13.5	15	12	12	17	11	10	6
Norway	2	2	3	5	3	7	7	9	5	10	12	10	11.5	12
Sweden	8	7	8	12	8	10	11.5	14	17	15	14.5	14	19	16
Finland	--	19	22	22	22	22	23	23	23	22	22	22	20	22
Spain	--	5	6	6	12	12	11.5	8	10	13	13	13	14	14
Portugal	--	12	16	15	16	16	9	17.5	8	8	9	9	9	11
Greece	--	--	10	9	14	11	6	11	13	14	14.5	15	11.5	13
Yugoslavia/ Slovenia	--	4	5	4	5.5	6	13.5	5	7	7	7	-- 6	-- 2.5	-- 1
Israel	--	--	14	16	17	13	8	13	15	9	19	20	17	18
Equation Results														
Adj. R^2	.429	.431	.575	.629	.635	.650	.631	.614	.650	.652	.609	.567	.627	.553
F-Ratio	3.45	4.60	8.45	10.32	10.59	11.21	10.42	9.74	11.23	11.30	9.57	8.21	10.26	7.81
p	.943	.987	.999	.999	.999	.999	.999	.999	.999	.999	.999	.999	.999	.999

Population significant addition to equation 1960-1980.
Wealth a significant addition to equation 1965-1988, 1992-1994.
EC membership a signficant addition to equation 1965-1994.
EFTA a significant addition to equation in 1960, 1970, 1973, 1982-1994.

1994b has purchasing power parity figures substituted for GNP per capita.

producers, the changes in rankings were more likely due to the fact that some other states had become more open while barriers in Denmark and Norway had remained in place.

Japan was initially a relatively high per capita importer of textiles, but by the 1980s, it had reached a point at which imports were at the predicted levels, notwithstanding the fact that Japan did not avail itself of the MFA opportunities. Obviously other barriers to imports had become effective. The United States, however, was consistently an above-average importer, even though it was a country that had used the MFA to limit imports of textiles. Canada and Australia were generally poor markets for textile imports, whereas New Zealand was a very active importer. The five Mediterranean countries were not good markets in the 1960s and 1970s, reflecting the fact that they themselves had significant textile industries. By the end of the 1980s, however, their imports had expanded. This expansion may have reflected the fact that they had begun to utilize foreign suppliers to provide some of the intermediate textile products that were necessary for other textile production or for production in other sectors. Portugal, in fact, had become an above-average importer in the later years of the analysis. Neighboring Spain, however, never became even an average per capita importer of textiles and as a consequence was a relatively poor market.

The results for clothing imports were different in some respects. The explanatory value of the equations was somewhat higher on the whole, particularly in the later years (see Table 6–4). Per capita income was almost always an important independent variable, as was membership in the EC and in EFTA. While EFTA membership had been generally an unimportant predictor for the analyses in the preceding chapters, it was quite important for predicting per capita imports of clothing. Population size, however, added little to the equations after 1976 when it failed to be a significant addition to the equations.

The ranks and standardized values (see Tables 6–4 and 6–5) indicated that France and usually Italy were far below predicted levels. Given the importance of the clothing industries in these two countries, it was perhaps not surprising that they had effective protective mechanisms in place to limit imports and to benefit domestic firms, including the EC/EU structure with its common external tariff and commercial policies. Germany, on the other hand, imported near predicted levels in most years. The United Kingdom also imported pretty much at anticipated levels. Among the smaller European countries, Belgium, the Netherlands, Ireland, and Switzerland were above-average per capita importers. Switzerland and Ireland, in fact, were consistently higher (two standard deviations above predicted levels), and either Belgium or the Netherlands (but not both in the same year) approached similar values. Austria was an average importer, while the Scandinavian countries, except Norway, were generally below-average importers. Norway in the 1970s was among the more active importers but slipped toward average per capita levels by the 1980s. Finland was consistently one of the worst markets on a per capita basis, always being at least one standard deviation below predicted import levels. The best rank achieved by Finland was nineteenth in 1965.

As in many other areas of imports, Japan started as a fairly good market and progressively became less open. The United States followed an opposite trend as it increasingly became a better market for imports of clothing. Even so, it was never so far above predicted per capita levels to the same extent as was true for Switzerland and some other countries. While it was a better importer than many states, the MFAs and other restrictions would

Table 6-5
Standardized Scores for Imports of Clothing for Industrialized Countries

Country	1960	1965	1970	1973	1976	1980	1982	1984	1986	1988	1990	1992	1994a	1994b
Japan	--	--	.945	.556	.324	-.262	-.148	-.286	-.324	-.671	-.335	-.599	-1.273	.163
United States	.775	.592	.183	.283	.427	.800	.737	.681	.771	1.132	.788	1.030	1.354	.666
Canada	-.126	-.758	-1.026	-.856	-.816	-.808	-.462	-.810	-.574	-.528	-.004	-.398	-.466	-.825
Australia	-.432	-.681	-.783	-.837	-.816	-.984	-.698	-1.184	-.910	-.532	-.402	-.588	-.688	-.875
New Zealand	-.755	-.752	-.760	-.981	-.812	-.733	-.763	-.690	-.445	-.580	-.096	-.143	.013	-.398
Germany	-.321	.025	-.089	-.062	-.272	-.195	-.244	.249	.401	.563	.745	.405	.314	.634
France	-1.489	-1.572	-1.616	-1.903	-2.086	-1.884	-2.056	-1.450	-1.310	-1.169	-1.258	-1.307	-1.358	-1.215
Italy	--	-.801	-.917	-.953	-1.029	-1.194	-.241	-1.444	-1.960	-1.937	-2.389	-2.286	-2.101	-2.178
Netherlands	1.685	2.338	2.300	1.843	2.103	1.636	.999	.854	1.101	1.099	.975	1.165	1.000	.908
Belgium/Lux.	.125	.011	.321	1.106	.875	.948	.868	.975	1.067	1.298	1.589	1.542	1.645	1.314
United Kingdom	-1.399	-.761	-.812	-.317	.511	.209	-.344	-.042	-.176	-1.447	-.339	-.445	-.446	-.635
Ireland	.537	.383	.421	.671	1.363	2.429	2.144	2.065	1.708	1.648	1.451	1.465	1.078	.983
Switzerland	1.185	1.382	1.775	1.992	.636	.791	1.850	-1.759	1.600	1.524	1.918	1.414	1.259	1.555
Austria	--	-.695	-.633	-.235	.259	.405	-.261	.567	.002	.161	.262	.506	.569	.327
Denmark	-.979	1.206	-.468	-.878	.176	-.574	-.179	-.186	-.037	.058	-.333	-.003	.182	.740
Norway	1.348	1.398	1.299	.822	.950	.610	.673	.340	.893	.170	-.237	-.302	-.703	-.510
Sweden	-.155	.427	.360	-.168	.436	.125	-.173	-.109	-.371	.071	-.237	-.302	-.703	-.510
Finland	--	-1.336	-1.133	-1.299	-2.055	-1.537	-2.186	-1.951	-2.206	-1.853	-1.808	-1.685	-1.244	-1.391
Spain	--	.681	.768	.752	.210	.061	-.172	.368	.173	-.043	-.207	-.150	-.238	-.214
Portugal	--	-.495	-.722	-.442	-.348	-.560	.002	-.683	.443	1.500	.156	.330	.259	.042
Greece	--	--	.258	.335	.043	.072	.691	.199	.093	-.062	-.232	-.359	.077	-.146
Yugoslavia/	--	.821	.883	1.088	.638	.642	-.179	.835	.510	.513	.306	--	--	--
Slovenia												1.020	1.360	1.870
Israel	--	--	-.558	-.518	-.640	-.002	.143	-.056	-.265	.266	-.358	-.628	-.677	-.772

1994b has purchasing power parity figures substituted for GNP per capita.

appear to have limited the potential of the U.S. market for imports of these products. Australia, New Zealand, and Canada had not been particularly good markets. While there were fluctuations, they usually imported below predicted levels, and even when they were above these expected levels, it was not by very much.

The Mediterranean countries were neither particularly good nor particularly bad markets. Yugoslavia (and especially Slovenia) was at times noticeably above average. Portugal was quite variable in different years, perhaps a reflection of its own clothing industry and its changes in membership from EFTA to the EC. None of the five countries would have been expected to be particularly good markets for the type of clothing produced by the NICs and other developing countries. In fact, it was more likely that indigenous plants in these countries were competing for the same foreign markets, especially those elsewhere in Western Europe (i.e., members of the EC and EFTA).[25]

One other pattern emerged from the analyses of imports of textiles and clothing. Most countries were not well-above-average importers or well below predicted levels for per capita imports of both commodities. For example, between 1970 and 1992, Finland, almost always a poor market for the imports analyzed in the preceding chapters, averaged a rank of 12.2 for textiles and 22.3 for clothing. New Zealand ranked 6.1 on average for textiles and 17.3 for clothing, while Australia ranked 13.4 and 18.2 respectively. Germany, on the other hand, had an average rank of 18.5 for textiles but 11.1 for clothing. Similarly, Sweden was 17.7 for textiles but averaged 11.8 for clothing. Some countries, of course, were well above predicted levels for both textiles and clothing. France and Italy were clear exceptions to the pattern of positive import levels in at least one area in that they were well below anticipated levels for both textiles and clothing. Most countries, however, were more open to either imports of textiles—often an intermediate good for clothing production—or imports of clothing. Clothing producers may have needed cheap imports of cloth or thread in order to be competitive globally or at least to be competitive within a customs area or even a national domestic market. At least some influences from comparative or competitive advantage obviously were operative in the industrialized countries.

Footwear

Shoes have faced restrictions similar to the import limitations placed on clothing and textiles. In fact, the footwear industry has often cooperated with textile and clothing manufacturers in the same country in seeking protection from imports.[26] The NICs, and more recently countries in Eastern Europe, have been among the exporters facing such barriers.[27] For shoes, the regression equations explained at least half of the variation through 1988, and slightly less thereafter (see Table 6–6). Wealth was the most important predictor variable in the equations, but EFTA membership

Table 6-6
Rankings for Total Imports of Footwear for Industrialized Countries

Country	1970	1973	1976	1980	1982	1984	1986	1988	1990	1992	1994a	1994b
Japan	7	11	13	18	19	19	20	21	21	21	22	19
United States	10	7	6	3	4	4	4	3	4	3	2	3
Canada	18	19	19	16.5	15	17	15	14.5	10	12	12	17
Australia	19	17	17	20	18	20	19	16	16	14	16	18
New Zealand	21	21	20	19	20	18	16	18.5	12	10	9	11
Germany	12	10	14	13	12	13	11	11	8	9	10	9
France	23	23	22	23	21	21	21	20	20	20	20	21
Italy	20	20	21	21	23	23	23	23	23	23	23	23
Netherlands	6	8	10	8	5	7	6	7	5	7	7	8
Belgium/ Luxembourg	2	1	2	2	2	2	2	2	2	2	3	5
United Kingdom	17	12	8	9	10	8	12	10	11	13	13	14
Ireland	9	3	1	1	1	1	1	1	1	1	1	1
Switzerland	1	2	3	4	3	3	3	4	3	5	4	4
Austria	16	13	5	5.5	7	5	5	6	7	6	6	7
Denmark	8	14	9	14	13	12	7	5	6	8	8	6
Norway	4	5	4	5.5	9	9	10	12	13	11	11	10
Sweden	13	18	18	16.5	17	14	18	14.5	17.5	17	18	13
Finland	22	22	23	22	22	22	22	22	22	22	21	22
Spain	5	6	11	12	16	10	13	18.5	19	19	19	20
Portugal	15	16	15	15	6	16	9	9	14	15	17	16
Greece	11	9	12	10.5	14	11	14	13	15	16	14	12
Yugoslavia/ Slovenia	3	4	7	7	8	6	8	8	9	--	--	--
										4	5	2
Israel	14	15	16	10.5	11	15	17	17	17.5	18	15	15

Equation Results

	1970	1973	1976	1980	1982	1984	1986	1988	1990	1992	1994a	1994b
Adj. R^2	.691	.656	.624	.556	.633	.563	.628	.613	.482	.461	.444	.442
F-Ratio	13.29	11.49	10.12	7.89	10.49	8.08	10.27	9.73	6.11	5.71	5.39	5.36
p	.999	.999	.999	.999	.999	.999	.999	.999	.997	.996	.995	.995

Population significant addition to equation 1970-1976.
Wealth a significant addition to equation 1970-1988, 1994.
EC membership a signficant addition to all equations except 1980.
EFTA a significant addition to equation in 1970-1973, 1982-1986, 1990, 1994b.

1994b has purchasing power parity figures substituted for GNP per capita.

was consistently important as well. Based on the fact that the regression coefficient was positive, EFTA members would thus appear to have imported shoes at higher levels, perhaps reflecting increased trade (i.e., trade creation) among the countries in that customs area.

Belgium, Ireland, and Switzerland were consistently excellent importers of shoes, leading the other countries with high standardized scores (see Table 6–7). From 1976, Austria also was a fairly good importer, although not at the level of these other smaller countries. Italy and France were significantly below predicted levels for these products as had been the case for both countries with the related clothing and textile industries, and by 1980 the scores for Italy were quite negative and were matched only by Finland in terms of the magnitude of the shortfall in expected per capita imports. Germany and the United Kingdom fluctuated

Table 6-7
Standardized Scores for Imports of Footwear for Industrialized Countries

Country	1970	1973	1976	1980	1982	1984	1986	1988	1990	1992	1994a	1994b
Japan	.975	-.102	-.238	-.627	-.639	-.776	-.875	-1.381	-.953	-1.109	-1.523	-.638
United States	.230	.586	.694	.937	1.031	.991	1.113	1.368	1.155	1.310	1.490	1.102
Canada	-.868	-.766	-.753	-.608	-.268	-.929	-.434	-.198	.153	-.166	-.143	-.558
Australia	-.917	-.618	-.729	-.901	-.612	-.929	-.786	-.266	-.327	-.278	-.321	-.594
New Zealand	-1.007	-.979	-.761	-.705	-.772	-.665	-.448	-.385	-.120	-.098	.100	-.246
Germany	.125	.026	-.285	-.154	-.092	-.114	.018	.064	.465	.136	-.049	.231
France	-1.698	-1.808	-1.487	-1.420	-1.268	-1.170	-1.032	-.960	-.920	-1.004	-1.031	-1.010
Italy	-.948	-.869	-1.045	-1.252	-1.683	-1.603	-2.211	-2.306	-2.747	-2.166	-1.874	-2.018
Netherlands	.788	.416	.343	.292	.380	.291	.541	.308	.676	.820	.567	.533
Belgium/Lux.	1.734	2.203	1.914	1.705	1.688	1.355	1.546	1.697	1.497	1.548	1.080	.869
United Kingdom	-.753	-.268	.463	.257	.030	.182	.010	.089	.016	-.268	-.187	-.336
Ireland	.366	1.290	1.983	2.733	2.682	2.716	1.979	1.962	1.769	1.612	2.543	2.578
Switzerland	1.999	1.877	1.090	.813	1.396	1.296	1.432	1.243	.543	.860	.937	1.070
Austria	-.724	-.378	.838	.789	.271	.799	.554	.511	1.313	1.179	.735	.606
Denmark	.409	-.462	.354	-.504	-.148	-.033	.496	.550	.565	.453	.439	.725
Norway	.868	.819	1.012	.793	.065	.128	.194	.075	-.192	-.111	-.081	-.167
Sweden	-.106	-.695	-.736	-.612	-.603	-.170	-.523	-.192	-.369	-.512	-.473	-.308
Finland	-1.298	-1.203	-2.006	-1.325	-1.489	-1.452	-1.721	-1.540	-1.339	-1.461	-1.151	-1.236
Spain	.833	.622	-.035	-.100	-.287	.100	.002	-.385	-.687	-.801	-.846	-.779
Portugal	-.712	-.605	-.317	-.562	.296	-.659	.330	.110	-.212	-.285	-.429	-.492
Greece	.220	.267	-.075	-.154	-.153	.096	-.164	-.080	-.288	-.365	-.243	-.281
Yugoslavia/ Slovenia	1.394	1.166	.494	.538	.003	.599	.446	.277	-.370	1.256	.744	1.382
Israel	-.630	-.518	-.718	-.044	.173	-.312	-.467	-.352	.371	-.554	-.285	-.433

1994b has purchasing power parity figures substituted for GNP per capita.

around the predicted levels, indicating that their relative import propensities were appropriate to their wealth. Denmark and Norway had variable ranks, but they came to be average per capita importers, while Sweden joined Finland as a relatively poor market for imports of footwear. The Mediterranean countries were not particularly good markets for shoes with the exception of Yugoslavia/Slovenia. The standardized

Table 6-8
Rankings for Total Imports of Travel Goods for Industrialized Countries

Country	1970	1973	1976	1980	1982	1984	1986	1988	1990	1992	1994a	1994b
Japan	6	7	14	17	16.5	20	19	21	14	17	19	3
United States	9	9	9	7	7	7	6	3	4	4	4	13
Canada	18	14	19	19	21	21	20	20	17	18	17	22
Australia	12	13	11	11	4	4	10	4.5	8	8	7.5	10
New Zealand	18	20	21	20	22	22	18	11	12	11	7.5	14
Germany	13	16	16	14	15	15	15	13	13	13	13	6
France	22	19	22	22	18	16	16	16	16	15	14	15
Italy	14	12	15	16	16.5	19	21	22	22	22	18	20.5
Netherlands	4	11	7	8	11	11	12	10	10	9	11	8
Belgium/ Luxembourg	2	2	3	4	3	2	2	2	2	2	2	4
United Kingdom	21	17	6	7	10	8	9	8	11	12	10	12
Ireland	7	5	2	2	2	5	4	6	3	10	6	5
Switzerland	1	1	1	1	1	1	1	1	1	1	1	1
Austria	10.5	6	4	3	6	6	3	7	5	5	9	9
Denmark	18	21	10	18	19	17	14	18	18	21	23	18
Norway	3	8	8	15	14	18	5	19	20	16	16	19
Sweden	20	22	16	21	20	14	23	15	21	20	20	17
Finland	23	23	23	23	23	23	23	23	23	23	22	23
Spain	8	4	13	12	13	10	11	14	15	14	15	16
Portugal	16	15	17	13	12	13	6	9	7	3	12	11
Greece	10.5	10	12	10	9	9	13	12	9	6	5	7
Yugoslavia/ Slovenia	5	3	5	5	5	3	7	4.5	6	-- 7	-- 3	-- 2
Israel	15	16	20	9	8	12	17	17	19	19	21	20.5

Equation Results

	1970	1973	1976	1980	1982	1984	1986	1988	1990	1992	1994a	1994b
Adj. R^2	.487	.543	.721	.682	.732	.703	.536	.641	.546	.559	.634	.490
F-Ratio	6.23	7.54	15.19	12.78	15.99	13.99	7.36	10.81	7.62	7.98	10.53	6.28
p	.998	.999	.999	.999	.999	.999	.999	.999	.999	.999	.999	.998

Population significant addition to equation 1970 and 1976.
Wealth a significant addition to all equations.
EC membership never a signficant addition.
EFTA a significant addition to equation in 1970.

1994b has purchasing power parity figures substituted for GNP per capita.

scores indicated that while they imported less than anticipated, they were not especially far from predicted levels.

Outside of Europe, Japan again started out a mediocre market and progressively declined as an importer relative to other countries. The United States began as an average market and improved to the point of being almost on a par with Belgium in terms of the extent of the excess imports above predicted levels. Given the overall size of the U.S. market, of course, its active import stance was tremendously important for producers in the developing world. Canada, Australia, and New Zealand were generally among the poorer markets for these imports, although by 1988 they had become average importers with their standardized scores approaching zero.

Table 6-9
Standardized Scores for Imports of Travel Goods for Industrialized Countries

Country	1970	1973	1976	1980	1982	1984	1986	1988	1990	1992	1994a	1994b
Japan	.688	.267	-.051	-.613	-.591	-.952	-.573	-1.098	-.288	-.596	-.871	1.167
United States	.216	.168	.266	.575	.601	.620	.556	.830	.497	.628	.729	-.202
Canada	-.822	-.307	-.642	-.723	-1.085	-1.113	-1.008	-.832	-.482	-.661	-.773	-1.294
Australia	-.010	-.284	.094	-.017	.771	.927	.227	.559	.249	.386	.448	-.024
New Zealand	-.823	-1.063	-1.086	-.855	-1.126	-1.241	-.553	.121	.031	.240	.451	-.238
Germany	-.214	-.418	-.376	-.250	-.261	-.333	-.179	-.153	-.013	.012	-.276	.286
France	-1.065	-1.048	-1.295	-1.082	-.653	-.381	-.274	-.405	-.426	-.471	-.345	-.254
Italy	-.383	.055	-.257	-.549	-.590	-.875	-1.249	-1.352	-1.468	-1.273	-.864	-1.092
Netherlands	.722	.132	.560	.192	.038	.020	.100	.126	.148	.326	.230	.174
Belgium/Lux.	.940	1.446	.964	1.102	1.149	1.178	1.124	1.552	1.658	1.600	1.602	1.048
United Kingdom	-1.050	-.448	.591	.669	.070	.471	.408	.425	.123	.029	.287	-.082
Ireland	.568	.550	1.271	1.814	1.469	.894	.710	.539	.496	.308	.530	.434
Switzerland	3.301	3.201	2.119	2.326	2.523	2.404	2.537	2.692	2.946	2.765	2.608	2.732
Austria	.035	.489	.929	1.132	.731	.728	.825	.524	.492	.592	.315	-.264
Denmark	-.824	-1.075	.159	-.372	-.723	-.450	-.154	-.585	-.522	-1.208	-1.680	-.640
Norway	.854	.243	.339	-.361	-.211	-.507	.585	-.710	-.590	-.478	-.630	-.683
Sweden	-.869	-1.161	-.331	-.926	-.896	-.230	-2.342	-.377	-.637	-1.157	-.914	-.552
Finland	-1.189	-1.367	-2.863	-2.131	-2.228	-2.402	-1.667	-2.204	-2.285	-1.776	-1.420	-1.531
Spain	.452	.591	.020	-.103	-.108	.223	.128	-.245	-.351	-.148	-.346	-.260
Portugal	-.674	-.326	-.361	-.221	.015	-.089	.493	.421	.363	.827	.221	-.063
Greece	.042	.143	.051	.029	.109	.273	.039	.115	.152	.474	.551	.202
Yugoslavia/	.695	.951	.755	.738	.749	.956	.546	.557	.476	--	--	--
Slovenia										.425	1.153	1.975
Israel	-.589	-.622	-.852	.080	.292	-.079	-.278	-.494	-.573	-.844	-1.008	-1.095

1994b has purchasing power parity figures substituted for GNP per capita.

Travel Goods

Luggage had a smaller total volume than many of the other products included in this chapter, but the developing countries have become increasingly important as exporters. Wealth was the great predictor variable for relative imports, and the equations themselves explained half to three-quarters of the variation in per capita imports (see Table 6–8). The particular importance of wealth levels in explaining relative imports for these goods was obvious from the differences in ranks and standardized scores for the industrialized countries for 1994a and 1994b (see Table 6–9). With wealth so important, the substitution of purchasing power parity for GNP per capita led to major changes in the positions of the countries.

Germany, France, and Italy were consistently below anticipated import levels. The shortfalls from predictions, however, were not as major as had been the case for many other manufactured goods, overall manufactures, or imports in general. Given the size of these three countries, there was clearly a relatively more open global market for these products than for many others. Finland and, at times, Sweden and New Zealand were countries below anticipated levels. In general, the Scandinavian countries were relatively poor markets for luggage compared to the other industrialized countries. The United Kingdom was again close to predicted levels (usually slightly above), further contributing to the market potential for sales of travel goods globally. The Netherlands, though slightly above predicted levels, was about average as well. Belgium, Switzerland, Ireland, and Austria were again very active per capita importers, being among the best markets for these types of goods.

In the case of travel goods, the Mediterranean countries were either average or better than average in terms of per capita imports. Even when these countries had middle range ranks, the ranks reflected per capita imports close to the predicted levels as could be seen with the standardized scores. Israel was the least active importer among this group. Yugoslavia/Slovenia was generally a good market, while Portugal and Greece were also good markets in selected years.

Japan and the United States followed the same pattern that was apparent for many other goods. Japan went from being a good importer to a relatively poor market, while the United States started in a position very similar to Japan but improved noticeably. The United States actually reached the same high levels in terms of the standardized scores that Belgium and

Switzerland had attained. Canada again proved to be a below-average per capita importer of goods important in the export mix of the developing world. Australia and New Zealand were not as consistently below expected levels as Canada was. By the early 1980s, Australia was often importing at levels above anticipated ones. New Zealand was initially one of the smallest relative importers but improved to predicted levels in the late 1980s. While these two countries had often been poor overall importers of many products, they clearly had been more open to imports of these goods.

Overall, the patterns for travel goods suggested relative openness in the global marketplace. While smaller in total volume than other categories (which may explain the lower import barriers), the developing countries had captured a large share of the world market, and all the larger markets except Japan were fairly open to imports of luggage. Even the industrialized countries in Oceania and the larger European countries had been importing at least at predicted levels. In addition to Japan, the Scandinavian countries were clearly the least open markets for these goods, but then they have been among the smaller markets.

Toys and Sporting Goods

Toys and sporting goods have been a rather disparate group of items. Many toys have been manufactured in Asian countries for export to the industrialized world. Sporting goods have been produced in multiple locations. Equipment for winter sports, such as skiing, is much more likely to be manufactured in developed countries and exported to other developed countries. Baseballs for the United States and Canada, however, have been produced in the Caribbean, primarily for export to North America. Materials for soccer (i.e., football to most of the world), could be produced almost anywhere with many potential producers given the global popularity of the game. By 1990, the developing countries were accounting for at least 45 percent of global exports in this SITC category, indicating that it had become an important area of manufacturing activity for them.

The import patterns for these products were similar to those for other manufactured goods. The regression equations accounted for high amounts of variation (at least half) through 1988 (see Table 6–10). Population (negative associations with imports as always) and wealth were the important predictors of per capita import levels. Trade area membership proved to be unimportant for this category of products. The standardized values were somewhat less consistent overall since there were only a few countries that were always one standard deviation above or below predicted levels (see Table 6–11). In effect, imports of these products were more variable by country from year to year than for most other products. The amount of money spent on toys or sporting goods in the different industrialized countries, of course, could have been very much in the discretionary realm for consumers, and somewhat adverse national

Table 6-10
Rankings for Total Imports of Toys and Sporting Goods for Industrialized Countries

Country	1970	1973	1976	1980	1982	1984	1986	1988	1990	1992	1994a	1994b
Japan	4	9	14	20	22	23	22	23	22	22	23	22
United States	8	8	5	3	2	3	4	2	2	2	2	2
Canada	10	6	8	9.5	5	9	16	12	6	6	3	7
Australia	16	15	13	12	11	14.5	19	16	13	12	12	18
New Zealand	19	18	19	19	21	16.5	12	6	9	9	8	10
Germany	20	23	22	23	23	22	20	21	20	16.5	20	20
France	23	20	20	21.5	17	20	17	19	19	18	20	20
Italy	12	11	11	15.5	15	16.5	21	22	23	19	22	23
Netherlands	2	5	7	7	7	11	10	1	8	4	4	4.5
Belgium/ Luxembourg	5	2	3	4	4	4	3	5	1	3	1	1
United Kingdom	22	13	10	6	14	7	11	11	10	8	10	11
Ireland	3	3	1	1	1	1	1	4	3	1	6	4.5
Switzerland	1	1	2	2	3	2	2	3	4	5	7	8
Austria	9	10	6	5	6	6	6	9	5	7	5	6
Denmark	14	17	4	11	9	5	5	8	7	11	16	12
Norway	18	16	15	9.5	12	19	8	13	12	14	11	14
Sweden	11	22	17	13	16	14.5	23	17.5	17	16	16	12
Finland	17	19	23	21.5	19	21	18	20	21	21	21	21
Spain	7	7	16	15.5	20	12	13	17.5	18	13	18	15
Portugal	15	12	9	14	10	8	7	7	11	10	15	16.5
Greece	13	14	18	17	18	13	15	15	15	15	9	9
Yugoslavia/	6	4	12	8	13	10	9	10	14	--	--	--
Slovenia										17	13	3
Israel	21	21	21	18	8	18	14	14	16	19	17	19
Equation Results												
Adj. R^2	.668	.683	.757	.560	.575	.724	.594	.603	.499	.433	.324	.538
F-Ratio	12.05	12.83	18.10	8.01	8.43	15.40	9.05	9.34	6.48	5.20	3.64	7.42
p	.999	.999	.999	.999	.999	.999	.999	.999	.998	.994	.976	.999

Population significant addition to equation 1970-1976, 1982-1988, and 1994b.
Wealth a significant addition to all equations.
EC membership a signficant addition in 1980.
EFTA never a significant addition to equation.

1994b has purchasing power parity figures substituted for GNP per capita.

economic conditions could have depressed imports for some nations while relative prosperity in a year could have led to increased purchases in others.[28]

The three large European initial EC members were again usually well below anticipated levels for per capita imports. Only Italy in the 1970s imported near expected levels, an openness to imports that did not persist. Even so, the deviations from anticipated levels were not as great for these goods as had been the case for other products. Japan, an above-average importer of note in 1970, quickly became much less open to imports, and beginning in 1982, the deviation from expectations was consistently a major one. As was frequently the case for other products, Finland was part of the group of countries that was regularly below anticipated per capita import levels.

Table 6-11
Standardized Scores for Imports of Toys and Sporting Goods for Industrialized Countries

Country	1970	1973	1976	1980	1982	1984	1986	1988	1990	1992	1994a	1994b
Japan	1.202	.252	-.260	-.820	-1.045	-1.540	-1.329	-1.927	-1.580	-1.884	-2.009	-1.331
United States	.133	.268	.632	.928	1.218	1.340	1.352	1.715	1.538	1.483	1.541	1.356
Canada	-.068	.643	.431	-.054	.350	.221	-.606	.023	.703	.866	1.403	.667
Australia	-.544	-.423	.046	-.154	-.142	-.474	-.908	-.426	-.357	-.069	-.087	-.557
New Zealand	-.811	-.850	-1.061	-.805	-.858	-.532	.087	.828	.531	.517	.559	-.003
Germany	-.830	-1.227	-1.445	-.974	-1.289	-1.449	-1.007	-1.335	-.880	-.910	-.787	-.434
France	-1.248	-.999	-1.106	-.884	-.587	-.770	-.668	-.791	-.760	-.646	-.907	-1.064
Italy	-.321	.121	.212	-.399	-.440	-.527	-1.141	-1.411	-1.804	-.844	-1.531	-1.947
Netherlands	1.620	.719	.554	.293	.231	-.007	.154	1.963	.535	1.121	1.069	1.149
Belgium/Lux.	.779	1.374	1.112	.625	.855	1.239	1.382	1.061	1.965	1.390	1.994	1.862
United Kingdom	-1.172	-.279	.264	.415	-.189	.312	.115	.032	.066	.529	.048	-.119
Ireland	1.318	1.284	2.405	3.688	3.529	2.745	1.764	1.108	1.486	1.535	.747	1.145
Switzerland	3.749	2.911	1.603	1.106	1.075	1.397	1.680	1.428	1.161	.988	.701	.550
Austria	.114	.237	.569	.598	.294	.547	.738	.063	.824	.771	.927	.960
Denmark	-.427	-.790	.701	-.085	-.011	.603	1.038	.143	.690	-.866	-.223	-.239
Norway	-.768	-.728	-.292	-.054	-.155	-.740	.296	-.043	-.289	-.188	-.063	-.253
Sweden	-.083	-1.071	-.574	-.311	-.472	-.477	-1.914	-.504	-.689	-.490	-.507	-.145
Finland	-.659	-.947	-1.727	-.889	-.726	-1.013	-.830	-.977	-1.007	-1.116	-1.089	-1.145
Spain	.294	.316	-.525	-.402	-.759	-.324	-.192	-.508	-.712	-.151	-.597	-.424
Portugal	-.532	-.227	.319	-.394	-.047	.245	.442	.254	-.007	.090	-.483	-.436
Greece	-.410	-.389	-.715	-.560	-.664	-.371	-.440	-.414	-.470	-.441	.095	.434
Yugoslavia/ Slovenia	.701	.862	.183	.077	-.186	.191	.199	.033	-.386	--	--	--
										-.608	-.211	1.299
Israel	-1.038	-1.058	-1.327	-.672	.018	-.615	-.209	-.313	-.561	-.844	-.590	-1.058

1994b has purchasing power parity figures substituted for GNP per capita.

The United States was a good market for these goods beginning in 1980, and it was on a level with the other countries that were the most active per capita importers. Ireland, Switzerland, Austria, Belgium, and the Netherlands in most years were also well above average importers, although Belgium did not have the margin of leadership in per capita imports of toys as it had in other product areas. In general, these smaller European countries and the United States formed a group of nations that regularly imported at levels well beyond those predicted by population and wealth.

Most of the other countries had less pronounced patterns. Except for 1970, the United Kingdom again fluctuated around predicted levels. Australia and New Zealand were often below predicted per capita levels in the earlier years, but they were close to anticipated levels in later years. Canadian ranks and standardized scores were highly variable, but they frequently were those of an above-average importer. Thus, toys and sporting goods were one area in which Canada was not among the least active importers. Denmark, Norway, and Sweden had fluctuating ranks and scores as well. Denmark was on occasion a good importer, Norway varied between average and below average, and Sweden was below average, sometimes marginally so and sometimes substantially so.

The Mediterranean five were generally below-average markets for these goods, although their per capita levels were never as far from the predicted levels as was the case for France, Finland, or Japan after 1980. Portugal and Yugoslavia were the states that were comparatively most open to these imports, at least in some of the years. Spain, Israel, and Greece, on the other hand, were average importers at best.

Watches and Clocks

Export shares of the developing countries for clocks, watches, and parts increased dramatically between 1970 and 1990. The developing world accounted for over a third of the total exports, and Hong Kong was second only to Switzerland as an exporter in 1990 (a situation that has probably changed since the retrocession of the British Crown Colony to Chinese rule). The regression equations for these items did not explain as much variation as was the case for other products. The variation explained approached half in 1976 and 1980, but it slowly declined thereafter, sometimes reaching points at which the equation results were not very useful at all (see Table 6–12). Wealth was the key variable in terms of explaining per capita imports at these modest levels.

What stood out in the analyses of the rankings and standardized scores for watches and clocks was the special position of Switzerland. Not only was Switzerland ranked first in per capita imports in every year, it was far in advance of whatever country was second in terms of its standardized scores for per capita imports (see Table 6–12 and 6–13). In effect, levels of Swiss imports were extremely higher than expected, and all the other

Table 6-12
Rankings for Total Imports of Clocks and Watches for Industrialized Countries

Country	1970	1973	1976	1980	1982	1984	1986	1988	1990	1992	1994a	1994b
Japan	4	10	15	20	19	17	17.5	21	18	19	21	10
United States	10	7	8	7	7	10	9	7	9.5	7	8	11.5
Canada	23	20	20	18	18	20	20	18	19	18	18	21
Australia	14	15	10	13	16	18	19	13	17	17	16	18
New Zealand	8.5	11	9	12	12	11	10	12	14	13	11	16.5
Germany	12.5	18	19	17	17	16	14	15	12.5	10	10	5
France	17	17	18	16	13	15	13	14	15	16	14	11.5
Italy	5	3	3	2	2	3	8	5	7	6	4	7
Netherlands	7	13	11.5	14	14.5	12	15	17	16	15	17	15
Belgium/ Luxembourg	3	4	5	10	9	8	7	10	6	11	13	14
United Kingdom	20	12	2	5	8	5	4	4	8	8	7	8
Ireland	11	14	4	4	5	6	11	8	9.5	9	9	9
Switzerland	1	1	1	1	1	1	1	1	1	1	1	1
Austria	15	16	17	11	14.5	13	16	16	12.5	12	15	16.5
Denmark	16	22	11.5	21	20	19	17.5	19.5	20	20	22	19
Norway	18	21	22	22	22	23	23	23	22	22	23	23
Sweden	22	23	23	23	23	22	21	19.5	21	23	20	20
Finland	19	19	21	19	21	21	22	22	23	21	19	22
Spain	2	2	14	3	3	2	2	2	3	4	5	4
Portugal	21	6	16	15	11	14	3	3	2	2	6	6
Greece	12.5	9	7	9	10	7	12	9	4	3	3	3
Yugoslavia/ Slovenia	6	5	6	6	6	4	5	6	5	--	--	--
										5	2	2
Israel	8.5	8	13	8	4	9	6	11	11	14	12	13
Equation Results												
Adj. R^2	.385	.311	.488	.473	.381	.362	.341	.341	.252	.250	.290	.227
F-Ratio	4.44	3.49	6.23	5.94	4.38	4.17	3.84	3.84	2.86	2.84	3.24	2.62
p	.989	.972	.998	.997	.988	.985	.980	.980	.946	.945	.964	.930

Population significant addition to equation 1970-1976, 1982-1988, 1992, and 1994b.
Wealth a significant addition to all equations.
EC membership a significant addition in 1980 and 1992.
EFTA never a significant addition to equation.

1994b has purchasing power parity figures substituted for GNP per capita.

countries imported near predicted levels or below them. Import levels for Switzerland were three to four standard deviations above predicted levels, whereas the other countries that were above the anticipated levels exceeded predicted per capita import levels only moderately. There were actually only a few countries that consistently had positive standardized scores. Spain and Yugoslavia/Slovenia were among the few, and the other Mediterranean countries were among the somewhat more active importers in many of the years. Among the other nations, the United Kingdom, the United States, and Ireland were frequently close to expected per capita levels. France, Germany, and Italy did not occupy the ranks of the least active importers for these goods, even though they had not been particularly good markets. All of the Scandinavian countries (and not just Finland) were consistently below predicted levels, as were Canada and

Table 6-13
Standardized Scores for Imports of Clocks and Watches for Industrialized Countries

Country	1970	1973	1976	1980	1982	1984	1986	1988	1990	1992	1994a	1994b
Japan	.355	-.076	-.209	-.752	-.562	-.374	-.472	-.954	-.450	-.809	-1.130	-.052
United States	.027	.002	.096	.179	.159	.078	.124	.263	.143	.281	.358	-.101
Canada	-1.090	-.716	-.671	-.434	-.485	-.664	-.730	-.803	-.648	-.720	-.572	-.897
Australia	-.187	-.223	-.064	-.169	-.300	-.570	-.494	-.052	-.288	-.213	-.184	-.397
New Zealand	.041	-.078	.051	-.162	-.062	.030	.122	.029	-.106	-.034	.018	-.320
Germany	-.165	-.432	-.506	-.364	-.342	-.353	-.121	-.135	-.100	.036	.025	.307
France	-.527	-.291	-.425	-.326	-.147	-.227	-.074	-.116	-.184	-.203	-.127	-.101
Italy	.312	.602	.600	.776	.683	.466	.140	.362	.172	.336	.498	.283
Netherlands	.005	-.137	-.133	-.217	-.206	-.097	-.125	-.251	-.213	-.196	-.286	-.286
Belgium/Lux.	.375	.329	.266	.024	.088	.145	.162	.100	.277	-.003	-.098	-.263
United Kingdom	-.672	-.128	.671	.439	.108	.318	.315	.453	.163	.171	.382	.191
Ireland	-.157	.197	.449	.660	.374	.308	.104	.196	.141	.078	.186	.172
Switzerland	4.074	4.010	3.946	3.712	3.835	3.859	3.906	3.690	3.816	3.643	3.575	3.707
Austria	-.293	-.247	-.256	.006	-.207	-.122	-.455	-.157	-.098	-.021	-.175	-.317
Denmark	-.415	-.844	-.132	-.778	-.697	-.531	-.477	-.893	-.733	-1.057	-1.230	-.757
Norway	-.530	-.855	-1.165	-1.282	-1.320	-1.524	-1.453	-1.479	-1.323	1.256	-1.443	-1.465
Sweden	-.870	-1.188	-1.305	-1.527	-1.424	-1.087	-.798	-.905	-.960	-1.283	-1.055	-.889
Finland	-.562	-.702	-1.027	-.734	-.908	-.969	-1.257	-1.190	-1.482	-1.117	-.929	-1.067
Spain	.932	.994	-.177	.731	.670	.739	.724	.771	.537	.574	.461	.461
Portugal	-.697	.071	-.255	-.270	-.016	.196	.392	.546	.631	.834	.446	.293
Greece	-.171	-.067	.153	.041	.080	.179	.044	.159	.421	.618	.643	.476
Yugoslavia/ Slovenia	.178	.235	.227	.353	.289	.452	.228	.334	.600	-- .439	-- .643	-- 1.212
Israel	.037	-.022	-.136	.094	.389	.142	.186	.035	.022	-.097	-.060	-.189

1994b has purchasing power parity figures substituted for GNP per capita.

Australia. As had been the case with most other manufactured goods, Japan started the period importing somewhat more than predicted but quickly became a poor market. No country was anywhere as far below predicted levels as Switzerland was above expectations.

Obviously much of the global trade in timepieces was explained by Swiss activity. Switzerland was a major exporter of these materials, but it

Table 6-14
Rankings for Total Imports of Electronic Items for Industrialized Countries

Country	1970	1973	1976	1980	1982	1984	1986	1988	1990	1992	1994a	1994b
Japan	3	11	15	21	23	23	23	23	23	22	23	22
United States	4	3	2	3	6	3	3	1	2	2	1	4
Canada	20	17	21	6.5	21	12	19	12	7	10	8	11
Australia	13	15.5	11	16	5	7	20	6	6	14	10	13.5
New Zealand	18	18	14	20	16	2	2	2	5	7	7	8
Germany	22	23	22	22	13	10.5	17	10	16	18	18	13.5
France	23	22	23	23	18	21	21	19	21	20	21	21
Italy	21	20	18	17	22	20	22	22	22	23	22	23
Netherlands	1	1	1	1	2	1	1	4	1	1	2	3
Belgium/ Luxembourg	7	4	6	2	12	10.5	5	7	4	3	3	5
United Kingdom	14	5	3	10.5	1	6	9	9	13	9	11	9
Ireland	8	8	5	4	8	15	14	13	8	5	14	16
Switzerland	2	2	16	9	10	9	4	8	3	4	12	10
Austria	12	12	10	8	19	18	16	15	9	6	17	19
Denmark	9	10	7	13	14	19	11.5	14	12	12	4	2
Norway	10	13	4	6.5	20	22	13	18	18	8	5	6
Sweden	17	21	9	19	4	14	15	16	10	19	9	7
Finland	16	14	20	15	11	4	10	3	19	21	15.5	17
Spain	6	7	17	12	9	8	7	11	17	16	15.5	15
Portugal	15	15.5	12	14	7	5	6	5	14	11	13	12
Greece	11	9	13	10.5	17	16	8	20	20	17	19	18
Yugoslavia/ Slovenia	5	6	8	5	15	13	11.5	21	15	--	--	--
										13	6	1
Israel	19	19	19	18	3	17	18	17	11	15	20	20
Equation Results												
Adj. R^2	.487	.590	.739	.705	.492	.581	.393	.123	.142	.535	.211	.319
F-Ratio	6.23	8.92	16.58	14.13	6.33	8.64	4.56	1.78	1.91	7.33	2.48	3.58
p	.998	.999	.999	.999	.998	.999	.990	.822	.848	.999	.919	.974

Population significant addition to equation 1970-1984 and 1992.
Wealth a significant addition to all equations.
EC membership a signficant addition in 1973.
EFTA a significant addition to equation in 1970.

1994b has purchasing power parity figures substituted for GNP per capita.

was also one of the major importers in absolute terms and very clearly the most important importer in per capita terms (and the level of imports predicted for Switzerland would have been relatively high since wealth was a key for import levels, and Switzerland had one of the highest per capita GNP figures). The Swiss watch industry underwent major restructuring when faced with import challenges from the developing world. One part of the restructuring was importing more components, including goods from the developing world, resulting in higher levels of intra-industry trade flows. Such intra-industry trade appeared to be quite high, especially since there were large Swiss imports from Hong Kong in the 1970s and 1980s. Changes in Swiss exports of these products also appear to have been related to production in Hong Kong.[29] The existence of high levels of intra-industry trade and the very special place of Switzerland in this product area

Table 6-15
Standardized Scores for Imports of Electronic Items for Industrialized Countries

Country	1970	1973	1976	1980	1982	1984	1986	1988	1990	1992	1994a	1994b
Japan	.615	-.202	-.240	-1.265	-1.830	-2.519	-2.281	-2.839	-2.511	-1.525	-2.258	-1.576
United States	.550	.750	.883	1.313	.720	1.314	1.608	1.570	1.710	1.454	1.706	1.450
Canada	-.589	-.297	-.998	.535	-.948	-.035	-.557	.295	.257	.135	.480	-.136
Australia	-.264	-.282	.101	-.402	.759	.578	-.733	.598	.595	-.194	.130	-.310
New Zealand	-.531	-.320	-.193	-.988	-.680	1.624	1.853	1.449	.797	.545	.574	.162
Germany	-1.289	-1.635	-1.702	-1.628	-.223	.170	-.480	.342	-.219	-.526	-.624	-.318
France	-1.542	-1.592	-1.745	-1.998	-.787	-1.052	-1.008	-.813	-1.138	-1.195	-1.058	-1.115
Italy	-.976	-.725	-.514	-.500	-1.026	-.808	-1.145	-1.115	-1.397	-1.190	-1.528	-1.743
Netherlands	3.515	3.230	3.051	2.507	.938	1.802	2.128	1.019	1.920	2.119	1.533	1.568
Belgium/Lux.	.292	.681	.517	1.392	-.066	.170	.654	.572	1.026	1.103	1.424	1.187
United Kingdom	-.293	.621	.816	.282	2.961	.710	.171	.411	.019	.254	.125	-.004
Ireland	.160	.162	.681	.567	.506	-.392	-.312	-.015	.214	.987	-.461	-.364
Switzerland	1.377	1.466	-.251	.290	.244	.181	1.109	.485	1.077	1.035	-.022	-.121
Austria	-.244	-.228	.168	.326	-.911	-.667	-.375	-.336	.172	.747	-.598	-.768
Denmark	.133	-.168	.472	-.168	-.292	-.799	-.210	-.183	.077	.031	1.385	1.607
Norway	.080	-.245	.709	.538	-.926	-1.113	-.267	-.796	-.546	.392	.755	.695
Sweden	-.498	-1.031	.432	-.621	.855	-.338	-.335	-.456	.167	-.868	.337	.651
Finland	-.377	-.256	-.989	-.341	.138	1.088	-.136	1.143	-.900	-1.347	-.486	-.470
Spain	.342	.328	-.454	.097	.263	.397	.390	.314	-.232	-.347	-.485	-.353
Portugal	-.299	-.282	-.128	-.208	.605	.892	.446	.801	.008	.048	-.274	-.245
Greece	.030	-.096	-.165	.279	-.739	-.520	.183	-.863	-1.096	-.476	-.678	-.587
Yugoslavia/ Slovenia	.430	.536	.438	.543	-.454	.089	-.212	-1.025	.157	-.081	.718	1.761
Israel	.561	-.421	-.889	-.549	.892	-.593	-.490	-.556	.156	-.300	-.695	-.970

1994b has purchasing power parity figures substituted for GNP per capita.

would probably also have been responsible for the lower levels of variance explained by the equations. One country occupied a particularly important place in the overall global market, and its trade overshadowed the effects that size, wealth, and customs area membership normally would have had to at least some extent.

Electronic Products

The results for electronic goods were highly variable. The regression equations explained over seventy per cent of the variance in 1976 and 1980 and only slightly more than ten per cent in 1988 and 1990 (see Table 6–14). Some of the variability was probably due to the revision of the SITC code in 1976, which would have affected trade reporting for these products in some cases. But since the explanatory value continued to decline well after any lingering effects due to the revision, the SITC changes were not the only factor. In addition to these trends, the ranks and standardized scores were frequently quite varied over time (see Tables 6–14 and 6–15). The tables indicated that the imports varied quite substantially for individual countries from year to year (note the Finnish scores and ranks for 1984 and 1988 and the Israeli ones for 1982 compared to earlier and later years). Wealth was the best predictor of per capita imports. Population was important in most years but not in 1988 and 1990, when the explanatory power of the equations were minimal.

The Netherlands and the United States ranked as the best importers for all the years analyzed. They were almost always at least one standard deviation above expected levels. From 1984 on, New Zealand was a very good market as well, while Belgium was usually well above anticipated import levels. Many of the other countries had quite variable levels of imports from year to year. Italy and France were again relatively poor markets, while Germany was in a few cases close to anticipated levels but was still generally a poor importer for these products. Except in 1982,[30] Israel was obviously a poor market as well. Japanese imports quickly declined in a relative sense, going from above average in 1970 to slightly below predicted levels to well below. No other country was a consistently poor market. The Mediterranean countries showed the same high variability as did many of the other industrialized nations. Clearly, imports of these items did not follow the standard pattern for other goods, nor did a single country dominate as had been the case with Switzerland for watches.

All Goods

A final analysis was undertaken utilizing per capita import totals for all the seven categories discussed above. Since total per capita imports (rather than average of the scores or ranks) were used, the ranks and the standardized scores reflected the effects of textiles and clothing, the two largest of the groups included. Each of them accounted for approx-

Table 6-16
Rankings for Total Imports of All Goods for Industrialized Countries

Country	1970	1973	1976	1980	1982	1984	1986	1988	1990	1992	1994a	1994b
Japan	11	7	11	17	16	18	18	20	19	20	22	3
United States	5	6	4	4	4	4	5	4	4	3	2.5	4
Canada	22	22	21	18	20	20	16	17	10	13	18	20
Australia	16	15	17	19	15	19	19	13	15	18	16	19
New Zealand	10	10	13	13	7.5	8	8	11	9	9	9	12
Germany	20	16.5	18	22	17	14	11	19	7	11	12	10
France	23	23	23	23	23	23	20	21	21	21	21	21
Italy	18	21	19	21	21	22	23	23	23	23	23	23
Netherlands	1	2	3	3	5	6	4	5	5	5	7	6
Belgium/ Luxembourg	4	1	2	2	2	2	2	1	2	1	1	1
United Kingdom	21	14	9	8	11	9	15	18	14	12	13	14.5
Ireland	3	4	1	1	1	1	3	3	3	4	5	5
Switzerland	2	3	7	5	3	3	1	2	1	2	2.5	3
Austria	12	9	5	6	6	5	6	7	6	6	6	7
Denmark	8	12	6	14	12	10.5	17	8	16	10	11	8
Norway	7	11	8	9	14	17	9	15.5	20	15	15	16
Sweden	14	20	12	15	19	15	22	15.5	18	19	19	18
Finland	15	16.5	22	20	22	21	21	22	22	22	20	22
Spain	9	8	14	11.5	18	10.5	13	14	17	17	17	17
Portugal	19	18	15.5	16	7.5	16	7	6	8	7	8	9
Greece	13	13	15.5	11.5	9.5	12	14	12	12	14	10	11
Yugoslavia/ Slovenia	6	5	10	7	13	7	10	9.5	11	--	--	--
										8	4	2
Israel	17	19	20	10	9.5	13	12	9.5	13	16	14	14.5

Equation Results

	1970	1973	1976	1980	1982	1984	1986	1988	1990	1992	1994a	1994b
Adj. R^2	.626	.715	.720	.691	.691	.678	.631	.635	.567	.510	.532	.512
F-Ratio	10.25	14.81	15.13	13.31	13.30	12.60	10.40	10.55	8.20	6.72	7.25	6.77
p	.999	.999	.999	.999	.999	.999	.999	.999	.999	.998	.999	.998

Population significant addition to equation 1970-1988 and 1994.
Wealth a significant addition to all equations except 1990.
EC membership a signficant addition except in 1970.
EFTA a significant addition to equation 1970-1973, 1982, 1986 and 1990.

1994b has purchasing power parity figures substituted for GNP per capita.

imately a third of the global exports of all seven categories, while the remaining five combined to total approximately a third (at least after 1980). In all cases the equations explained at least half of the variation in per capita imports (see Table 6–16). Wealth was important in every year except 1990, population except in 1990, 1992, and EC/EU membership except in 1970, while EFTA membership in most years was a significant addition. All four variables had a role to play in explaining per capita import levels. As expected, wealthier countries imported more per capita, larger countries imported less per capita, and countries in trade areas imported more.

The patterns for the residuals were similar to many of the patterns already noted above (see Table 6–17). Japan imported at predicted levels in the 1970s and then became a below-average market. Canada and Australia

Table 6-17
Standardized Scores for Imports of All Goods for Industrialized Countries

Country	1970	1973	1976	1980	1982	1984	1986	1988	1990	1992	1994a	1994b
Japan	.114	.432	.161	-.567	-.513	-.658	-.615	-.995	-.578	-.851	-1.387	-.219
United States	1.037	.670	.781	1.161	1.147	1.066	1.020	1.407	.949	1.200	1.451	.926
Canada	-1.488	-1.175	-1.225	-.663	-.804	-1.068	-.567	-.523	-.029	-.307	-.667	-1.135
Australia	-.453	-.489	-.664	-.698	-.486	-.925	-.674	-.335	-.306	-.473	-.437	-.742
New Zealand	.222	.133	-.069	-.349	.144	.376	.359	-.030	.116	.012	.247	-.177
Germany	-.718	-.716	-.833	-1.378	-.552	-.026	.015	-.859	.498	-.057	-.140	.206
France	-2.062	-2.021	-2.036	-1.670	-1.840	-1.530	-1.164	-1.061	-1.244	-1.226	-1.262	-1.212
Italy	-.627	-.872	-.886	-.862	-.858	-1.391	-1.773	-1.672	-2.168	-2.059	-1.743	-1.906
Netherlands	2.343	1.638	1.523	1.338	.625	.576	1.046	1.052	.719	.964	.689	.643
Belgium/Lux.	1.064	1.912	1.626	1.805	1.776	1.734	1.778	2.007	1.954	2.020	2.218	1.931
United Kingdom	-1.187	-.346	.432	.275	-.069	.110	-.006	-.529	-.256	-.292	-.261	-.448
Ireland	1.232	1.496	1.945	2.385	2.389	2.027	1.164	1.407	2.052	1.606	1.453	1.646
Switzerland	1.282	1.558	.516	.867	1.727	1.725	1.996	1.407	2.052	1.606	1.453	1.646
Austria	.038	.258	.776	.820	.362	.933	.622	.532	.682	.870	.798	.615
Denmark	.266	-.180	.653	-.361	-.113	-.074	-.594	.146	-.344	-.048	-.084	.322
Norway	.484	-.002	.447	.127	-.246	-.501	.260	-.410	-.639	-.352	-.362	-.457
Sweden	-.451	-.858	-.053	-.501	-.721	-.414	-1.595	-.405	-.540	-.633	-.746	-.546
Finland	-.458	-.715	-1.399	-.797	-1.318	-1.316	-1.332	-1.465	-1.544	-1.537	-1.177	-1.295
Spain	.233	.323	-.279	-.252	-.583	-.069	-.060	-.358	-.457	-.429	-.546	-.473
Portugal	-.687	-.728	-.369	-.548	.139	-.479	.473	.569	.470	.650	.424	.297
Greece	-.141	-.235	-.374	-.251	-.014	-.092	-.212	-.265	-.187	-.334	-.055	-.141
Yugoslavia/	.631	.734	.306	.330	-.174	.448	.215	-.021	.083	--	--	--
Slovenia										.582	1.044	1.767
Israel	-.582	-.818	-.980	-.211	-.018	-.218	.007	-.024	-.210	-.414	-.283	-.452

1994b has purchasing power parity figures substituted for GNP per capita.

were consistently among the poorer markets, while New Zealand hovered around the expected levels. At the very least, in low years the United States was a good market for all these goods combined and oftentimes was an excellent market. The United States, however, never had imports of these goods at high enough per capita levels to distinguish it as the best relative market for these products in total.

In Europe, France and Italy were very poor markets throughout the period. Germany was well below predicted levels through 1980, but in later years it was often close to predicted levels, indicating that it had become pretty much of an average market overall. After being a poor market in the 1970s, the United Kingdom showed a similar pattern in that it was consistently near anticipated levels. The Netherlands, Belgium, Switzerland, Ireland, and Austria were consistently good markets for these goods. Belgium, Ireland, and Switzerland were almost always well above predicted levels. The Scandinavian countries were sometimes good markets in the early years, but they quickly become poorer markets in most years. Finland was clearly one of the least open markets for these goods in this group of countries, just as it has been for most of the products in the individual analyses and for all manufactured products.

The Mediterranean countries were for the most part near anticipated levels. Portugal and Yugoslavia were the two countries that most frequently imported at higher than expected levels, although Portuguese imports in the 1970s were considerably below expected levels. Spain, Greece, and perhaps most especially Israel were likely to have imported less than predicted. The general trend of imports near predictions was constant whether the countries were in EFTA, whether they had joined the EC/EU, or whether they were outside both these trade areas. Customs area membership did not appear to have any major additional effects on their trends in terms of import levels for these industrializing states. It was clear that none of these five countries ever was a consistently good market for the goods in question, but at the same time, they were never among the very poor markets.

Summary

The analyses of the selected manufactured products that have been important as exports for the developing world showed that most of the industrialized countries were at least fair markets for some of the products that were likely to have originated in the developing world. The results were broadly similar to those that were generated for manufactures in general, although there were some differences. Italy, France, and Germany were generally inferior markets for all manufactured goods. Germany was, however, somewhat more open for the products analyzed above. Recently the textile and clothing sectors in Germany, which had previously been supporting protection, began to accept liberalization, in part because of the advantages that could be gained as a consequence of intra-industry trade with Eastern Europe, where production facilities located in these countries could provide materials in a cost-effective fashion. Lower labor costs in Eastern Europe led to greater competitiveness, increased profits, and greater exploitation of existing markets.[31] Italy, on the other hand, was actually more open to manufactures in general than it was to imports of these particular goods. France and Finland were the two countries that were consistently well below predicted import levels. They had the most closed markets of the countries that were included in the analyses. Finnish entrance into the EU is unlikely to lead to major changes in rankings and comparative openness since France's limited import levels have still been present after many years of membership. Japan became a poor market for the SITC categories used, as had been the case for manufactures in general. Notwithstanding the geographic proximity of Japan to the Asian NICs, the Japanese market was among the most closed. Clearly, the possibilities and potential of intra-industry trade and complementary trade between Japan and the Asian NICs was not being exploited. It has been suggested that Japan has increasingly shifted to imports from developing countries rather than advanced ones, particularly for labor-intensive goods,[32] but the above analysis has not supported that argument. Australia and Canada were generally poorer markets as well, but they showed some signs of relative improvement. They were also generally more open than Japan, so their proximity to the Asian producers had some impact (as it obviously did for the United States as well). New Zealand became more open with time, indicating that its liberalizing policies had not only encouraged trade but had helped the country catch up to states that had established liberal importing patterns in earlier years.

The United States was not the most open industrialized country for these imports. The presence of MFA marketing agreements, VERs, other quota arrangements, and bilateral pressure on individual developing countries all had an effect in leading to reduced imports. But either the United States undertook fewer efforts to limit imports in these areas or the efforts that it did undertake were less effective.[33] The comparative openness of the

United States was quite important for the developing countries given the overall size of the U.S. market. The United Kingdom was the other large market that was usually reasonably open to these imports. The size of the British market meant that its average per capita import levels were important in absolute terms for producers in the developing world.

There has been an important geographic aspect to the imports. The United States, Canada, Japan, and the Oceanic countries imported a large percentage of the goods in question (at high or low levels, as the case might be) from Asian or Latin American sources. The European countries were much more likely to import these goods from European countries that produced them (including East European producers).[34] EU commercial provisions also have encouraged offshore production or purchases in East European locations or in the Mediterranean countries rather than from other parts of the developing world.[35] Thus, the openness of the U.S. and British markets was in fact quite important to producers in the developing world.

The same smaller European countries were generally as open for these selected manufactures as they had been for manufactures in general. Belgium, Ireland, and Switzerland were the farthest above predicted per capita import levels. Austria and the Netherlands were usually good markets as well, even though the Netherlands declined somewhat over time in terms of relative imports. These smaller countries represented wealthy countries such as Switzerland and not-so-wealthy ones such as Ireland. Ireland was a peripheral country in the European and EC/EU context but was an active importer, even though other peripheral countries such as Italy, Greece, and Spain were not so active. Thus, peripheral status by itself did not suffice to explain low per capita import levels (or high ones). The Scandinavian countries were poor markets for the above goods, more so than was the case for manufactured goods in general. Their imports of labor-intensive products were less than their relative levels of other manufactured goods, at least compared to the countries in this sample. Remaining domestic producers of clothing, shoes, textiles, etc., were obviously being protected in some fashion, or the level of protection remained unchanged while other countries were removing barriers to imports, or, perhaps most likely, the Scandinavian countries lowered protection much more slowly than other countries did. The five Mediterranean countries were most noticeable by being about average markets for the goods in question, notwithstanding the fact that they would have been producing many of the same goods themselves.

Chapter 7

Imports and Domestic Production
of Selected Manufactured Products

The preceding two chapters analyzed per capita imports of manufactured goods by the 23 states without reference to domestic production. While the results clearly indicated the extent of relative openness in many areas, both for manufactures in general and for products important to the developing world, the analyses ignored the size of the potential import competing sector in these countries. Given the tenets of comparative advantage, such concerns would not be especially important for overall per capita imports of manufactured products, since, as noted earlier, every industrialized country would have advantages for some products and disadvantages for others, and mutually beneficial trade could occur as a result. By definition, industrialized states would import some industrial products from each others. For specific product categories, however, nations would have potentially different needs and import levels. Countries with sizable sectors producing particular goods could either have protected against imports or engaged in intra-industry specialization. Both of these approaches could be associated with local employment in the sector but differential openness to imports. In other cases, some countries might have lacked a domestic sector in a particular product area of manufacturing and thus would have been open to imports in this particular area. Yet other countries might have lacked a domestic industrial sector and had low import levels as well due to a lack of local demand for the products in question. In this chapter, therefore, imports in five product areas will be analyzed to determine influences on per capita import patterns among the industrialized countries.

Data Utilized

Information on imports by various sector categories was readily available from the same sources used in the preceding chapters. Information on domestic production was contained in various issues of the *Yearbook of Industrial Statistics*.[1] This data source had information on output in factor values or for total output in local currencies for as many as 25 categories of manufacturing activities (the categories used and the information available varied somewhat from country to country).[2] Regardless of which measure of output was used for the national statistics, it was possible to express output for a particular industry as a percentage of the total manufacturing sector. World Bank sources[3] in turn had data on the percentage of total GNP accounted for by the manufacturing sector (as well as other broad areas of activity).[4] By combining these two sets of data it was possible to calculate total output values in industrial sectors in a standardized fashion for the industrialized countries on a per capita basis.

One problem with the domestic manufacturing data bases was the prevalence of missing or aggregated data. In some cases national statistics aggregated the data for various industries. Thus, the production and import data did not correspond in some cases, preventing the inclusion of some countries in the analysis of particular manufacturing sectors. There were also missing data. Switzerland has had virtually no national industrial statistics available, either for the manufacturing sector in total or for individual sectors of production.[5] As a consequence, one of the more interesting industrialized nations was not available for inclusion in the analyses to follow. Ireland and New Zealand also frequently lacked the necessary data for inclusion. Other countries had missing data for particular years, representing an apparent lacunae in national statistics. Ultimately, the number of industrialized countries included varied both by year and by the industrial sectors that were being analyzed.

Five industrial sectors were chosen for the specific analyses that followed, representing a diversity of trade situations and opportunities. Textiles and clothing were chosen because of their importance to developing countries and the presence of the MFA (in effect a continuation of the analyses from the previous chapter). The iron and steel industry was selected as well given its importance in the industrial base of developed countries. This sector also represented one product area that has been important for some countries of the developing world as well as developed ones. Finally, both the entire transportation industry and the subset for the production of automotive vehicles were chosen. The transportation sector was chosen because of incomplete reporting by countries for automotive output.[6] Some major producers consistently did not have such information in their national statistics. Automobiles and related products, of course, have been an important source of trade controversies and protection, and an analysis of the sector would be enlightening. Analyses of overall production of transport equipment (rail, road, sea, and air) provided a useful surrogate since automotive products were the largest portion of the total output in this sector. Of course, for some countries, ships or locomotive construction could have been relatively more important; consequently, the transportation figures must be used with the information available for automotive production and imports with some care.

Given the incomplete nature of the data and the preliminary nature of the analyses in this chapter, only four years were used—1960, 1970, 1980, and 1988.[7] The data available for 1960 were the least complete, while coverage improved in later years.[8] Data were available for 1990, but they were much less complete than similar data for 1988. For example, there were no production data reported for the United States in 1990. The earlier year of 1988 was consequently a far better choice given the greater coverage in that year.

Possibilities

There were four combinations that were possible for individual nations in specific years—and changes could have occurred over time in terms of where a nation was located. (These four possibilities are outlined in Figure 7–1). A particular country could have lacked an indigenous domestic production capacity while still maintaining at least average demand for a product. In such cases the country would have had above average per capita imports (controlling for other factors) and below average per capita domestic production (Quadrant I in Figure 7–1). A number of European countries, for example, have neither domestic auto plants nor even local assembly operations.[9] Given that there would have been demand for autos, imports would have been a necessity. Another possible combination would have been that a particular country was heavily involved in intra-industry trade in a specific sector. In such cases, there would have been significant local production, much of which would have been for export, as well as imports of goods that were part of the production process or that served a particular portion of the national market (Quadrant II of Figure 7–1). It was also possible, at least in some circumstances, that a country might have an especially high demand for a product, leading to above-average production and high imports without a great deal of intra-industry activity. Countries like Greece and Norway with their large merchant fleets could have both imported and produced ships in order to fill their needs.

A third possibility would have been a country with important domestic capacity and very limited imports (Quadrant III). Such a situation could have represented a number of circumstances. The domestic industry could have been so competitive that imports could not penetrate the domestic market, a somewhat unlikely prospect for competitive industries given the importance of intra-industry trade for successful operations. Another obvious possibility would have been the presence of significant protective barriers. Imports would have been limited, but the domestic capacity could also have been lower. If the protection had been necessary for the domestic industry to survive, then export possibilities would be limited as well (unless, of course, significant subsidies were being provided to the industry in question). Given the different possible

Figure 7-1
Possible Relationships Between
Production and Imports

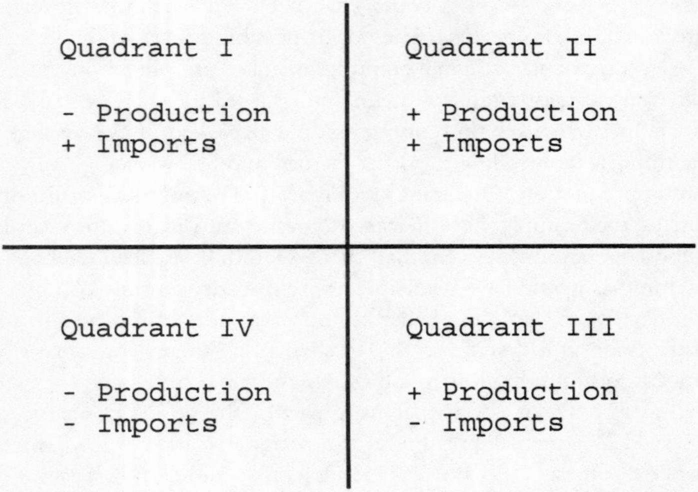

Quadrant I	Quadrant II
- Production + Imports	+ Production + Imports
Quadrant IV	Quadrant III
- Production - Imports	+ Production - Imports

interpretations for this category, any conclusions would be less definitive and would need to rely on evaluations drawing upon additional information. The final possibility would have been the case of products for which the country in question had very limited demand, whether from domestic production or from imports. In these cases, a country would be a below-average importer and producer (Quadrant IV). Austria, for example, would have little need for ships, unlike Norway or Greece (but not zero need given traffic on the Danube). An indigenous industry would be unlikely to develop unless it was totally for export, a relatively unlikely occurrence. Similarly, imports would be low as well. Another example might be particular kinds of clothing materials, which could be in much less demand in some countries compared to others given prevailing climatic conditions.

In order to determine the relative levels of imports and production within the five categories of manufactured products, multiple regression was again used. A series of regression equations was used for each of the four years. One equation included all the countries with available data for imports on a per capita basis, as was done in previous chapters. A second equation included manufactured output per capita in the industrial sector as an independent variable with the other independent variables as predictors of imports levels. Given the incomplete data for countries, the number of observations was always fewer than 23 for this equation. An equation for imports per capita as the dependent variable and with population, wealth, and EC or EFTA membership as independent variables was run for only those countries for which information on the domestic production levels had been available. The results from this equation could then be compared to the one with domestic production in order to determine how much domestic production increased and aided in predicting imports in comparison to the standard variables used. Finally, an equation with domestic production as the dependent variable was calculated with population, wealth, and EC/EU and EFTA membership in years as the independent variables. It was expected that a larger population size would be associated with more domestic production since the presence of a larger market would have facilitated economies of scale for the local firms. Customs union membership should also have been positive since the membership would in effect have provided important linkages with larger markets. Similarly, greater wealth should also have encouraged more domestic production, all other things being equal, by generating higher levels of demand. With the regression equations it was then possible to have residuals from selected equations available for additional analysis. The analysis of the residuals could then be used to determine which quadrants of Figure 7–1 particular countries occupied for specific years.

Results

The above set of equations was run for imports and domestic production of (1) textiles, (2) clothing, (3) iron and steel, (4) transportation equipment, and (5) road vehicles for 1960, 1970, 1980, and 1988, except for road vehicles in 1960. In that year there were data on domestic output of automobiles for only six countries. The residual values for per capita import predictions were taken from the total set of twenty-three countries. Thus, the figures for textiles and clothing corresponded to the ones in the tables in chapter six. Even though these equations included countries for which data on domestic production were missing, the use of the total country set provided for greater confidence in the validity of the standardized figures. Also, in some cases, aspects of domestic production could be inferred for countries where production was not known (i.e., France had and contin-

Table 7-1
Multiple Regression Equations Results for Production and Import Levels of Textiles

| Year | n | Independent Variables | | | | | R^2 | Adjusted R^2 | F-Ratio |
		GNP per capita	Population	EC	EFTA	Domestic Production			
1960									
Imports a	23	.602**	-.681**	-.026	-.079	--	.495	.383	4.412*
Imports b	18	.610**	-.691**	.131	.151	-.342	.630	.476	4.092*
Imports c	18	.594*	-.756**	.012	-.008	--	.541	.399	3.825*
Dom. Prod.	18	.186*	.893***	.118	.104	--	.937	.918	48.665**
1970									
Imports a	23	.747***	-.255	.117	.151	--	.550	.450	5.507**
Imports b	21	.632**	-.692**	.271	.235	-.030	.710	.613	7.333**
Imports c	21	.630***	-.702***	.256	.230	--	.709	.636	9.747**
Dom. Prod.	21	.058	.325	.479+	.166	--	.303	.128	1.736
1980									
Imports a	23	.499**	-.507**	.212	.138	--	.611	.524	7.054**
Imports b	20	.588***	-.536**	.227	.114	.177	.765	.681	9.114**
Imports c	20	.564***	-.500**	.322+	.156	--	.741	.671	10.703**
Dom. Prod.	20	-.135	.204	.538	.234	--	.220	.012	1.058
1988									
Imports a	23	.311	-.508	.310	.231	--	.508	.399	4.651**
Imports b	18	.075	-.470	.211	.363	-.086	.501	.293	2.409+
Imports c	18	.098	-.508+	.186	.365	--	.496	.340	3.192*
Dom. Prod.	18	-.267	.435	.293	-.014	--	.275	.052	1.233

+ $p = .90$ * $p = .95$ ** $p = .99$ *** $p = .999$ for inclusion of variable in equation or for the F-ratio value for the equation.

ues to have important levels of domestic auto production while Switzerland does not).

Textiles

It was clear from the previous chapter that governments have had significant restrictions on imports of textiles in many cases. For textiles, the equations for all four years indicated that domestic production did not contribute to explaining per capita imports of the materials (see Table 7–1). Equations without the domestic production variable had virtually the same explanatory power as those equations that did have it, including the equations with the same subset of countries with domestic production and without such production (equations b and c in the table).[10] Interestingly enough, except for 1980, the equations with all 23 countries explained less in terms of per capita imports than the equations that had a smaller set of observations. The missing countries were obviously more aberrant importers of textiles in some sense. The missing countries included a number of the smaller ones, and they included the larger-than-predicted importers such as Belgium and Switzerland in 1988, Ireland in 1980 and 1988, and New Zealand in 1970 as well as countries importing well below anticipated levels—France and Greece in 1960, Spain in 1980, and Yugoslavia in 1988. Except in 1960, domestic production was not particularly a function of size, wealth, or customs union membership. In 1960, however, for the 18 countries with data available for all the variables, population size and to a less extent wealth were both positively associated with higher production.

The comparison of the residuals for production and imports per capita indicated that most states were either producers or importers. Japan moved from being an above-average importer and below average producer in 1960 to the opposite pattern in later years. Other countries had above average production and limited imports (Germany for 1970, 1980, and 1988; Israel for 1960 and 1970; Portugal in 1960 and 1970). There were some indications that intra-industry trade was present for the United States in 1960 and 1970, Belgium in 1970 and 1980, Austria in all four years, and Portugal in 1988 since there were both greater per capita production and larger per capita imports than anticipated. In the case of Austria, Belgium, and Portugal, it was a fairly safe assumption that important portions of the production were destined for export given the relatively small domestic markets. Other countries like the Netherlands,

Norway, and the United States in the later years relied heavily on imports to supplement below average domestic production. Countries such as Canada, Sweden, Yugoslavia, and France appeared to have relatively low overall demand (relative to the other countries that were included), being both below average importers and producers. Not surprisingly, the Mediterranean countries generally were above predicted production levels for textiles and correspondingly less active as importers with the exception of Portugal in some years.

The country results in Table 7–2 were mixed at best. There were relatively few patterns. Part of the reason for the volatility was the fact that the regression equations explained virtually none of the variation in domestic production in 1970, 1980, and 1988. As a consequence, the residuals accounted for virtually all the variation in this production, which would have been due to a variety of factors, including protection but hardly restricted to it. The unexplained variance for per capita imports

Table 7-2
Rankings for Production and Imports of Textiles

Country	1960 Imports	1960 Production	1970 Imports	1970 Production	1980 Imports	1980 Production	1988 Imports	1988 Production
Japan	.828	-2.642	-.744	-.081	-.245	1.201	-.401	2.054
United States	.081	.812	1.519	.236	1.136	-.472	1.132	-1.015
Canada	-1.289	-.818	-1.558	-.316	-.789	-.253	-.443	-.189
Australia	1.045	.091	-.210	1.329	-.318	.129	-.113	-.308
New Zealand	2.397	.072	1.161	--	.626	.044	.330	-.377
Germany	.199	1.346	-.907	.914	-2.352	.915	-2.540	.453
France	-1.180	--	-1.856	-.571	-.889	-.204	-.646	-.393
Italy	-.629	--	-.205	-1.082	-.427	-.250	-.720	1.694
Netherlands	1.202	-.566	1.743	-1.086	.612	-1.889	.707	-1.480
Belgium/ Luxembourg	.047	-.780	1.225	1.774	2.406	1.732	2.509	--
United Kingdom	-.203	.768	-1.173	.305	.145	-.753	.308	-.796
Ireland	.429	1.093	1.639	-.712	1.793	--	.993	--
Switzerland	-1.926	--	-.075	--	.310	--	.931	--
Austria	.405	.373	.655	.314	1.147	2.085	.984	1.289
Denmark	1.103	-.501	.789	.260	.014	-.161	.307	.242
Norway	.893	-.526	-.060	-1.245	-.532	-.638	-.843	-.782
Sweden	.243	-1.237	-.812	-.840	-.628	-1.123	-.555	-.410
Finland	-.413	.528	.307	-.565	.377	-.561	-.535	-.141
Spain	-.529	.283	-.364	-.777	-.714	--	-.755	-1.094
Portugal	-.515	1.122	-.450	2.108	-.471	.210	.654	1.267
Greece	-.706	--	-.384	-.224	-.708	1.320	-.419	-.054
Yugoslavia	-.299	--	.175	-1.132	-.239	-.938	-.737	--
Israel	-1.544	.581	-.369	1.341	-.202	-.395	-.149	--
Adjusted R^2	.383	.918	.450	.128	.524	.012	.399	.052

was also comparatively high in all four years. Clearly, a complex of factors had been at work in the areas of both textile production in the developed countries and their imports. One probable factor in at least some cases would have been increasing specialization on the part of the producers focusing on specific types of textiles and niche production. Such production strategies would have been independent of size or wealth, and even to some extent of customs area membership, and were perhaps more reflective of established locational advantages that existed for specific countries.

Clothing

As was obvious from the discussion in chapter six, clothing, like textiles, has been an area of trade suffering from a multitude of restrictions. The results for clothing were a little more consistent than had been the case for textiles, and the explanatory value of the equations was higher (see Table 7–3). The equation results for all countries (or for most of them in 1960) and the subset for which domestic production data were available

Table 7-3
Multiple Regression Equations Results for Production and Import Levels of Clothing

| Year | n | Independent Variables | | | | | R^2 | Adjusted R^2 | F-Ratio |
		GNP per capita	Population	EC	EFTA	Domestic Production			
1960									
Imports a	14	.524	-.590+	.384	.692*	--	.605	.429	3.446+
Imports b	11	.462	-.690	.202	.709*	-.391	.838	.676	5.170
Imports c	11	.208	-.313	.233	.777**	--	.800	.666	5.982
Dom. Prod.	15	.314	.564*	.363	.176	--	.629	.481	4.241*
1970									
Imports a	23	.609***	-.394*	.347*	.387*	--	.653	.575	8.454**
Imports b	21	1.105**	-.462*	.519**	.207	-.615	.740	.653	8.537**
Imports c	21	.631**	-.438*	.374*	.319	--	.633	.542	6.908**
Dom. Prod.	21	.770***	-.038	.236	-.182	--	.718	.648	10.188**
1980									
Imports a	23	.601***	-.260+	.304+	.277	--	.714	.650	11.208**
Imports b	20	.624***	-.241	.332+	.296+	.020	.744	.653	8.148**
Imports c	20	.627***	-.241	.343+	.295+	--	.744	.676	10.899**
Dom. Prod.	20	.161	-.017	.579	-.027	--	.435	.285	2.289+
1988									
Imports a	23	.515*	-.235	.345*	.412+	--	.715	.652	11.304**
Imports b	17	.456*	.013	.522**	.502*	-.452*	.817	.733	9.793**
Imports c	17	.468+	-.189	.368+	.512+	--	.677	.569	6.283**
Dom. Prod.	17	-.028	.447	.342	-.023	--	.316	.088	1.388

+ p = .90   * p = .95   ** p = .99   *** p = .999 for inclusion of variable in equation or for the F-ratio value for the equation.

were similar in all years. In 1970 and 1988, the addition of domestic production enhanced the explanatory value of the equations. Production and imports were negatively associated in some of the years, as would be expected. In 1960 and 1980, however, the per capita domestic production was unrelated to per capita imports. Nor was there any major loss in explanatory value of the equations when domestic production was excluded in these two years. The importance of the other variables in the equations was mixed. Each of them was important in some years but not in others. Per capita domestic production was partially explained by the independent variables in the equation, much more so than had been the case for textiles. In 1960, per capita output was most influenced by larger market size. In 1970, wealthier countries had enhanced output in the apparel sector. In 1980 and 1988, the explanatory value of the equations was lower, and none of the independent variables stood out in terms of predicting domestic output.

Table 7-4
Rankings for Production and Imports of Clothing

Country	1960 Imports	1960 Production	1970 Imports	1970 Production	1980 Imports	1980 Production	1988 Imports	1988 Production
Japan	--	-.771	.945	-1.396	-.262	-.531	-.671	.336
United States	.775	-.745	.183	.437	.800	.644	1.132	-.591
Canada	-.126	.802	-1.026	-1.369	-.808	-.090	-.528	.848
Australia	-.432	.313	-.783	1.150	-.984	.489	-.532	.365
New Zealand	-.755	-.206	-.760	--	-.733	.262	-.580	--
Germany	-.321	1.705	-.089	1.284	-.195	.381	.563	.511
France	-1.489	--	-1.616	.920	-1.884	-.274	-1.169	.592
Italy	--	--	-.917	-.844	-1.194	-.760	-1.937	1.601
Netherlands	1.685	--	2.300	-1.552	1.636	.872	1.101	-2.048
Belgium/ Luxembourg	.125	-1.704	.321	.191	.948	.447	1.067	--
United Kingdom	-1.399	2.189	.209	.434	.209	-.869	-1.447	-.479
Ireland	.537	.303	2.249	.087	2.429	--	1.648	--
Switzerland	1.185	--	.791	--	.791	--	1.524	--
Austria	--	--	.405	1.170	.405	1.898	.161	.859
Denmark	-.979	-.582	-.574	.359	-.574	-1.149	.058	-.516
Norway	1.348	-.688	.610	-.979	.610	-1.136	.170	-1.298
Sweden	-.155	-.644	.125	-1.285	.125	-1.525	.071	-1.087
Finland	--	.039	-1.537	.930	-1.537	1.512	-1.853	1.580
Spain	--	.265	.768	-.317	.061	--	-.043	-.447
Portugal	--	.274	-.722	-.592	-.560	-.677	1.500	.383
Greece	--	--	.258	-.279	.072	-.480	-.062	-.609
Yugoslavia	--	--	.883	-.162	.642	-.829	.513	--
Israel	--	--	-.558	1.813	-.002	1.809	.266	--
Adjusted R^2	.429	.481	.575	.648	.650	.285	.652	.088

A comparison of the standardized scores in Table 7–4 indicated that some of the possible relationships from Figure 7–1 were present. Ireland, Austria, Belgium in 1980, Germany in 1988, and the United States in 1970 and 1980 appeared to be involved in intra-industry trade given above average per capita imports and per capita production. France, Finland, Australia, the United Kingdom in 1960, Italy in 1988, and Portugal in 1988 all had well above average production and imports well below predicted levels, indicating either the presence of protection or demand that was being met by locally competitive producers. The Netherlands, Norway, and the United States in 1988 were clearly meeting demand via imports given the well below average local production. The Mediterranean countries produced apparel at lower than expected levels in most cases. As a consequence, they were much more likely to import clothing at higher than predicted levels than they were to have been producing such goods above expected levels. Of course, the less industrialized countries of Southern Europe might have been importing less expensive items of clothing, even if in considerable volume, or lighter clothing appropriate to warmer climates, which would be less expensive than the more substantial apparel that would be needed in more northern nations. No country was consistently below anticipated levels in both production and import levels. Of course, clothing would be a necessary manufactured good from whatever source it originated.

Iron and Steel

There have been many efforts by governments to support national firms in this sector. World steel production has faced a crisis in that there has been extensive surplus capacity in the global industry by the 1980s.[11] Prior to this time in the 1960s, the weight and shipping costs involved for iron ore, coal, and steel resulted in production being geographically limited to sales in the same region. With the construction of larger freighters, however, it became possible beginning in the 1970s for profitable shipments at greater distances (i.e., from Japan to the United States).[12] This problem for the steel industries of the developed states was exacerbated by increasing competition in global markets from the NICs.[13] The United States instituted a trigger price mechanism, in effect a quota, to control imports of foreign steel. Various European nations attempted to limit long-term protection because it hindered the competitiveness of domestic steel-consuming sectors, but they did provide a variety of short term support.[14] While subsidies avoided some of the problems of introducing higher costs for other sectors in the European countries, the various efforts to help declining domestic steel industries have failed with high costs being exchanged for limited benefits.[15]

There was some relationship between per capita domestic production of iron and steel and per capita imports of such goods. Domestic production was negatively related to imports (see Table 7–5). This independent variable was a significant addition to the equations in 1980 and 1988 Even in 1960 and 1970, the equations with the domestic production variables had more explanatory value than the equivalent equations without this variable. The equations with all 23 countries did less well in terms of explaining imports than did the equations with the smaller set of countries and with domestic production as an independent variable. The amount of variation explained with the equations for per capita domestic production generally had declined over time. Customs union membership was not an important factor, while wealth was the best predictor of levels of domestic production.

The comparison of the standardized scores revealed some patterns (see Table 7–6). Australia and Austria were consistently active producers with

Table 7-5
Multiple Regression Equations Results for Production and Import Levels of Iron and Steel

Year	n	Independent Variables GNP per capita	Population	EC	EFTA	Domestic Production	R^2	Adjusted R^2	F-Ratio
1960									
Imports a	23	.444*	-.691***	-.011	.081	--	.486	.372	4.254*
Imports b	15	.652*	-.732*	.288	.303	-.438	.628	.422	3.045+
Imports c	15	.510+	-.700*	-.007	.173	--	.531	.343	2.826+
Dom. Prod.	15	.540*	.654*	.192	.080	--	.653	.514	4.701*
1970									
Imports a	23	.531*	-.606**	.262	.105	--	.499	.388	4.486**
Imports b	18	.716**	-.612**	.343	.269	-.293	.707	.585	5.789**
Imports c	18	.523*	-.609**	.214	.331	--	.682	.584	6.973**
Dom. Prod.	18	.364*	.140	.521	.060	--	.469	.305	2.869+
1980									
Imports a	23	.601***	-.435**	.266+	.229	--	.768	.717	14.907**
Imports b	19	.764***	-.343*	.460**	.395*	-.501**	.827	.761	12.438**
Imports c	19	.580**	-.472*	.242	.237	--	.704	.619	8.306**
Dom. Prod.	19	.366	.256	.436+	.314	--	.508	.368	3.617*
1988									
Imports a	23	.578**	-.452*	.423*	.182	--	.716	.653	11.335**
Imports b	17	.753***	-.407*	.451**	.396*	-.495***	.877	.822	15.756**
Imports c	17	.546*	-.508*	.395+	.268	--	.772	.629	7.791**
Dom. Prod.	18	.418	.203	.113	.260	--	.366	.154	1.729

+ $p = .90$ * $p = .95$ ** $p = .99$ *** $p = .999$ for inclusion of variable in equation or for the F-ratio value for the equation.

limited imports, reflecting the presence of protected industries, perhaps most clearly in Australia, where protection of the steel sector had been part of the broader pattern of protection. Israel, Norway, and Denmark were importing countries that lacked any particular indigenous capacity. The United States, notwithstanding its own domestic capacity, also fit the same pattern as these three smaller countries. Sweden was the one country that consistently seemed to be involved in intra-industry trade in this sector, as might have been expected given the Swedish reputation for the production of specialty steel (as well as for steel in general). Belgium in 1970 and Yugoslavia in 1980 were two other examples of countries that might have been involved in such intra-industry trade, at least for some points in time. The Mediterranean countries were more likely to have imported more per capita than predicted than they were to have produced large amounts of iron or steel domestically. Some countries underwent changes over time. In 1960, the United Kingdom imported relatively little and trailed only West Germany in terms of its standardized positive production value. In

Table 7-6
Rankings for Production and Imports of Iron and Steel

Country	1960 Imports	1960 Production	1970 Imports	1970 Production	1980 Imports	1980 Production	1988 Imports	1988 Production
Japan	.815	1.401	.249	.840	-1.099	1.998	-1.011	2.351
United States	.400	-.855	.523	-.561	1.353	-1.262	1.395	-1.551
Canada	-1.616	.461	1.240	-.656	-1.272	-.195	-.372	-.356
Australia	-1.236	.408	-1.390	1.337	-2.159	.971	-1.164	.389
New Zealand	.258	--	.754	--	.450	-.403	-.199	--
Germany	-.025	2.118	-.423	2.002	-1.137	1.559	-.807	.850
France	-.552	--	-.638	-1.601	-1.013	-.506	-1.461	.055
Italy	-.157	--	-.385	-.978	-.209	.067	-1.364	1.045
Netherlands	1.415	--	.390	--	.668	--	2.960	1.050
Belgium/ Luxembourg	-.681	-.212	1.009	.596	1.112	-.364	.538	--
United Kingdom	-1.150	1.723	-.681	.480	-.207	-.484	-.714	-.132
Ireland	.655	--	-.275	--	.665	--	-.250	--
Switzerland	1.534	--	-2.581	--	.361	--	.542	--
Austria	-1.382	-.046	-.652	1.041	-1.198	1.797	-.253	.346
Denmark	1.006	-.522	1.582	-1.444	1.279	-1.784	1.161	-1.621
Norway	.459	-.411	1.494	-.431	1.482	-.794	.115	-1.225
Sweden	.607	-.301	.427	1.050	.265	.010	.406	.646
Finland	.764	.167	1.177	-.426	-.432	-.167	-.838	.242
Spain	-.970	.034	.173	.281	-.584	--	-.014	.295
Portugal	-1.074	-.422	-.509	-.309	-.499	-.854	.524	-.130
Greece	1.820	--	-.393	--	.447	.078	-.051	-.153
Yugoslavia	-.744	--	.181	-.344	.791	.587	.434	--
Israel	-.145	.188	1.160	-.359	.936	-.254	.424	--
Adjusted R^2	.372	.514	.388	.305	.717	.368	.653	.154

1970, the signs for the United Kingdom were the same, but the scores were much closer to anticipated levels. By 1980 and 1988, however, the United Kingdom was slightly below anticipated levels in terms of both imports and production, indicating that changes occurred in the method of meeting domestic demand. Japan began as an active importer with a low domestic capacity in 1960, was apparently involved in intra-industry activity in 1970, and then became a larger than anticipated domestic producer and an importer that was well below the predicted per capita levels.[16] Successful industrialization had obviously led to changing relationships in terms of domestic production and imports for Japan as well.

The results for the iron and steel sectors were similar to those for textiles and clothing. The positions for countries were quite dynamic. The whole industry was in flux, as might be expected for products that were part of a sector with surplus capacity on a global level. Countries changed positions relative to each other in terms of both imports and production, and there were probably some shifts in comparative advantage that had been occurring for the nations in question.

Table 7-7
Multiple Regression Equations Results for Production and Import Levels of Transport Equipment

Year	n	GNP per capita	Population	EC	EFTA	Domestic Production	R^2	Adjusted R^2	F-Ratio
1960									
Imports a	22	.545**	-.651**	-.031	.155	--	.558	.454	5.363**
Imports b	18	.650+	-.674*	-.092	.207	-.096	.561	.362	2.813+
Imports c	18	.575	-.634*	-.110	.191	--	.557	.410	3.776
Dom. Prod.	17	.240	.706***	.240	.196	--	.755	.673	9.230**
1970									
Imports a	23	.752***	-.747***	-.072	-.160	--	.593	.502	6.549**
Imports b	20	.981**	-.717**	-.186	-.171	-.248	.619	.483	4.549*
Imports c	20	.772***	-.743***	-.185	-.131	--	.602	.503	6.055**
Dom. Prod.	20	.789***	.179	.067	-.049	--	.806	.754	15.563**
1980									
Imports a	23	.537+	-.398+	.128	-.041	--	.425	.297	3.329*
Imports b	19	.675+	-.393	-.098	-.014	-.152	.410	.183	1.805
Imports c	19	.584*	-.438+	-.136	-.022	--	.634	.232	2.358
Dom. Prod.	19	.599**	.297	.251	.056	--	.668	.574	7.059**
1988									
Imports a	23	.630*	-.388+	.023	.134	--	.552	.452	5.540**
Imports b	18	.492	-.415	-.117	.178	.031	.454	.227	1.999
Imports c	18	.513+	-.409	-.117	.168	--	.454	.286	2.702+
Dom. Prod.	18	.669+	.196	-.002	-.295	--	.546	.407	3.914*

+ $p = .90$ * $p = .95$ ** $p = .99$ *** $p = .999$ for inclusion of variable in equation or for the F-ratio value for the equation.

Transportation Equipment

The equations for transport equipment were reasonably consistent through time with some decline in the amount of variation explained in 1988 (see Table 7–7). The equations for imports with all 23 countries included and the equations for the smaller set of observations in this case were similar. There was no improvement in the explanatory value with the smaller set of observations. Domestic production had virtually no effect in terms of predicting per capita imports. Imports were greater with smaller populations and greater wealth, as expected. Membership in the EC/EU and EFTA had no effect whatsoever on per capita imports. The per capita level of domestic production was positively associated with larger population size in 1960 and with relative wealth in later years. Length of membership in the EC and EFTA had no apparent influence on the relative level of domestic production.

Table 7-8
Rankings for Production and Imports of Transport Equipment

Country	1960 Imports	1960 Production	1970 Imports	1970 Production	1980 Imports	1980 Production	1988 Imports	1988 Production
Japan	1.058	-.586	.350	-.043	-.846	1.089	-1.965	1.065
United States	.261	-.676	.427	-.900	.920	-1.182	.988	-1.121
Canada	.003	.445	1.275	.340	1.869	.873	2.825	1.023
Australia	-.299	.534	-1.108	1.776	-.928	.146	-.744	-.470
New Zealand	-.760	-.170	-.561	--	-.057	.066	-.456	-.465
Germany	-.590	-.000	-.874	1.694	-1.173	2.238	-.561	1.849
France	-.810	--	-1.141	.165	-1.159	.427	-.540	.298
Italy	-.055	--	-.095	-.212	-.311	-.380	-.585	-.211
Netherlands	.520	--	.352	-1.647	-.247	-1.661	.175	-1.097
Belgium/ Luxembourg	.935	--	1.758	--	3.043	--	1.908	--
United Kingdom	-1.303	3.467	-.402	1.405	.315	.125	.513	.023
Ireland	-.040	.292	.021	-.555	.544	--	-.173	--
Switzerland	-.589	--	-.220	--	.261	--	-.048	--
Austria	-.708	-.660	-.210	-.374	.317	-.766	-.229	-.314
Denmark	.343	-.802	-.495	-1.710	-1.318	-1.995	-1.112	-1.867
Norway	3.624	-.742	2.933	.672	.147	.397	1.078	-1.000
Sweden	-.475	-.885	-1.746	.756	-.551	.918	-.064	1.735
Finland	-.092	.050	.003	-1.133	-.113	-.823	-.764	-.435
Spain	-.288	-.004	-.342	.097	-.700	--	-.039	.656
Portugal	-.892	-.376	.125	.585	-.065	.235	.523	.392
Greece	--	--	.760	-.560	.750	-.248	-.229	-.059
Yugoslavia	-.111	.148	-.249	.485	-.369	.347	-.314	--
Israel	.269	-.033	-.563	-.840	-.329	.196	-.190	--
Adjusted R^2	.454	.673	.502	.754	.297	.574	.452	.407

A comparison of standardized scores indicated that the United States was noticeably inclined toward per capita imports above expected levels and that it had domestic production below anticipated levels (see Table 7–8). Germany, France, Sweden, and the United Kingdom in 1960 and 1970 were active producers and below average importers, indicating the possibility of protection being present. Canada and Norway in some years appeared to be the countries most actively involved in intra-industry trade in these products. Japan followed a transition similar to that for iron and steel. In 1960 it was an active importer and below average producer; in 1970 it was close to expected levels in both areas; then it became a producer above expected levels and an importer well below predicted per capita levels. There were a number of countries that seemed to have had below average total demand with negative standardized scores for both imports and domestic production (or at least their demand was relatively low compared to countries with higher demand). New Zealand, the Netherlands, Austria, Denmark, and Finland in 1980 and 1988 all fit into this category. The five Mediterranean countries all were usually near anticipated levels for both imports and production.

The results for many nations for transport equipment showed greater consistency than had been the case with the other types of products analyzed above, notwithstanding the fact that road, rail, sea, and air equipment were included in the SITC category. The inclusion of ships would explain Norway's intra-industry involvement. Norway built ships and imported other products, although Norway also imported ships since the considerable domestic demand could not be met by local production. The size of the Norwegian merchant fleet placed this country in a category of its own in terms of high demand. The domestic production below expected levels for the United States would have reflected limited production in some areas (rail stock, ships), higher production in others (commercial aircraft), and variable production in yet other areas (road vehicles). An analysis of imports and production in the automotive sector in the next section will provide more insight into the interactions that were occurring in this broad sector.

Road Vehicles (Automobiles)

Imports of automobiles (and other road vehicles) have been particularly controversial in international trade. European nations have had a long history of protecting the automotive sector with tariffs, quotas, investment aid, local content requirements, rules of origin, technology policy, and other measures.[17] The United States has had domestic content regulations as well, and efforts have also been made to reduce imports of Japanese parts for use in U.S. plants producing Japanese autos (or American ones) and to increase usage of components produced in the United States.[18] The problem of high levels imports of parts into the United States from Japan has been exacerbated by the fact that firms in Japan in turn have imported very few U.S. produced parts.[19] Both European nations and the United States have negotiated VERs with Japan. The U.S. quota, however, was for one-quarter of its domestic market, whereas France and Italy had quotas restricting Japanese imports to just 3 percent of their domestic markets.[20] In 1991, Japan and the EC negotiated a VER for the EC in general, but there were limits on imports of Japanese cars for specific national markets as well. This VER clearly demonstrated the presence of protectionist objectives of the individual member states that had domestic production or assembly facilities. It also demonstrated that these countries were quite capable of gaining their objectives in the form of EC commercial and trade policies.[21]

The importance of automotive industries to particular countries has also been demonstrated by other kinds of aid provided through bailouts or

Table 7-9
Multiple Regression Equations Results for Production and Import Levels for Automobiles

Year	n	Independent Variables			EFTA	Domestic Production	R^2	Adjusted R^2	F-Ratio
		GNP per capita	Population	EC					
1970									
Imports a	23	.800***	-.708***	-.013	-.250	--	.592	.501	6.533**
Imports b	16	.765*	-.737*	.093	-.207	.130	.635	.453	3.481*
Imports c	16	.846**	-.717*	.061	-.248	--	.629	.494	4.666*
Dom. Prod.	16	.622*	.154	-.239	-.316	--	.649	.522	5.091*
1980									
Imports a	23	.507*	-.342*	.176	.000	--	.402	.270	3.030*
Imports b	14	.606	-.432	.068	-.038	.024	.447	.102	1.294
Imports c	14	.621	-.428	.060	-.047	--	.447	.201	1.818
Dom. Prod.	14	.614	.154	-.341	-.351	--	.510	.292	2.337
1988									
Imports a	23	.610*	-.360	.051	.022	--	.406	.274	3.075*
Imports b	14	.425	-.462	-.027	-.003	.150	.281	-.169	.624
Imports c	14	.565	-.494	-.083	-.129	--	.272	-.052	.840
Dom. Prod.	14	.933*	-.215	-.370	-.837*	--	.619	.450	3.663*

+ $p = .90$ * $p = .95$ ** $p = .99$ *** $p = .999$ for inclusion of variable in equation or for the F-ratio value for the equation.

nationalizations of failing companies. Automotive production has also been fairly concentrated, with large scale production in a few countries—the United States and Canada, Japan, the United Kingdom, Germany, France, Italy, and Sweden (and more recently Korea and quite briefly Yugoslavia—when there was a Yugoslavia). Major subsidiary operations or assembly plants in the industrialized world have included Australia, Spain, and Portugal among those countries with important domestic interest groups desirous of restricting imports. Other countries, on the other hand, have not had major domestic groups seeking to limit imports since there has been minimal domestic activity.

The equations for automotive imports and manufactures indicated that local manufacturing had no influence on levels of imports (see Table 7–9). This conclusion must be tempered by the fact that Germany,

Table 7-10
Rankings for Production and Imports of Automobiles

Country	1970 Imports	1970 Production	1980 Imports	1980 Production	1988 Imports	1988 Production
Japan	.288	.067	-.780	1.857	-1.965	1.254
United States	.388	-.627	.920	-1.041	.988	-.820
Canada	2.353	1.070	2.014	.873	2.825	.219
Australia	-1.280	1.694	-.700	-.012	-.744	-1.402
New Zealand	-.198	--	-.124	-.262	-.456	--
Germany	-1.124	--	-1.338	--	-.561	--
France	-1.363	--	-1.083	--	-.540	.800
Italy	--	--	-.917	-.844	-1.194	-.760
Netherlands	.267	-.000	-.282	-.009	.175	-.829
Belgium/ Luxembourg	2.399	--	3.051	--	1.908	--
United Kingdom	-.179	1.708	-.023	-.027	.513	-.083
Ireland	.432	.067	.948	--	-.173	--
Switzerland	.519	--	.347	--	-.048	--
Austria	.645	-.123	.611	-.045	-.229	.360
Denmark	-.260	1.708	-.023	-.027	.513	-.083
Norway	-.546	-1.400	-.480	-1.700	1.078	-1.526
Sweden	-1.536	.796	-.386	1.472	-.064	1.935
Finland	.394	-.695	-.178	-.783	-.764	-.797
Spain	-.234	-.111	-.510	--	-.039	--
Portugal	.712	.894	.077	1.019	.523	.271
Greece	-.570	-.977	-.334	-.716	-.229	-.084
Yugoslavia	-.023	--	-.178	--	-.314	--
Israel	-.956	-1.084	-.164	-.644	-.190	--
Adjusted R^2	.501	.522	.270	.292	.274	.450

Italy, and France (except in 1988) were countries for which domestic production data were unavailable. The absence of such major producers was quite important for analyzing relationships. The number of observations available was quite limited except for total imports. In these cases, wealth was most important for explaining import levels. Wealth was also important in explaining per capita levels of domestic production. It was interesting that EFTA membership in 1988 was significantly associated with such production in a negative fashion, even though such a relationship was absent in 1980 (when the membership of EFTA was the same).

From the comparisons of imports and production, Canada and Portugal were clearly involved in intra-industry trade (see Table 7–10). In the case of Canada, the Autopact with the United States explained both the above-average imports per capita and per capita production. The Autopact has long provided for sectoral free trade in automotive parts and final products between the two countries. The Autopact, of course, has been much more important for Canada than the United States given the disparity in size between the two countries. The intra-industry effects were also much larger given the size of the Canadian economy (one-tenth that of the United States). The arrangement has also probably been quite important for U.S. producers since it has given them a significant edge in the Canadian market vis-à-vis their Japanese and European rivals. In the case of Portugal it would have been the presence of assembly plants,[22] with some products destined for export. The lower Portuguese GNP per capita relative to other industrialized countries explained the fact that levels of domestic activity were higher than expected. Among the other countries, Finland, Israel, and Greece would appear to have had relatively lower-than-average overall demand.

Japan in 1980 and 1988, France, and the United Kingdom in 1970 clearly produced beyond anticipated levels and consequently had lower imports. The lower imports clearly reflected the presence of domestic competition, but protection was present as well. Germany and France in earlier years would also appear to have fit into this category. They were well above predicted levels as producers of transport equipment, of which road vehicles served as the most important group, and clearly below average importers of these products. Italy, however, would seem to have been near predicted levels of imports and was also only slightly below anticipated per capita production of transport equipment, as can be seen in Table 7–8. The United States, notwithstanding its large automotive sector, was below anticipated production levels and was above predicted import levels as a consequence (although the higher import levels could also have reflected the trade creating effects of the Autopact on the United States).

Summary

The above analyses generated results that were indicative rather than definitive ones, given the missing data, but they still shed additional light on import patterns in at least some economic sectors. It is important to note that the patterns were variable for different countries in different years and that there were often differences for various industries for the same countries. There were obviously dynamic aspects in the industrial activities of the developed countries. Clearly, as expected, smaller countries did not produce all items and frequently imported them. In some cases they relied on imports since they lacked the domestic capacity to produce the items for themselves. In other cases it was clear that intra-industry trade had clearly been important for the economic activities of at least some countries. Canada and the automotive industry was just the clearest such example of these kinds of circumstances. The categories used with the trade statistics and national reports of industrial activity were by nature quite broad (apparel still ranged from designer gowns to inexpensive off-the-rack clothes), making more definitive conclusions difficult. Import levels were affected by local production in specific areas. Domestic production figures were of limited explanatory value in terms of explaining imports, indicating that protection was very likely a factor that interfered in trade levels. The variables included were also not particularly important in terms of explaining the relative levels of domestic production. Interestingly enough, any effects of membership in EFTA or the EC/EU were indirect in nature since the trade area variables were usually insignificant additions to the equations. Other factors obviously were quite relevant. Comparative advantages and locational advantages related to earlier comparative advantages would have been possible causes for such discrepancies. Individual company decisions could have played a role as well. They might have kept existing plants running even when comparative advantage or locational advantages would have suggested shifting to manufacturing locations elsewhere because the existing plants would still have had some value in the short term in generating returns on the initial investments. Ultimately, all the industrialized countries imported some goods and exported others, as would be expected, but the influences involved were quite complex.

Protection was clearly present in the patterns seen above in some cases and was less obviously present in other cases. Different countries did limit imports in the industries in question in order to safeguard domestic production and employment. Strange had suggested that steel and textiles, as well as shipbuilding, were more prone to protection because the firms in these sectors were national firms. Local automobile production, however, was less likely to have been protected because the automobile firms were multinational ones.[23] The above results indicated that while intra-industry trade was perhaps more prevalent for automobiles, protectionism was still present for this industry as well.

The analyses indicated that for the categories selected the same general patterns were frequently present in this chapter as in the previous ones. Japan was a better relative importer in earlier time periods and very poor in later ones. France, Germany, and Italy—to a lesser extent, in some cases—were also not very active importers. The United States, on the other hand, was among the more active importers of these particular goods, notwithstanding local production. The Netherlands and Belgium would appear to have fallen into the category of active importers as well. In addition, other smaller industrialized countries fit into this group for the most part. The five Mediterranean countries generally were close to expected levels of production and imports, with the exception of textiles in those cases in which they had competitive export industries with access to the European markets (at least within the advantages for greater access provided by the EC/EU or EFTA frameworks).

Chapter 8

Import Levels of the Developing Countries

The preceding four chapters have dealt with per capita import levels of the industrialized nations of the world. Wealth and size explained significant portions of their per capita imports, and memberships in customs unions and trade areas also had some explanatory value. It was also clear that other factors, including protectionist activities and the presence of local producers, influenced the level of imports. Domestic policies in the industrialized countries were clearly important impediments to imports, including the levels of imports of manufactured goods that have been such a large portion of trade among industrialized states. By way of comparison, the present chapter considered total per capita imports and per capita imports of manufactured products in the developing world to determine whether similar factors influenced imports of the developing countries and whether similar patterns of revealed protection were obvious in the developing world or whether the import patterns for these countries were different.

Inward versus Outward Orientations

Even though most developing countries have used protection for some domestic sectors, one factor clearly affecting the level of per capita imports for different developing countries has been the relative openness of their economies. The Uruguay Round provided for some liberalization of their tariff policies for developing countries. They bound their tariffs with a commitment not to raise them; however, they bound them at relatively high levels, and most of these countries are unlikely to lower them significantly any time soon.[1] There has been a long-standing and ongoing debate in the developing world and elsewhere among political leaders, practitioners, and academics about the most appropriate policies that should be followed in regard to trade and economic development. Many studies of economic growth have found that growth has been associated with economies that were more open to trade, while countries that had been more closed on average lagged behind in terms of economic gains.[2] The association between greater growth and greater trade that has been present could reflect a virtuous circle whereby export growth contributes to economic growth, which in turn contributes to increases in exports and so forth.[3] Liberalization of trade policies also has resulted in greater growth in states, and in comparisons of countries more liberal trade policies have been associated with greater growth.[4] It has also been suggested that trade can be beneficial for developing countries by promoting technological change that could in turn lead to a shift in resources toward the production of more sophisticated goods by industries in the developing world.[5] There have been other studies, however, that have found few indications that more open economies have grown more rapidly or that countries developing at a faster rate were more likely to have been involved in trade or to have higher levels of imports,[6] or that the gains in growth have not been consistent over time.[7] The weight of opinion has favored freer trade as a tool for development. It was possible of course that developing countries best able to grow were also those countries that were best able to take advantage of free trade policies, the possibilities that were present with trade, or other factors that influenced the rate of growth.[8] It has also been suggested that freer trade and openness would generate greater income inequality in developing countries, but there has been little evidence of such effects.[9] Some indications have been seen that low income groups have actually benefited the most from trade liberalization.[10] It was still possible, however, that there would have been increasing inequality in at least some states with the advent of greater openness, even if there had been no such general pattern.[11]

Even though liberal trade has been associated with greater growth for the most part, developing countries have frequently protected domestic sectors. In some cases political leaders sought to limit imports because they perceived that the industrialized countries were using trade (and other economic activities) to control and dominate the economic life of the developing world and that they used their position to exploit the resources of developing countries.[12] These views in their Marxist, neocolonial, and dependency variations all have argued against liberal trade policies for developing countries. The possibilities of trade among the developing countries themselves have also been limited since for the most part their economies have not been complementary. Yet there has been little evidence that autarkic growth has been possible or that countries that limited trade and economic contracts with the industrialized countries have benefited as a consequence of this choice. The decline and then collapse of the relatively autarkic, centrally planned economies of Eastern Europe and the old Soviet Union have been obvious recent examples of the inadequacies of such policies for long-term growth—albeit growth with greater equality or inequality in income distribution.

In other countries of the developing world, the emphasis has been on the support of infant industries. Developing countries generally have used protective devices to support their infant industries or to generate revenues. Further, it has been the manufacturing area in developing states that has frequently had the greatest amount of protection provided by state policies.[13] Governments have also supported infant industries as part of policies of import substitution industrialization (ISI). Protecting the infant industries has long been justified as a necessary measure so that the new firms can develop to the point at which they can effectively compete with foreign producers at least in their domestic market. The creation of such infant industries was also deemed to have been necessary to permit the country to advance beyond being simply a producer of raw materials and a consumer of manufactured goods that were produced elsewhere. The ISI policy has been geared toward creating an industrial base for a more diverse and self-sustaining economy, and the starting point for such an industrial base would have been domestic production that replaces manufactured goods that were previously imported. With the production of these goods, the industrialization process would be started. Government-supported ISI has been and still is considered by some to be a viable option for developing countries.[14] If governments in developing nations were simply to focus on current comparative advantage, their countries might suffer long term losses since the current advantages have normally been in low technology areas. When governments selectively encouraged industries with potential future comparative advantage, national welfare can be increased in the long run.[15] What has frequently occurred, however, is that the ISI industries and the infant industries have not become competitive with the foreign producers. They have continued to need subsidies, tariff protection, quota limitations, or other forms of aid in order to survive. Further, once the firms have become established behind protective walls or via subsidies, owners and workers in the industries have frequently been able to combine in order to lobby and exert pressure on the government in power to continue the support.[16]

These groups seeking protection have often been better organized than other groups in society, and their continued support for the governments in power has been exchanged for the continuation of the protection. The exchange has been advantageous for the workers and owners and for the government leaders, but the end result has been inefficient and subsidized industries.[17] Overall, ISI made sense as a policy when it was formulated, and it appealed to the desire of political leaders to manage their economies. Faulty implementation and conflicting interests ultimately limited its effectiveness.[18] Even when such policies have been successful, there has been a limit to the extent that ISI was possible. The opportunities for production for the local market have been limited, and once the easy substitution possibilities are exhausted, problems usually set in.[19]

To date, the results for countries that have attempted to follow an ISI policy have been poor. Countries in Latin America have frequently chosen to follow this approach, especially the ones with larger domestic markets such as Brazil, Mexico, and Argentina. Such large internal markets at least provided an opportunity for economies of scale and more efficient production. Yet these Latin American countries have lagged behind the NICs of East and Southeast Asia in terms of growth.[20] There was a time when these nations were ahead of their Asian counterparts in terms of wealth and economic performance, but they have now been passed. India followed a similar policy, resulting in an economy that has been among the most protected and regulated in the world.[21] While the size of the domestic market undoubtedly aided the industrialization process, it was costly for the economy as a whole. As a consequence, the Indian standard of living has also fallen behind many other developing states with the passage of time.[22]

The economic advances of the NICs, such as Hong Kong, Singapore, Taiwan, and (South) Korea point to the advantages that an outward orientation can presumably bring. The outward orientation has been designed to lead to involvement and interaction with the global economy ultimately permitting involvement with the system of comparative advantage. An outward orientation would also permit the developing state to become involved in intra-industry trade, which could serve as a continuing basis for industrialization. With the exception of Hong Kong, these countries did provide protection for domestic industries at some points, and they fostered infant industries as well. This support for industry, however, was not designed to substitute for imports; rather, it was designed to create industries that would be competitive in global markets. The protection that was provided was thus an essential part of an outward-oriented policy.[23] Those sectors that could not demonstrate an ability to compete globally would quickly lose government support.[24] In these Asian countries it was thus necessary to plan for production directed toward the global market because domestic markets were so much smaller than those in the Latin American countries. Singapore's brief flirtation with ISI is instructive. This period of import substitution began when the city was about to join the Malaysian Federation and when there was going to be a sufficiently large domestic market for such an approach to at least be conceivable.[25] The withdrawal of Singapore from the federation ended all efforts to consider producing primarily for a domestic market. Overall, in the NICs there was some ISI type of protection provided in many of these countries, and even sectors producing for the global market might have had a guaranteed (i.e., protected) domestic market, but the primary purpose of government policy was to provide temporary protection in order that favored industries would reach the point of being able to export and to be competitive in the global marketplace.

It would be expected that different developing countries would have had varying levels of protection. This protection would at least partially have reflected domestic policy preferences. The resulting protection, if at all effective, would consequently have affected import levels. The Asian NICs should have been relatively more open, although not totally so given the need to build the industries that would eventually export to foreign markets. Population and wealth should also have been factors in the levels of per capita imports. For developing countries a large domestic population actually might have been a factor influencing government policy in favor of ISI, just as large populations in the industrialized countries were linked to lower relative import levels.

Analyses

In order to analyze the patterns among the developing countries, forty-one nations were chosen, representing all regions of the world. In South America, Argentina, Brazil, Colombia, Chile, and Uruguay were included. Mexico, Costa Rica, El Salvador, and Nicaragua from Central America and Jamaica and Trinidad and Tobago from the Caribbean were also included. All the larger Latin American states were thus part of the data set, as well as many of the smaller ones. In East and Southeast Asia, Hong Kong, Singapore, (South) Korea, Taiwan (for the years for which comparable data were available),[26] Indonesia, Thailand, Malaysia, the Philippines, and Fiji were included. Thus, the four Asian NICs (the Four Tigers or Four Dragons, as they have been variously known) were present in addition to other countries, many of which are considered to have the potential to be the NICs of the future. In South Asia, India (the largest continuing free market economy), Pakistan (first the unified Pakistan and then the former West Pakistan sans Bangladesh), Sri Lanka, and Mauritius were the countries chosen from the region.

A number of countries in sub-Saharan Africa were also selected. They were Kenya, the Malagasy Republic, Zambia, South Africa, Gabon, Cameroon, Nigeria, Benin (formerly Dahomey), the Ivory Coast, and Senegal. Many other countries from this region of the world could not be included because of a lack of complete data for various periods. The incomplete data were at times the result of inadequate data collection or reporting, but in other cases they were a direct consequence of internal turmoil (continuing civil wars in Chad and Angola, governmental collapse in Zaire and Somalia). In the Middle East and North Africa, Morocco, Tunisia, Egypt, Jordan, Syria, and Turkey were included. The major oil exporters that had large reserves and small populations were intentionally excluded. The revenues from petroleum production were the basis of trade and the source of revenue for imports, meaning that protection was not an issue. Malta was also included as nearby small nation in the Mediterranean.

These 41 countries ranged from the very small to the very large in terms of population. They included countries relatively well off compared to others in the developing world and some that had lower standards of living. None of the very poor countries of the world were included since data were often lacking for them. It was possible that the exclusion of countries in turmoil in Africa, the Middle East, or other parts of the world could have had an impact on the results. Collapsing countries were unlikely to have effective import barriers and thus would have been more open economies by default. Still, the lack of data prevented their inclusion. Similarly, the Communist governments in the developing world with their centrally planned economies could not be included given their different reporting categories and missing data. Overall, however, this set of countries provided a reasonable sample of the developing states for analysis.

Regression analyses were again used to control for the effects of the key variables and to generate the residual values that then provided an indication of the levels of protection present in the various developing countries. Population and GNP per capita were used as the control variables in the equations. Greater wealth was expected to be positively associated with per capita imports, while larger populations should have facilitated relatively lower per capita imports. Membership in free trade areas was not included in the regression equations. There have been far too many such arrangements in the developing world to include all of them, and most of them have been quite ineffective. Due to a lack of economic benefits and results, most of them have not had very long lives as functioning organizations. Members have come and gone in the various groups, and countries have switched from one trade organization to another. The trade areas have also become moribund due to the inability of the members to reach agreement on economic decisions such as the location of new production facilities or on the list of items that would no longer be eligible for protection. Sometimes political difficulties have undermined such arrangements. The demise of the first Central American Common Market was a consequence of the political difficulties and rivalries attendant upon the Sandinista assumption of power in Nicaragua. Mexico's membership in NAFTA will obviously be a potentially important exception to the presumed unimportance of trade area memberships. This free trade arrangement should lead to significant increases in imports for Mexico and has already led to liberalization of Mexican trade and economic politics. The NAFTA arrangement, however, postdates the years under study here. The free trade area recently agreed to by Singapore and New Zealand would be another potential exception.[27] Of course, by the 1990s Singapore no longer was a representative developing country since its GNP per capita income and standard of living were higher than some of the West European countries. In any event, none of the trade areas formed among developing countries has had the staying power of the EC/EU or even EFTA.

The regression analyses were undertaken for 1960, 1965, 1970, 1975, 1980, 1985, 1990, and 1994 to determine the basic relationships present and changes over time. The regressions were used with both total per capita imports and per capita imports of all manufactured goods as the dependent variables. Ranks and standardized scores were derived for each of these 8 years for the 41 countries, or at least for those countries for which there were data available for the years in question. If import substitution industrialization policies have been in effect in some of the countries included, there might have been differences between the per capita levels of total imports and total manufactures. ISI could actually have increased imports of raw materials while being designed to decrease imports of manufactured goods.

Results

The regression results for both total imports and imports of manufactured goods for the eight years are contained in Table 8–1. A number of clear patterns emerged. First, the results were very similar for both sets of regression with little differences between them. It also was obvious that the

Table 8-1
Equations Results for Developing Countries

Year	Population	GNP/Capita	Adjusted R^2	F-Ratio
All Imports				
1960	-.448	3.373**	.218	6.570*
1965	-.089	3.702***	.264	8.168***
1970	-.284	4.482***	.340	11.056***
1975	-.065	5.689***	.455	17.248***
1980	.138	6.036***	.480	19.029***
1985	.255	8.018***	.621	32.980***
1990	.427	12.875***	.818	84.305***
1994	.663	14.618***	.863	108.533***
Manufactures				
1960	-.969	3.448***	.257	7.758**
1965	-.911	3.782***	.286	9.007***
1970	-.389	4.488***	.344	11.245***
1975	-.073	6.180***	.498	20.356***
1980	.170	6.654***	.531	23.101***
1985	.282	8.706***	.660	38.883***
1990	.485	13.446***	.831	91.869***
1994	.703	14.760***	.866	110.592***

** $p = .99$ for t-value for inclusion of variable in the equation or for the equation.
*** $p = .999$ for t-value for inclusion of variable in the equation or for the equation.

Table 8-2
Rankings for Developing Countries for All Imports

Country	1960	1965	1970	1975	1980	1985	1990	1994
Argentina	41	41	40	39	39	39	36	35
Brazil	37	33.5	35	35	36	35	35	28
Chile	40	40	38	30	33	31	29	27
Uruguay	38.5	36	39	37	37	32	32	33
Colombia	34	38	32	31	29	30	24	18.5
Mexico	38.5	39	37	38	38	37	33	32
Nicaragua	29	28	31	25	8	11	3	2.5
Costa Rica	35	22.5	29	28.5	30	25	26.5	24.5
El Salvador	32	5	30	15.5	16.5	18	18	15
Jamaica	23.5	14.5	16	32	19	10	21	12
Trinidad	3	2	3	3	34	40	34	29
Hong Kong	2	3	2	2	21	2	28	20
Singapore	1	1	1	1	1	1	1	1
Taiwan	12	31	--	--	--	--	--	--
Korea	28	20.5	25	20	35	34	38	34
Malaysia	10	27	12.5	21	25	29	25	17
Thailand	19	18.5	19	17.5	14.5	20	23	22
Philippines	33	29	18	19	14.5	14.5	13	10
Indonesia	20	9	8.5	13	13	17	11	14
Fiji	5	6	6	28.5	24	27	22	18.5
India	6	7	5	6	11.5	19	19	21
Pakistan	15	12	14	7.5	4	9	8	8
Sri Lanka	9	8	7	11	2	8	6	6
Mauritius	8	37	10	7.5	16.5	16	26.5	23
Kenya	13	13	12.5	9.5	5	6	4	4
Zambia	7	10	26	23	11.5	5	--	--
Malagasy Rep.	17	16	15	17.5	9	7	2	2.5
South Africa	36	33.5	36	36	32	36	31	26
Nigeria	14	11	11	26	26	28	7	5
Gabon	31	20.5	34	40	40	38	--	31
Benin	16	25	8.5	9.5	6	3	5	--
Cameroons	23.5	17	17	15.5	20	21	17	--
Senegal	27	18.5	21	14	7	4	9.5	7
Ivory Coast	21	22.5	22	22	27	14.5	12	--
Morocco	22	30	23.5	24	22.5	12.5	15.5	13
Egypt	25	25	28	12	10	12.5	9.5	9
Tunisia	26	25	27	27	22.5	23	20	16
Jordan	11	14.5	20	4	3	22	14	11
Syria	18	32	23.5	33	28	33	15.5	--
Turkey	30	35	33	34	31	26	30	24.5
Malta	4	4	4	5	18	24	37	30

explanatory value of the equations increased tremendously through time. Perhaps with general economic advances through time, factors common to the countries began to have more importance for trade. Wealth was the only important addition to the equations, and by the 1990s this variable was explaining four-fifths of the variation.[28] Population was never a significant addition, notwithstanding the range of population sizes present in the sample of countries.[29] Clearly, for this very diverse group of developing countries, the relative per capita import levels had not been sensitive to population size. It was possible that the small industrial bases of most of these countries mitigated against any size effect appearing in a consistent fashion in the analyses. In effect, most of these countries, at least in the early years, had not reached a level of economic development and industrialization at which size would have been important in predicting production and therefore imports.

The results in Table 8–1 suggested that in the 1960s the import patterns for the developing countries were different from those of the industrialized countries. Over time, with increasing integration into the international trade system, their economic patterns became more similar to those of the industrialized states. Thus, with economic growth and development, these states may eventually reap greater benefits from membership in trade areas, and larger population bases could come to play a much greater role in their import patterns as had been the case for the developed states in most of the years analyzed in chapters 3 and 4.

The rankings for total per capita imports are contained in Table 8–2, while the standardized scores are found in Table 8–3. For these data the rankings were somewhat misleading for many of the years. In 1960, for example, there were only a handful of countries that imported appreciably more than anticipated. Singapore was so much above predicted levels that it dwarfed the second-ranked country in terms of standardized scores. A good many of the developing countries were near their predicted levels. There were some countries, however, that were poor per capita importers, although the negative standardized scores represented comparative values among the group of countries, not absolute ones.

In 1960 and 1965 Singapore, Hong Kong, Malta, and Trinidad were clearly well above predicted levels of imports, with Singapore most clearly so. In later years these other small island territories slowly declined in terms of their standardized scores, and Trinidad and Malta even became very poor per capita importers in some of the later years. Thus, except in the case of Singapore, increasing wealth in these islands led to a relative decline in imports. Insularity was thus not a guarantee of above average

Table 8-3
Standardized Scores for Developing Countries for All Imports

Country	Year							
	1960	1965	1970	1975	1980	1985	1990	1994
Argentina	-1.613	-2.512	-2.447	-1.430	-1.271	-1.748	-1.592	-3.044
Brazil	-.686	-.530	-.625	-.979	-.909	-.603	-1.248	-.640
Chile	-1.196	-1.309	-1.245	-.208	-.654	-.308	-.487	-.595
Uruguay	-.818	-.616	-1.548	-1.199	-1.136	-.371	-.883	-1.157
Colombia	-.542	-.754	-.362	-.216	-.230	-.258	.007	.165
Mexico	-.816	-1.028	-1.184	-1.397	-1.164	-.972	-.939	-.955
Nicaragua	-.319	-.225	-.283	-.043	.322	.322	.735	.829
Costa Rica	-.496	-.131	-.165	-.184	-.356	-.015	-.048	-.265
El Salvador	-.207	.734	-.192	.130	.165	.190	.213	.377
Jamaica	-.165	-.063	.054	-.342	.129	.336	.389	.464
Trinidad	1.115	2.283	1.114	.869	-.672	-3.149	-1.296	-.669
Hong Kong	1.825	2.125	2.276	1.011	.066	.890	-.148	.105
Singapore	5.090	4.001	4.273	4.721	5.212	4.202	3.665	2.786
Taiwan	-.152	-.257	--	--	--	--	--	--
Korea	-.283	-.116	-.074	.070	-.683	-.514	-2.687	-2.494
Malaysia	.134	-.160	.099	.013	-.119	-.177	-.030	.260
Thailand	-.037	-.112	-.000	.119	.197	.126	.039	-.001
Philippines	.528	-.242	.007	.106	.194	.285	.425	.517
Indonesia	-.049	.052	.170	.221	.238	.212	.452	.394
Fiji	.578	.468	.294	-.182	-.082	-.083	.054	.163
India	.393	.424	.343	.336	.260	.160	.202	.078
Pakistan	.010	-.033	.094	.291	.393	.364	.586	.638
Sri Lanka	.266	.067	.189	.259	.477	.431	.632	.681
Mauritius	.274	-.690	.164	.296	.164	.242	-.044	-.041
Kenya	.079	-.041	.097	.269	.366	.452	.664	.797
Zambia	.290	.026	-.085	-.002	.256	.461	--	--
Malagasy Rep.	-.023	-.085	.077	.120	.307	.444	.769	.834
South Africa	-.641	-.530	-.863	-1.142	-.489	-.727	-.814	-.471
Nigeria	.064	-.010	.116	-.073	-.131	-.099	.623	.693
Gabon	-.481	-.118	-.517	-2.225	-1.761	-1.684	--	-.867
Benin	-.167	-.146	.046	.132	.118	.087	.253	--
Cameroons	-.007	-.092	.170	.274	.348	.485	.656	--
Senegal	-.037	-.112	-.000	.119	.197	.126	.039	-.001
Ivory Coast	-.102	-.130	-.052	.005	-.152	.280	.440	--
Morocco	-.131	-.249	-.066	-.025	.013	.303	.273	.425
Egypt	-.207	-.149	-.136	.233	.066	.305	.476	.579
Tunisia	-.238	-.149	-.122	-.111	.017	.038	.182	.280
Jordan	.103	-.063	-.010	.661	.429	.054	.389	.505
Syria	-.025	-.283	-.062	-.425	-.180	-.383	.268	--
Turkey	-.388	-.579	-.383	-.637	-.447	-.038	-.624	-.262
Malta	.656	1.155	.860	.514	.151	-.010	-1.712	-.774

or below average per capita import levels. Of course, increasing liberalization in other countries would have had an impact on the relative positions of the islands.

There were some clear regional patterns. The countries in South America were poor relative importers, well below anticipated levels. This trend lasted throughout the period of analysis. Only Colombia (by 1970) had approached import levels near those that were predicted, but the other countries were frequently well below anticipated levels, especially Argentina. Mexico had a pattern that was similar to the South American countries. The small Central American countries and the two Caribbean islands were less obviously closed to imports. Except for Trinidad in 1960 and 1965 and Nicaragua in 1990 and 1994, however, none of these countries had been especially active importers. Small size as well as links to the Central American Common Market (CACOM) for Nicaragua, Costa Rica, and El Salvador had not led to increased imports. The original CACOM had been largely trade diverting rather than trade creating.[30] Trade diversion, of course, would not have generated noticeably higher levels of imports, it would simply have changed the sources of the products.

The results for the East Asian NICs were somewhat surprising. Singapore was overwhelmingly open to imports. Hong Kong was a very active importing territory for 1960 to 1975, but less active in later years. By 1994, in fact, Hong Kong had fallen to the point at which per capita imports were almost at predicted levels—perhaps an early reflection of the economic and political doubts caused by the looming incorporation of the city into China. For the two years for which there were data for Taiwan, the country was near predicted levels, as was Korea through 1975. Neither of these countries had been a particularly active importer in any year and by the 1990s Korea was clearly below expected levels. In fact, in 1994 only Argentina ranked lower. Obviously Korea and Taiwan had had some protective mechanisms in place, and they had not been the open economies that they have at times been portrayed to be. The nearby nations in Southeast Asia were either average importers or somewhat above predicted levels. Malaysia and Thailand were close to anticipated levels in almost every year. Indonesia was above predicted levels in some years. Indonesian imports clearly increased after the replacement of the Sukarno regime by the military in the mid-1960s. There were major efforts at liberalization by the military, but it has been somewhat difficult to judge the effects of these changes in import policy amid all the other political and economic changes that had been occurring in these years.[31] Whereas Sukarno had provided protection for domestic sectors, the new Indonesian leaders utilized state mechanisms to create an outward–oriented and more diversified economy for the country.[32] The Philippines was also fairly open to imports in some of the years, as was Fiji in 1960 and 1965. Generally speaking, all of these Southeast Asian countries had been relatively more active than Korea (and maybe Taiwan as well), an unexpected result.

Perhaps equally surprising were the results for South Asia, countries considered to be less open than other areas due to either early ISI policies or lower levels of liberalization in later years.[33] India, frequently considered to have been a prototypical closed economy, imported more than predicted in all of the selected years (even if not substantially so). Pakistan, a country that has liberalized its trade slowly over the years in a steady fashion,[34] was at anticipated levels in the early years and progressively more active as an importer in later years. Sri Lanka followed a similar pattern to that of Pakistan, even though shortly after independence Sri Lanka had followed protectionist policies. In 1965, in fact, the economy was largely considered to be a closed one.[35] Imports may have remained relatively higher than predicted even with protectionist policies and with the controls in the equations because Sri Lankan income levels had fallen to levels similar to those of neighboring countries.[36] By the mid-1970s more liberal policies had been established, leading to somewhat higher relative import levels for the country.[37] The pattern for Mauritius was more variable, as might be expected for a small island state, but was generally near anticipated import levels. The import levels may have reflected the fact that Mauritius had consciously pursued outward-oriented, export-led policies.[38]

With two exceptions, the African countries were active importers, even though these states have not been countries in which liberalization policies have been widely pursued.[39] In some cases, government economic and trade policies have clearly limited imports.[40] Ultimately, of course, in sub-Saharan Africa the relatively underdeveloped infrastructures, the lack of opportunities for scale economies, poor technological fits, and high transport costs have all been natural barriers to trade and growth that have overshadowed government policies.[41] Of course, limited development combined with limited wealth would have led to relatively low predicted levels of per capita imports, perhaps making it more possible for these countries to exceed predictions. In general, these states usually imported near anticipated levels or better. The relative import levels for Africa demonstrated that they were increasing over time for the most part as well. The two countries that were exceptions were Gabon and South Africa. Gabon's per capita wealth increased with the discovery and exploitation of petroleum, but import levels would appear not to have kept pace. (Of

Table 8-4
Rankings for Developing Countries for Imports of Manufactures

Country	Year							
	1960	1965	1970	1975	1980	1985	1990	1994
Argentina	40	41	40	39	38.5	39	36	35
Brazil	32	35.5	35	36	35	35	34	28
Chile	37	40	38	30	33	31	29	27
Uruguay	39	38	39	37	36.5	32	32	33
Colombia	31.5	37	30	29	28	30	23	19
Mexico	36	39	37	38	36.5	37	33	32
Nicaragua	20	12	26	20	8	10	3	3
Costa Rica	10	8	8	23	30	24	28	24
El Salvador	21	3	6	11	17.5	18	19	16
Jamaica	9	10	5	33	22	17	26	14
Trinidad	4	5	31	31	38.5	40	35	29
Hong Kong	1	2	2	2	2	2	9	11
Singapore	2	1	1	1	1	1	1	1
Taiwan	31.5	29.5	--	--	--	--	--	--
Korea	33	27	28.5	24.5	34	34	38	34
Malaysia	15	14	19	22	23	26	24	17
Thailand	22	23	21	16	16	20.5	22	22
Philippines	35	28	22	19	17.5	13.5	14	10
Indonesia	24	16	9.5	10	14.5	15	11	15
Fiji	5	13	7	28	26	29	25	20
India	6	7	4	5	14.5	19	20	21
Pakistan	23	20	16	7	5	9	8	8
Sri Lanka	16	6	14	12.5	3	8	7	6
Mauritius	8	35.5	11	6	20	16	27	23
Kenya	11	21	12.5	8	6.5	6	4	4
Zambia	--	11	19	18	12.5	4	--	--
Malagasy Rep.	19	24	17	17	9.5	5	2	2
South Africa	12	15	36	35	31	36	31	26
Nigeria	13	18	12.5	24.5	24	27	6	5
Gabon	29	9	33	40	40	38	--	31
Benin	25.5	26	9.5	9	6.5	3	5	--
Cameroons	3	25	15	14	19	22	15	--
Senegal	28	32.5	23	15	11	7	12	7
Ivory Coast	17	17	19	21	27	12	13	--
Morocco	27	32.5	24	27	25	13.5	17.5	13
Egypt	30	29.5	32	12.5	12.5	11	10	9
Tunisia	25.5	19	28.5	26	21	23	21	18
Jordan	18	22	25	3	4	28	17.5	12
Syria	14	31	27	32	29	33	16	--
Turkey	34	34	34	34	32	25	30	25
Malta	7	4	3	4	9.5	20.5	37	30

course, the petroleum revenues were in government hands rather than in the hands of individuals, and it would seem that the government was frugal in its expenditures on imports.) In the case of South Africa, increasing international isolation of the apartheid regime and the imposition of economic sanctions obviously played a role in reducing the import levels (and the available sources of imports and the types of imports). South Africa thus was consistently a lower ranked country, but interestingly enough there some indications of improvement in import levels in the 1990s when apartheid and minority rule were in the process of being dismantled.

The Middle Eastern countries started out as somewhat below predicted levels of per capita imports. The significant protectionist practices in Turkey were particularly obvious in the form of high negative residuals for many of the years.[42] Over time, however, the per capita import levels rose compared to the other states, even if not to levels well above those anticipated. Eventually, however, Turkish imports were close to the expected levels. Jordan's high ranks and reasonably high standardized scores for 1975 and 1980 reflected the high incidence of re-exports to Iraq during this period when other trade routes had been limited by the Iran-Iraq war. Malta's pattern was similar to that of Trinidad, going from an especially good importer to a relatively poor one. Increases in wealth in Malta (and Trinidad) were not matched by a corresponding increases in import levels.

The rankings and standardized scores for only imports of manufactured goods were similar, but there were some important differences (see Tables 8–4 and 8–5). Singapore was still the country most above predicted levels throughout the period, but not to the extent that had been the case for overall imports. Until 1990 Hong Kong was also very active in terms of importing manufactured goods. In the 1990s, imports were still higher than anticipated but not to the extent that had been present in earlier years. Taiwan for the years available and Korea had not been active importers of these goods in any years, and they were relatively less active importers of manufactured imports than they had been of imports in general. (The standardized scores for manufactured products were never higher—i.e., less negative—than the similar scores for all imports.) The other Southeast Asian nations and Fiji were average markets in most years. Fiji was much better than average in 1960. After a period of below average imports, Fiji moved more toward slightly positive residuals, reflecting the effects of the liberalization of trade and economic policies after 1987.[43] The Philippines began as a market in which manufactured imports had been below predicted levels but improved over the years. The South Asian countries usually imported at or above predicted levels. Indian imports were always above predicted levels, even if only by a small amount. Even so, through 1975 India was among the relatively best per capita importers,

Table 8-5
Standardized Scores for Developing Countries for Imports of Manufactures

Country	Year 1960	1965	1970	1975	1980	1985	1990	1994
Argentina	-1.658	-2.556	-2.418	-1.449	-1.287	-1.871	-1.633	-3.032
Brazil	-.914	-.702	-.643	-1.055	-1.042	-.691	-1.302	-.649
Chile	-1.040	-1.523	-1.257	-.297	-.633	-.326	-.486	-.590
Uruguay	-1.383	-.936	-1.642	-1.392	-1.280	-.440	-.922	-1.166
Colombia	-.547	-.495	-.203	-.192	-.211	-.245	.040	.186
Mexico	-.824	-.978	-1.150	-1.469	-1.282	-1.009	-.959	-.972
Nicaragua	-.207	.185	-.145	.089	.382	.323	.776	.850
Costa Rica	-.028	1.233	.177	.027	-.291	.043	-.082	-.245
El Salvador	-.211	-.360	.342	.228	.201	.189	.237	.387
Jamaica	.383	.298	.349	.458	.039	.229	-.002	.427
Trinidad	1.658	1.189	-.215	-.323	-1.287	-3.316	-1.451	-.694
Hong Kong	3.176	3.016	2.942	1.430	1.082	2.355	.536	.487
Singapore	2.937	3.366	3.977	4.762	4.794	3.290	3.210	2.502
Taiwan	-.547	-.357	--	--	--	--	--	--
Korea	-.557	-.279	-.195	-.006	-.884	-.619	-2.930	-2.673
Malaysia	-.157	.021	-.000	.031	-.046	-.082	.021	.295
Thailand	-.216	-.154	-.011	.131	.207	.140	.061	.008
Philippines	-.756	-.336	-.027	.094	.196	.273	.435	.512
Indonesia	-.249	-.049	.133	.250	-.178	.244	.495	.414
Fiji	1.110	.145	.262	-.241	.151	-.182	.013	.131
India	.607	.522	.366	.345	.280	.172	.198	.071
Pakistan	-.227	-.124	.044	.290	.442	.388	.628	.661
Sri Lanka	-.175	.558	-.071	.197	.526	.458	.677	.706
Mauritius	.542	-.071	.095	.328	.138	.237	-.043	-.075
Kenya	-.046	-.134	.086	.284	.409	.486	.717	.829
Zambia	--	.281	-.001	.104	.326	.505	--	--
Malagasy Rep.	-.203	-.176	1.037	.117	.367	.488	.832	.865
South Africa	-.052	-.003	-.727	-.980	-.516	-.513	-.871	-.449
Nigeria	-.131	-.095	.088	-.002	-.064	-.098	.686	.730
Gabon	-.322	.420	-.237	-1.755	-1.750	-1.651	--	-.860
Benin	-.291	-.232	.130	.256	.408	.516	.709	--
Cameroons	2.230	-.189	.054	.180	.186	.126	.295	--
Senegal	-.308	-.154	-.011	.131	.207	.140	.061	.008
Ivory Coast	-.189	-.052	.001	.051	-.178	.294	.459	--
Morocco	-.301	-.433	-.122	-.082	-.077	-.273	.280	.429
Egypt	-.426	-.360	-.229	.197	.327	.299	.500	.596
Tunisia	-.287	-.100	-.011	-.075	.011	.042	.192	.284
Jordan	-.192	-.138	-.135	.753	.503	-.162	.279	.452
Syria	-.144	-.399	-.153	-.411	-.230	-.513	.287	--
Turkey	-.614	-.672	-.196	-.658	-.521	-.162	-.667	-.266
Malta	.554	1.198	1.037	.584	.365	.133	-1.705	-.836

even if it trailed far behind Hong Kong and Singapore.

The South American countries were below average importers of manufactured goods. Only Colombia had a trend toward greater relative openness for these products. Mexico was similar to the other South American countries in that it was less open for the years in question. The Central American countries, however, demonstrated a greater propensity to import manufactured goods than had been the case with overall imports. Jamaica was generally also more open than average to such imports. Trinidad had a turnaround in relative imports of manufactured goods, as had been the case with imports in general, going from being well above average in per capita terms to being below predicted levels.

With the exception of South Africa and Gabon, the African countries were also active importers for manufactured goods, and even Gabon and South Africa were more open (or not as closed) to imports of manufactured products than they had been for imports in general. It might have been expected that these countries would have been relatively more open to such imports since their indigenous manufacturing bases were quite small (South Africa being a partial exception). In most cases, any existing demand for manufactured goods would have to have been met by imports. Even a country such as Nigeria that successfully used tariffs to encourage industrialization, including plants created by foreign investment,[44] still had to be overall a relatively active importer of manufactured goods. While the overall absolute levels of these imports were not high given the lower GNP per capita levels in these countries, they were relatively high when compared to the other countries. The Middle Eastern countries were more variable in their patterns, but they frequently imported manufactured goods at levels that were less than predicted. Turkey always had negative standardized scores as did Syria in six of seven years. Tunisia approached anticipated levels in most years, while Egypt and Morocco had patterns that were indicative of progressively greater openness through the years. Malta showed the same turnaround pattern for manufactured goods as had been the case for all imports, going from being above predicted per capita levels to being below them.

Summary

The results for the developing countries were different in many respects from the similar analyses for the industrialized states. A great number of the developing countries were actually quite close to the predicted levels, with countries such as Singapore or Argentina being outliers. As might have been expected for smaller economies, there was greater volatility in relative per capita import levels over time. Drought and famines, depressed commodity prices (or higher ones), and variable petroleum costs would all have affected import propensities in particular years. In addition, population size did not have any noticeable effect on import levels for the developing countries. It was possible that the imports were more specific to wealth in the developing world, with more imports occurring with the presence of greater resources in particular countries. Except for Switzerland and the special case of watch imports, no developed country was so far ahead of its neighbors in terms of standardized scores for per capita imports as consistently as was the case for Singapore with the developing states. Compared to the industrialized countries, it would appear that in the developing world influences on imports were less complex, and that it was only relative wealth that explained significant amounts of basic variation in most years. Levels of protection would have been relevant for some of the remaining unexplained variance, as had been the case for the industrialized world. It would appear that it may be a few or even many years before the import patterns for the developing world are similar to the ones found for the developed world.

There were also some obvious political effects apparent in some of the results for particular countries. Limits placed on trade with South Africa by the governments of many countries reduced the potential for imports by that state. South Africa was forced, therefore, to adopt some import substitution industrialization, especially in areas related to armaments production, due to the trade sanctions that had been imposed by most of the rest of the world. These industries were not especially efficient ones, but they were ones that were essential to the preservation and continuation of the minority regime. Jordan's upsurge in imports during the Iran-Iraq war due to re-exports to Iraq was another example of import levels being influenced by international political factors. Egypt went from being a less active per capita importer to a more active one after it had broken its strong ties with the Soviet Union and reoriented its foreign policy towards the United States and the West. One consequence of the political changes was an increase in imports that would be compatible with the more open economic structure that was favored by Anwar Sadat. Changes in regimes also influenced the trade policies of other countries. The Indonesian economic policies shifted dramatically with the fall of Sukarno and the assumption of power by the military. The downturn in import levels in Hong Kong in the 1990s was also not surprising given the uncertainty surrounding the forthcoming reunification with mainland China.

It was also apparent that the Asian NICs were not uniformly open to imports. The cities of Hong Kong and Singapore were extremely open during the periods of rapid export expansion, but Korea and apparently Taiwan, were not especially open economies. Korean trade liberalization has been slow on the whole, and has even been held in abeyance at times in which there have been balance-of-payment difficulties.[45] Even Singapore toyed with the idea of ISI briefly as noted above. When all was said and done, however, export promotion and import substitution have not always been automatically antithetical to each other,[46] although frequently import substitution has tended to preclude export promotion as a result of protectionist groups gaining significant influence in government policy-making circles. What has been necessary for a successful outward orientation was that the protection that was being provided to those industries was linked to sectors that were geared towards producing exports that would be competitive in the global marketplace. Korea and Taiwan would appear to have successfully managed strategic planning at a level at which both industrialization and exporting have been encouraged.

The near-NICs of Southeast Asia had been much more open than either Korea or Taiwan, even though they have often been seen as countries that have had more state involvement and protection. The relative openness that these states demonstrated may have explained the relatively rapid growth of Thailand, Malaysia, Indonesia, and even the Philippines in recent years, at least until the recent Asian financial crisis. Initially these states had provided protection for many sectors.[47] Eventually, the protectionist policies were reduced, and these countries moved towards the more trade-neutral policies pioneered by Korea and Taiwan, policies that overcame distortions that occurred with the earlier protectionist programs that created biases against exports.[48]

The presence of significant protection in Latin America was obvious with the results. Countries in the region were consistently among the least active per capita importers. The low rankings were on the one hand an indication that these countries imported less than expected given their relatively high levels of GNP per capita, particularly when compared to South Asia or Africa. Their average wealth would have permitted greater imports had these governments and populations desired more open systems. One factor that has made successful efforts at trade liberalization in the region more difficult has been the lack of sufficient long-term political will to open up these economies. Liberalization efforts would be followed by the reestablishment of protection, especially in Argentina.[49] In other cases, protection was so deeply imbedded in the economic system that there were redundancies. Lowering tariffs did not lead to effective liberalization because other restrictions were still in place.[50] Brazil has been generally seen as having been more successful with liberalization than Argentina, yet the Brazilian ranks and standardized scores were very close to those of Argentina. Brazil followed an export-oriented policy based on export promotion rather than import substitution;[51] therefore, the low levels of imports were consistent with an outward-looking economy. Open trade policies were associated with greater growth in Brazil and greater efficiency in some economic sectors.[52] Brazil's first experiments with liberalization eventually ended in failure, and the efforts at liberalization were not renewed.[53] Colombia also attempted export promotion with less attention to any reform of import substitution policies.[54] Obviously in this case, notwithstanding the emphasis on exports and internal opposition to liberalization of the import sector, liberalization of imports did occur based on the rankings and standardized scores for Colombia.

In South Asia the relative openness of the countries combined with low GNP per capita. These states could have been caught in a vicious circle. They were importing at relatively high per capita levels but lower absolute levels of imports given their general lack of wealth; they then protected local industry, inducing inefficiency and slower growth, which meant that their per capita imports compared to the other developing countries were relatively high given their lower per capita wealth. Sri Lanka's active import trade reflected its availability to producers of apparel due to underutilized MFA quotas.[55] The presence of unused quotas attracted investment in the clothing facilities, but this investment failed to create backward linkages to the local economy or to lead to a more diversified economic base.[56] One consequence of this export activity was that higher levels of per capita imports were necessary since raw materials for the clothing plants had to be imported. The multinationals involved in the production preferred to use their own external sources for the materials in question rather than relying on Sri Lankan sources.[57] As a consequence, Sri Lankan per capita imports were comparatively high while the government still followed protectionist policies elsewhere in the domestic economy that were designed to stimulate indigenous industrialization. The end result was active trade, slow growth, and limited industrialization, although the apparel sector has provided important employment and foreign exchange earnings for the country.[58]

A number of these countries analyzed above as well as other developing countries have undertaken trade liberalization programs with varying results. Argentine efforts at trade liberalization have generally been considered inadequate.[59] The consistent rankings for Argentina in the above analysis would suggest that these conclusions are correct. While Brazil may have liberalized somewhat more effectively, the import levels were still relatively low. India's later attempts at liberalization have been another example of prior ineffective policies. While India has not been as closed as has usually been thought, greater openness still seems to be necessary for development. The continuing need for liberalization has resulted from the failure of ISI policies to work as well as was hoped.[60] Countries like Chile and Turkey also undertook trade liberalizations. Chile's liberalization under the Pinochet regime has generally been considered a success in terms of improving growth and an example of what liberalization could accomplish for other countries.[61] Turkey went from an extreme ISI approach in which imports were restricted,[62] and while the results for Turkey have been less obvious than those for Chile, the liberalization has generally been seen as successful.[63] Notwithstanding the positive results seen by those who have analyzed these liberalization attempts, there was no indication that per capita imports increased as a consequence of such policy changes. Import levels may have kept up with greater wealth, obscuring benefits. While the liberalization undoubtedly did occur, it is important to remember that the measures utilized to analyze protection were indeed comparative ones. These countries remained among the least open relative to the other states included because the other countries maintained their open systems or adopted even more liberal trade policies than had existed before. Thus, countries that opened up their domestic markets later were still relatively less open than other states. Late liberalization could have left states at a disadvantage in terms of participating in the international trade system, especially when compared to states that have been participating in the trade system more completely for longer periods of time. Mexico more recently has been following policies of trade liberalization with encouraging results.[64] The results would not be apparent in the data analyzed above since the Mexican efforts have been recent, but if the indications for other countries hold true for Mexico, it will remain relatively one of the least open because the move to liberalization came later in time. Of course, membership in NAFTA will be quite likely to offset some of the disadvantages of a later commitment to liberalization.

When all is said and done, there have been clear differences in the levels of revealed protection present. Liberalization efforts have not always had immediately obvious effects in the positions of countries present. And countries with higher levels of imports have not always been among the more rapidly growing countries. Lall has argued that overall free market approaches have not always been effective and government interventions have not always failed.[65] India and Mexico have been examples of governmental interventions that have not been especially successful since the interventions have not been integrated with other policies. A related possibility that would explain Indian imports would be that India had become sufficiently industrialized early enough, notwithstanding lower per capita GNP figures, to import relatively more than other countries. Korea, on the other hand, would appear from the above results to be a case of successful intervention. Hong Kong and Singapore were examples of positive results generated with free market approaches. Openness, however, works only when international and domestic circumstances are favorable.[66] Barriers to imports have not been sufficient to explain either the failures in Latin America, nor has the absence of barriers been a factor explaining the successes in East Asia.[67] And sometimes even with favorable circumstances it is still possible that openness can be a less effective policy. The levels of revealed protection, however, provided a starting point for assessing the relevance and impact of government interventions combined with other factors. To date it has been clear that the most important influence on import levels has been wealth. Developing countries with higher per capita GNP have been able to import relatively more—or states that were able to import more have had higher GNP per capita wealth figures. Export promotion and outward trade orientation appear to have been successful for countries that have already achieved a basic level of economic development, but such policies may not work for countries that are poorer.[68] A virtuous circle of importing and economic growth may well exist— importers grow and therefore can import more, helping them to grow, etc. If such a virtuous circle exists, it has favored and continues to favor the haves and may have limited and continues to limit the have-nots, perhaps most particularly the smallest have-not countries.

Chapter 9

Conclusions: Protectionism Revealed

The preceding chapters identified some important influences on per capita import levels, and they provided some indications of the extent of protectionist practices in various countries. All the analyses were comparative ones, since the measures used were derived relative to other states. Per capita imports for the individual countries were above or below predicted levels when compared to the other similar nations in the data sets. While all of the industrialized countries were undoubtedly more open in 1994 than in 1960, since there had been extensive global liberalization and world trade had expanded significantly, some countries were clearly still more open than others. If protection had provided advantages, and there is at least the possibility that a country can benefit from imposing protection, especially if no one else utilizes protectionist practices,[1] then the comparative openness of countries in terms of national import patterns continues to be important. The knowledge of the relative openness of markets will be relevant to understanding the trade and economic policies as well as the international economic activities of various countries. The analyses and the results that they generated indicated that this comparative approach to the idea of revealed openness or protection was indeed useful, and the import levels for different states were put into an appropriate perspective as a consequence. Comparisons over time also provided insights into changes that were taking place in individual countries, changes among the countries, and changes in different product categories.

The Industrialized Countries

Individual industrialized countries had different patterns for different years and different results for particular types of manufactures. Import patterns for either textiles or clothing, for example, tended to have somewhat different rankings and standardized scores for most of the developed nations. The results from the products considered in chapters 5, 6, and 7, however, indicated that there were some obvious national characteristics. In Europe, France, Italy, and Germany were normally the countries that imported below expected per capita levels. Frequently these countries were among the poorest relative importers for all kinds of manufactured goods, although there were some instances of particular product areas where Italy and Germany were better markets. Germany, for example, was often an average per capita importer for the manufactured goods considered in chapter 6. Of these three larger European countries, France was most consistently the least open.[2] France has continued its statist approach to trade policy issues even in the changing international economic context,[3] and the continuation of this approach with the provision of protection was one likely explanation for the lower imports. The United Kingdom, the other large European country, was quite open to imports of raw materials and was usually more open to imports of manufactured goods as well. Overall, the United Kingdom was near predicted levels, generally more so in later years. Historically, the United Kingdom never developed the statist institutions and traditions of France, Italy, or Germany, and the British were long ardent supporters of free trade. Of course, free trade was in the best interests of the United Kingdom when it was in the forefront of the industrial revolution and the major trader in the international economy with many comparative advantages. The previous free trade orientation of the United Kingdom, however, may have been one factor in its relative national openness to imports, a circumstance most noticeable when the rankings and scores for the United Kingdom are compared to the patterns for the other large European states.

Among the smaller European countries, the five industrializing Mediterranean states were generally near predicted per capita levels for most imports. There were some obvious sectoral differences apparent in the analyses of the manufactured goods analyses in chapters 6 and 7, but even here the countries often met the anticipated levels of per capita imports, even in product areas in which they would have been expected to be competing for shares in the European markets if not in the broader global markets. Intra-industry trade is one possible explanation for these types of patterns with higher imports, and there were indications that such trade had been occurring in areas such as textiles and clothing. All five of these states had periods of extensive government involvement—conservative authoritarian regimes in Spain and Portugal, the military regime in Greece, the garrison state and the heavy state economic involvement in Israel, and the modified central planning system in Yugoslavia. Yet import policies were relatively trade friendly, at least by the 1980s.

Among the smaller European countries, the Scandinavian nations were frequently among the poorer importers. Finland in particular was usually far below predicted levels. The extent of Finnish import barriers might have been exaggerated to some extent because a large portion of Finnish trade used to be with the old Soviet Union. The Soviet Union favored barter trade and state trading arrangements, trade methods that could have obscured the extent and the actual value of trade. The values could have been understated for the two countries due to the nominal accounting methods used. If Finnish imports from the Soviet Union has been undervalued by a third and Finnish exports to the Soviet Union were undervalued by a similar proportion, neither country gained from the accounting process, even though total trade figures would be understated as a consequence. Even so, at best Finland would have had import levels similar to those for the other Scandinavian countries and would never have been a good relative importer. Norway was at times an active importer for some products, especially in the earlier years of the 1960s, but increasingly Norwegian imports came to reflect the general patterns for Sweden and Denmark (and even Finland).

The other smaller West European countries, however, were quite good importers. Belgium was frequently the most active importing state, oftentimes by a significant margin. The Netherlands, Switzerland, Ireland, and Austria were also frequently well above anticipated per capita import levels. In the specific area of watches and related items, Switzerland was a preeminent importer, and very heavily involved in intra-industry trade. Switzerland and Austria showed indications that they were becoming more open over time, whereas the Netherlands was relatively less active as an importer in later years when compared to the earlier ones. All of these other smaller countries, however, were clearly quite different from the Scandinavian ones in terms of import propensities.

The differences between these two groups of small European countries was obviously not related to size, although the Scandinavian countries have somewhat smaller populations on average. Neither group was noticeably wealthier than the other. Sweden and Switzerland were among the wealthiest in terms of GNP per capita, and the other countries in the groups shared similar wealth levels in comparison with each other. Similarly, many countries in both groups were corporatist in their policy orientations. Sweden, Norway, and Austria have been among the most corporatist states in the world, while Belgium and Finland have been much less so, and Switzerland, Denmark, and the Netherlands have been in the middle.[4] Thus, corporatist practices or their absence would not explain the differences in import propensities. These countries, however, did have different historical patterns of state involvement in the economy. Although Ireland has had protectionist trade policies at times (as have virtually all the other countries of the world), the economic heritage for that state has been the free trade tradition of the United Kingdom. The Netherlands, like the United Kingdom, has a free trade history, and Belgium as a former part of the Netherlands, albeit briefly, shared some of the same patterns.[5] Switzerland has had an almost antistatist tradition with national decentralization and the local autonomy of the cantons.[6] The Scandinavian countries, on the other hand, modernized and industrialized under stronger state systems. Sweden in the later nineteenth century (and Norway was then associated with Sweden in a dynastic union) was led by the government in its modernization efforts. Sweden was, in effect, one of the late industrializing countries. Finland as part of Czarist Russia (even with some limited autonomy as a Grand Duchy) was part of a state that was one of the classic late industrializers; the government became heavily involved in the economy in order to help the country catch up with the major countries of West Europe. Thus, it would appear that historical traditions had a role to play in explaining the import levels for these smaller European countries just as it had for the larger ones.

The European Union as a single market (more or less) will be much more likely to reflect the revealed protectionist preferences of Germany, France, and Italy rather than the preferences of the smaller members such as Ireland or Belgium. Only the United Kingdom has the size and prestige to serve as a center for opposition to protectionist forces within the EU. The lukewarm support that the United Kingdom has had for many aspects of closer economic integration has made it a much less effective spokesman on this issues (and others). The United Kingdom would seem to have expended its efforts on achieving greater national benefits (smaller contributions to EU funds, greater access to regional funds, the continuation of a national currency instead of the euro) than in generating greater openness in the EU as a whole. The EU-wide VER on Japanese automobiles noted in chapter 7 has been one obvious example of the success of protectionist forces, including in this case groups within the United Kingdom. European countries will remain active traders and importers, but considerable trade activity will be concentrated among the EU countries themselves rather than with non-members. Part of the high import levels for Belgium or Ireland, of course, have reflected intra-EU trade and increases in intra-industry trade involving other member states, but this intra-industry trade has not been restricted to members. The EU framework, however, has still provided protection for many producers within the customs union at the expense of producers in non-member countries.

Elsewhere in the world Japan also presented a very consistent import pattern. In the 1960s, when the country was reindustrializing, it was an extremely active per capita importer of goods all types, including manufactured products. Imports were obviously essential for the rebuilding and reindustrialization process. Once industrialization had quickened, however, Japan became increasingly less open to imports in general, especially to imports of all types of manufactured goods. By the 1990s Japan was a relatively poor market in per capita terms for most products. Arguments in the United States and elsewhere that the Japanese domestic market has been protected are supported by the results of the above analyses. Factor endowments and comparative advantages cannot explain the relatively low volumes of Japanese imports, since by definition Japan has to have had comparative disadvantages and lower factor endowments in some product areas. Yamamura has argued that Japan had increasingly adopted a mixture of strategic and free trade practices.[7] The results in the earlier chapters have indicated that the elements of free trade practices, even if greater than in the past, have lagged far behind such practices in other industrialized countries. Those who point to the changes in Japanese import policies have been correct, just as those who point to the continuing difficulties of exporting to Japan have been correct. Japan may be more open than it was in the past, but it has still been less open than other nations in the present.

In Oceania, Australia was also among the less open nations in many product areas. Since liberalization in trade policies had clearly occurred, it would appear that Australia had remained relatively less open even after the changes in trade and economic policies. New Zealand, on the other hand, had become somewhat more open through time in both absolute and relative terms. The customs union between Australia and New Zealand increased imports for both states, especially for New Zealand since imports from Australia increased proportionately more due to the smaller size of the New Zealand economy. The customs union has ultimately been supportive of greater trade openness, but only because the governments of the two countries sought broader liberalization with the appropriate trade and economic policies by conscious choice.[8] New Zealand and Australia will probably always have somewhat lower comparative levels of imports given their geographical location somewhat distant from other major economic areas of the world. The rise of the NICs and near-NICs in Southeast Asia, however, has provided sources of materials, markets, and opportunities for intra-industry trade. Connections with these areas of Asia will become more and more important, notwithstanding the recent Asian financial crisis.

In North America, Canada was generally among the poorer relative markets. There were some indications of greater openness in some areas in the later years, and the Autopact with the United States clearly facilitated substantially important intra-industry trade in the automotive sector. First, the Canada–United States trade area encouraged such trade, and NAFTA will be having similar effects in other sectors. The overall Canadian market for imports will have increased as a consequence of these trade area arrangements. Of course, if controls for NAFTA are used in future analyses, as was the case with the EC/EU and EFTA, then Canada will be likely to remain a relatively poor market in many areas compared to other industrialized countries.

The United States proved to be a very good to excellent market for most products, particularly in the later years of the analyses. As the United States became more active in the global economy, it became an increasingly better market, with relative import levels higher than anticipated levels in the 1990s compared to levels in the 1960s. Given that the United States has been the largest single national market in the world, this relative openness has been very important for other countries participating in the international economy. The United States has been especially important because its trade openness for the years analyzed was not part of a broad trade area like the European countries and the EU. Thus, this propensity to import presented opportunities for exporters everywhere. The openness was apparent for manufactured products important to the developing world that were analyzed in chapter 6. The NAFTA arrangement in the future will undoubtedly lead to some increases in import and intra-industry trade, but the United States had already been the most important market for both Mexican and Canadian products prior to the free trade arrangements; therefore, dramatic changes are unlikely for the United States.[9] It was instructive that the United States was an open market even though clear barriers to imports have been adopted, as noted in chapter 2. The United States was indeed not without protectionist sin, and it would have been an even better market if these obstacles to imports had not existed. What the above results have suggested, however, is that protectionist measures in the United States have been ineffective or inadequate in deterring imports compared to other nations. The measures of revealed protection provide an indication of ineffective obstacles to imports as well as the absence of such barriers. Since the United States has lacked a statist tradition of any kind, nothing like the experiences and patterns that have been present for Japan or some of the European countries, it has been much less able to create and maintain effective barriers to imports. This lack of statist mechanisms opened the U.S. market to more imports, for better or worse. Since the large U.S. market has been important for other countries, including developing ones, this situation bodes well for the future of global trade, especially given the relatively weaker per capita import levels for Japan and many of the EU countries.

Ultimately, the democratic, industrialized countries have to respond to domestic groups when job losses or industrial downturns are threatened. Economic and trade policies thus will reflect both political and economic concerns,[10] and governments have sought to protect citizens against adverse economic conditions. The smaller Western European countries have had extensive systems of social insurance that have permitted them to support free trade *and* to deal with its consequences.[11] It would appear that the provision of greater economic benefits and security has gone hand-in-hand with increasing global liberalization. The existence of such programs may be an important precondition for the progressive reduction of barriers to imports in all the industrialized countries. Relative openness, of course, still remains an important consideration.

The Developing World

Chapter 8 indicated that for the most part the developing countries were different in terms of their import propensities. Many of these countries were near predicted levels with regularity. There were only a few countries that were extremely open and a few, especially in Latin America, that were much more closed. For the most part, the developing countries were less active in the global economy. Their markets, collectively or individually, were small, thereby placing constraints on domestic demand levels, even in the larger states. In any event, developing countries will not opt for total trade liberalization in the future in most cases. The domestic industrialization process in these states will continue to require protective devices at some level to permit domestic industries to be created. Tariffs will remain important for the developing countries, since they provide a source of revenue that is easy to collect and that has low administrative costs.[12] The developing countries for the most part also lack sufficient social insurance programs to protect their citizens against the adverse consequences of freer trade, thereby necessitating their reliance on the policy possibilities inherent with protection.[13]

Since it was clear that not all the successful NICs were open to imports, the analyses did not determine whether development preceded trade or whether development followed trade or what factors were relevant for the association between trade and development. Even Singapore provided no positive indication of the direction of the linkage between trade and development. It has reached the stage at which it has much more in common with developed countries. It also has had the wherewithal to provide programs for its population to mitigate the adverse consequences of trade policies. Its relative imports, as a consequence, have been high compared to those of the other developing countries and the industrialized states as well.[14]

Whether or not trade will be associated with growth or possibly fuel continued growth for the developing countries remains to be seen. The near-NICs of Southeast Asia were open, and they have grown, but the reasonably open but poorer South Asian countries have not done nearly as well. The various African countries have had quite different growth rates with the same general levels of openness. China as a potential NIC will be an intriguing element in international trade. China has sufficiently industrialized to permit at least the possibility of export-led growth. Massive increases of Chinese exports of the types analyzed in chapter 6, however, could very well hinder export activities in other countries. These other producers could simply be overwhelmed by Chinese production. Of course, large volumes of Chinese exports could also lead to increased protectionist pressures in the developed world, resulting in less open markets in general, to the detriment of not only China but other producers as well. Such a situation would limit the potential for other developing countries to replicate the experiences of the Asian NICs of the past.

Revealed Protectionism in the Future

The use of the concept of revealed protection or revealed openness in this volume was justified by the results achieved. Continued analyses based on revealed protection will be beneficial in the future as well. Countries will continue to provide protection to sectors threatened by import competition. The logic of democratic politics suggests that political leaders need to respond to popular demands. Even leaders in non-democratic systems often find it useful to respond to public pressures. Generally, though not always, politicians in all types of systems are more likely to respond to domestic interests than to foreign ones.

Governments will also continue to find ways of providing protection for threatened domestic industries. The rules developed for GATT have been circumvented by a variety of mechanisms, including the MFA, VERs, and other non-tariff measures. The rules establishing the WTO have eliminated some of the past non-tariff barriers, but they will not be able to prevent the use of all such devices.[15] There will always be loopholes, or at least the possibility of a country arguing that there was a loophole in the regulations that permitted the protectionist action that was undertaken. If the United States or the EU presents such an argument forcefully, other members are likely to acquiesce. Similarly, the WTO is unlikely to be successful in opening Japanese markets to imports.[16] Ultimately, the presence of such loopholes is useful. They provide a method for governments to deal with pressures from unhappy voters. The loopholes have permitted politicians to meet domestic pressures, institute protection, and to still keep the international trading system and its functioning organizations reasonably intact.[17] The WTO is quite likely to follow a similar pattern to GATT, with governments of the member countries finding opportunities to play to domestic groups by limiting at least some imports, albeit with different loopholes.

Currently there still are trade restricting measures that can be used by governments that are consistent with WTO rules.[18] Contingent protection measures are a major example. They have remained available to governments in part because domestic interest groups in major countries have supported their continued availability.[19] Contingent protection has been prevalent in the global trading system and is likely to persist because the antidumping and countersubsidy statutes have been so flexible.[20] These measures have become more prevalent because liberalization has removed other measures that could be used to protect the domestic economy, and "countries in the cold wind of competition feel more secure if they have some trade weapons up their sleeve to be used as a last resort."[21] Contingent protection measures also provide administrative discretion for government officials, including targeting particular countries or particular products. Such discretion can be particularly effective in countries in which statist practices are well established. These protective devices also provide discretion for domestic producing interests. In prosperous times, the use of such actions have been fewer. When there is a global economic downturn, filings increase. Thus, in a way, their use responds to international economic circumstances. Such countervailing duties or antidumping penalties can provide a respite for industries facing temporary problems. They then can function as a specialized safeguard in this fashion, but one instituted by the domestic producers rather than the government. Of course filings may also represent the continuing failures of domestic firms to adjust to import penetration or to become competitive in global markets or in their domestic ones. The subsidy and dumping regulations have also provided opportunities for collusion between domestic and foreign firms that lead to increased profits for both groups.[22]

The current WTO agreements dealing with subsidies are weak, and definitional criteria have been difficult to establish.[23] Even were the WTO to want to do away with this type of protection, it lacks the necessary mechanisms to eliminate it.[24] Thus, there will clearly be a need for continued refinement of codes on contingent protection within the WTO framework in the years to come. The recent efforts to start a new round of multilateral negotiations (the Seattle Round?) to deal with continuing issues have been just one indication of remaining problems and controversies.

All countries will continue to trade and import, and all countries will face at least occasional problems with imports. Thus, protection in whatever form will remain for the immediate future. The methods used to deter imports may be increasingly opaque and difficult to overcome. The obvious barriers to imports for the Japanese market are low—it has been the less obvious barriers that have limited the level of imports. As a consequence, it will remain necessary and useful to utilize measures that focus on actual imports and that reveal the level of barriers that remain after accounting for size, wealth, the relevant customs union membership, and whatever other factors might become important in the future. Such comparative measures could be especially important if it is the differences in the margins of protection in different countries that are more important than the absolute levels. If a few countries have low levels of protection while all the other countries practice virtually unfettered free trade, then the margin of advantage could still be significant, even though the obstacles to trade are low. The effects on imports could be as important as when some countries have very high barriers while most other countries only had high tariffs and other obstacles to imports. The relative advantage remains important, not just the actual levels of particular barriers to imports that are in place. While not all of the remaining deficit in imports that are found to be present in particular countries with the derivation of measures of revealed protection would be due to protectionist devices, large and continuing imports below predicted per capita levels would undoubtedly owe part of their presence to the existence of effective import barriers.

Notes

Chapter 1: Introduction

1. Leonard Gomes, *Foreign Trade and the National Economy: Mercantilist and Classical Perspectives* (New York: St. Martin's, 1987), p. 3.

2. Paul Kennedy, *The Rise and Fall of the Great Powers: Economic Change and Military Conflict from 1500 to 2000* (New York: Random House, 1987), p. 161.

3. Stalin and other Communist leaders who feared the influence of the West were correct in a sense. Communism collapsed when the centrally planned economies opened themselves to the West. The global recession in the aftermath of higher petroleum prices limited the Western markets for goods from Eastern Europe and the Soviet Union, disrupted their economies, and eliminated the sales of the exports that were expected to pay off Western loans. Of course, it was the dismal performance of the Communist economies in previous years that had led the political leaders to hope to strengthen public support by greater openness to the West. The timing proved to be less than ideal (at least from the perspective of the governing Communists).

4. Henry Thompson, "Do Tariffs Protect Specific Factors," *Canadian Journal of Economics,* Vol. 22, No. 2 (1989), pp. 406–12.

5. James A. Brander, "Rationales for Strategic Trade and Industrial Policy," in Paul R. Krugman (ed.), *Strategic Trade Policy and the New International Economics* (Cambridge, MA: MIT Press, 1987), pp. 23–46, and Greg Mastel, *Antidumping Laws and the U.S. Economy* (Armonk, NY: M. E. Sharpe, 1998), p. 5

6. H. Peter Gray, "Free International Economic Policy in a World of Schumpeter Goods," *International Trade Journal,* Vol. 12, No. 3 (1998), p. 341.

7. Jonathan J. Pincus, *Pressure Groups and Politics in Antebellum Tariffs* (New York: Columbia University Press, 1977), p. 1.

8. Bernard M. Koekman and Michel M. Kostecki, *The Political Economy of the World Trading System: From GATT to WTO* (Oxford: Oxford University Press, 1995), p. 72.

9. Young Whan Kihl and James M. Lutz, *World Trade Issues: Regime, Structure, and Policy* (New York: Praeger, 1985), p. 176. This customs post still exists due to historical accident. Poiters was guaranteed permanent status as a customs post to commemorate Charles Martel's victory in 732 over the invading Muslim armies at the spot.

Chapter 2: Variables Influencing International Trade

1. Winifred Ruigrok, "Paradigm Crisis in International Trade Theory," *Journal of World Trade,* Vol. 25, No. 1 (1991), pp. 77–89. Cf. also John H. Dunning, "What's Wrong—and Right—with Trade Theory?" *International Trade Journal,* Vol. 9, No. 2 (1995), pp. 163–66.
2. David Lazer, "The Free Trade Epidemic of the 1860s and Other Outbreaks of Economic Discrimination," *World Politics,* Vol. 51, No. 4 (1999), pp. 479–80.
3. C. Fred Bergsten, "Globalizing Free Trade," *Foreign Affairs,* Vol. 75, No. 3 (1996), pp. 105–20.
4. Lazer, "The Free Trade Epidemic of the 1860s."
5. Kym Anderson and Hege Norheim, "History, Geography and Regional Economic Integration," in Kym Anderson and Richard Blackhurst (eds.), *Regional Integration and the Global Trading System* (New York: St. Martin's, 1993), pp. 19–51; Jeffrey A. Frankel, Ernesto Stein, and Shang-Jin Wei, "Regional Trading Arrangements: Natural or Supernatural?" *American Economic Review,* Vol. 86, No. 2 (1996), pp. 52–56; L. R. Klein and Pingfan Hong, "'Fortress Europe' and Retaliatory Economic Warfare," in Dominick Salvatore (ed.), *Protectionism and World Welfare* (Cambridge: Cambridge University Press, 1993), pp. 396–418; Shelton A. Nicholls, "Measuring Trade Creation and Trade Diversion in the Central American Common Market: A Hicksian Alternative," *World Development,* Vol. 26, No. 2 (1998), pp. 323–355; and Per Magnus Wijkman, "The Existing Bloc Expanded? The European Community, EFTA, and Eastern Europe," in C. Fred Bergsten and Marcus Noland (eds.), *Pacific Dynamism and the International Economic System* (Washington, D.C.: Institute for International Economics, 1993), pp. 135–58.
6. James Harrigan, "Openness to Trade in Manufactures in the OECD," *Journal of International Economics,* Vol. 40, No. 1/2 (1996): 32–33, and Edward Mansfield and Rachel Bronson, "Alliances, Preferential Trading Arrangements, and International Trade," *American Political Science Review,* Vol. 91, No. 1 (1997): 94–107.
7. Paul Krugman, *EFTA and 1992,* Occasional Paper No. 23, European Free Trade Association (Geneva: EFTA, June 1988), and Constantinos Syropoulos, "Customs Unions and Comparative Advantage," *Oxford Economic Papers,* Vol. 51, No. 2 (1999), pp. 239–66.

8. Brigitte Levy, "Globalization and Regionalization: Main Issues in International Trade Patterns," in Khosrow Fatemi (ed.), *International Trade in the 21st Century* (Kidlington, Oxford: Pergamon, 1997), p. 71.

9. Pravin Krishna, "Regionalism and Multilateralism: A Political Economy Approach," *Quarterly Journal of Economics,* Vol. 113, No. 1 (1998), pp. 227–51, and David Palmeter, "Rules of Origin in Customs Unions and Free Trade Areas," in Kym Anderson and Richard Blackhurst (eds.), *Regional Integration and the Global Trading System* (New York: St. Martin's, 1993), pp. 326–43.

10. Helen Milner, "Industries, Governments, and Regional Trade Blocs," in Edward D. Mansfield and Helen V. Milner (eds.), *The Political Economy of Regionalism* (New York: Columbia University Press, 1997), pp. 77–106.

11. Barry Bracewell-Milnes, *Eastern and Western European Economic Integration* (New York: St. Martin's, 1976), p. 116, and F.V. Meyer, *International Trade Policy* (New York: St. Martin's, 1978), p. 180.

12. Ronald J. Wonnacott, "Free Trade Agreements: For Better or Worse," *American Economic Review,* Vol. 86, No. 2 (1996), pp. 62–66.

13. Khosrow Fatemi, "International Trade in the 21st Century: Problems and Prospects," in Khosrow Fatemi (ed.), *International Trade in the 21st Century* (Kidlington, Oxford: Pergamon, 1997), p. 5.

14. Barry Bosworth, Susan M. Collins, and Yu-chin Chen, "Accounting for Differences in Economic Growth," *Brookings Discussion Papers in International Economics,* No. 115, (October 1995), p. 40; Donald V. Coes, "Brazil," in Demetris Papageorgiou, Michael Michaely, and Armeane M. Choksi (eds.), *Liberalizing Foreign Trade: Vol. 4, The Experience of Brazil, Colombia, and Peru* (London: Basil Blackwell, 1991), p. 12; Michael Michaely, Demetris Papageorgiou, and Armeane M. Choksi, *Liberalizing Foreign Trade: Vol. 7, The Experience in the Developing World* (Cambridge: Basil Blackwell, 1991), p. 118; and Stephen D. Krasner, "State Power and the Structure of International Trade," *World Politics,* Vol. 28, No. 3 (1976), pp. 317–43.

15. Yair Aharoni and Seev Hirsch, "Enhancing Competitive Advantage in Technology-Intensive Industries," in John H. Dunning and Khalil A. Hamdani (eds.), *The New Globalism and Developing Countries* (Tokyo: United Nations University Press, 1997), p. 282.

16. Aharoni and Hirsch, "Enhancing Competitive Advantage," p. 282.

17. Aharoni and Hirsch, "Enhancing Competitive Advantages," and John H. Dunning, *Multinational Enterprises and the Global Economy* (Reading, MA: Addison Wesley, 1993), "The Theory of International Production," *International Trade Journal,* Vol. 3, No. 1 (1988), pp. 45–47, "Towards an Eclectic Theory of International Production: Some Empirical Tests," *Journal of International Business Studies,* Vol. 11, No. 1 (1980), p. 10, and "What's Wrong—and Right—with Trade Theory?" pp. 163–202.

18. Ronald Rogowski, *Commerce and Coalitions: How Trade Affects Domestic Political Alignments* (Princeton: Princeton University Press, 1989).

19. Gary R. Saxonhouse and Robert M. Stern, "An Analytic Survey of Formal and Informal Barriers to International Trade and Investment in the United States, Canada, and Japan," in Robert M. Stern (ed.), *Trade and Investment Relations among the United States, Canada, and Japan* (Chicago: University of Chicago Press, 1989), p. 313. Donald R. Davis, "Critical Evidence on Comparative Advantage: North-North Trade in a Multilateral World," *Journal of Political Economy,* Vol. 105, No. 5 (1997), pp. 1051–60, argues that technology and factor endowments do combine to explain trade among countries in the developed world.

20. Krasner, "State Power and the Structure of International Trade," and Daniel Trefler, "The Case of the Missing Trade and Other Mysteries," *American Economic Review,* Vol. 85, No. 4 (1995), pp. 1029–46.

21. Nancy H. Chau, "Dynamic Stability and International Trade under Uncertainty," *Economica,* Vol. 65, No. 259 (1998), pp. 381–99.

22. Dimitri Mardas, "Intra-Industry Trade in Manufactured Products between the European Economic Community and the Eastern European Countries," *Journal of World Trade,* Vol. 26, No. 5 (1992), pp. 5–23, and Damien J. Neven and Lars-Hendrik Roller, "The Structure and Determinants of East-West Trade: A Preliminary Analysis of the Manufacturing Sector," in L. Alan Winters and Anthony J. Venables (eds.), *European Integration: Trade and Industry* (Cambridge: Cambridge University Press, 1991), pp. 96–119.

23. Richard A. Brecher and Ehsan U. Choudhri, "The Factor Content of Consumption in Canada and the United States: A Two-Country Test of the Heckscher-Ohlin-Vanek Model," in Robert C. Feenstra (ed.), *Empirical Methods for International Trade* (Cambridge, MA: MIT Press, 1988), pp. 5–17.

24. James Harrigan, "Factor Endowments and the International Location of Production: Econometric Evidence for the OECD, 1970 - 1985," *Journal of International Economics,* Vol. 39, No. 1/2 (1995), pp. 123–41.

25. Marcus Noland, "Has Asian Export Performance Been Unique," *Journal of International Economics,* Vol. 43, No. 1/2 (1997), pp. 79–101, and Reza M. Ramazani and Keith E. Maskus, "A Test of the Factor Endowments Model of Trade in a Rapidly Industrializing Country: The Case of Korea," *Review of Economics and Statistics,* Vol. 75, No. 3 (1993), pp. 568–72.

26. Don P. Clark, "Determinants of Intraindustry Trade between the United States and Industrial Nations," *International Trade Journal,* Vol. 12, No. 3 (1998), pp. 345–62; Elhanen Helpman and Paul R. Krugman, *Market Structure and Foreign Trade: Increasing Returns, Imperfect Competition, and the International Economy* (Cambridge: MIT Press, 1985), p. 2; Edward R. Leamer, "Factor-Supply Differences as a Source of Comparative Advantage," *American Economic Review,* Vol. 83, No. 2 (1993), p. 439; Mardas, "Intra-Industry Trade in Manufactured Products," p. 18; and Peter A. Petri, "Market Structure, Comparative Advantage, and Japanese Trade Under the Strong Yen," in

Paul Krugman (ed.), *Trade with Japan: Has the Door Opened Wider?* (Chicago: University of Chicago Press, 1991), pp. 51–82.

27. Michael J. Gilligan, "Lobbying as a Private Good with Intra-Industry Trade," *International Studies Quarterly,* Vol. 41, No. 3 (1997), pp. 455–74; H. Peter Gray, "Free International Economic Policy in a World of Schumpeter Goods," *International Trade Journal,* Vol. 12, No. 3 (1998), pp. 323–44; and Ruigrok, "Paradigm Crisis in International Trade Theory."

28. Robert C. Gilpin, "The Implications of the Changing Trade Regime for U.S.-Japanese Relations," in Taskashi Inoguichi and Daniel I. Okimoto (eds.), *The Political Economy of Japan: Volume 2, The Changing International Context* (Stanford: Stanford University Press, 1988), pp. 138–70.

29. J. P. Hayes, *Making Trade Policy in the European Community* (Houndmills, Basingstoke: Macmillan for Trade Policy Research Centre, University of Reading, 1993), p. 156, and James R. Markusen, "Comment," in Robert M. Stern (ed.) *Trade and Investment Relations Among the United States, Canada, and Japan* (Chicago: University of Chicago Press, 1989), pp. 353–59.

30. Gray, "Free International Economic Policy," p. 341.

31. Steven Tolliday, "Competition and Maturity in the British Steel Industry, 1870 - 1914," in Etsuo Abe and Yoshitaka Suzuki (eds.), *Changing Patterns of International Rivalry: Some Lessons from the Steel Industry* (Tokyo: University of Tokyo Press, 1990), pp. 22–23.

32. Peter J. Katzenstein, "Japan, Switzerland of the Far East?" in Taskashi Inoguichi and Daniel I. Okimoto (eds.), *The Political Economy of Japan: Volume 2, The Changing International Context* (Stanford: Stanford University Press, 1988), pp. 279–80, and Markusen, "Comment," p. 358.

33. Jung-en Woo, *Race to the Swift: State and Finance in Korean Industrialization* (New York: Columbia University Press, 1991).

34. Shu-Chin Yang, "Open Industrialization in East Asia and the Quest for Regional Cooperation: An Overview," in Shu-Chin Yang (ed.), *Manufactured Exports of East Asian Industrializing Economies: Possible Regional Cooperation* (Armonk, NY: M. E. Sharpe, 1994), pp. 12–3.

35. William J. Baumol and Ralph E. Gomory, "Inefficient and Locally Stable Trade Equilibria under Scale Economies: Comparative Advantage Revisited," *Kyklos,* Vol. 49, No. 4 (1996), pp. 509–40; Gottfried Haberler, "Strategic Trade Policy and the New International Economics," in Ronald W. Jones and Anne O. Krueger (eds.), *The Political Economy of International Trade: Essays in Honor of Robert E. Baldwin* (Cambridge, MA: Basil Blackwell, 1990), pp. 25–39; Paul Krugman, "Import Protection as Export Promotion: International Competition in the Presence of Oligopoly and Economics [*sic*] of Scale," in Henryk Kierzkowski (ed.) *Monopolistic Competition and International Trade* (Oxford: Clarendon Press, 1984), pp. 180–93; and Kelvin Lancaster, "The 'Product Variety' Case for Protection," *Journal of International Economics,* Vol. 31, No. 1/2 (August 1991), pp. 1–26.

36. Partha Dasgupta and Joseph Stiglitz, "Learning-By-Doing, Market Structure and Industrial and Trade Policies," *Oxford Economic Papers,* New Series, Vol. 40, No. 2 (1988), pp. 246–68; Harald Sander, "Deep Integration, Shallow Regionalism, and Strategic Openness: Three Notes on Economic Integration in East Asia," in Franz Peter Land and Renate Ohr (eds.), *International Economic Integration,* Studies in Contemporary Economics (Heidelberg: Physica-Verlag, 1997), p. 226; Donald J. Wright, "Permanent *versus* Temporary Infant Industry Assistance," *Manchester School of Economic and Social Studies,* Vol. 63, No. 4 (1995), pp. 426–34.

37. Gilpin, "The Implications of the Changing Trade Regime," p. 163.

38. Levy, "Globalization and Regionalization," pp. 71–72.

39. Robert O. Keohane, "The Theory of Hegemonic Stability and Changes in International Economic Regimes, 1967 - 1977," in Ole R. Holsti, Randolph M. Siverson, and Alexander L. George (eds.), *Change in the International System* (Boulder, CO: Westview Press, 1980), pp. 131–62; Stephen D. Krasner, "State Power and the Structure of International Trade," and "American Policy and Global Economic Stability," in William P. Avery and David P. Rapkin (eds.), *America in a Changing World Economy* (New York: Longman, 1982), pp. 29–48; David A. Lake, "International Economic Structure and American Foreign Economic Policy, 1887–1934," *World Politics,* Vol. 35, No. 4 (1983), pp. 517–43; and Beth V. Yarbrough and Robert M. Yarbrough, "Cooperation in the Liberalization of International Trade: After Hegemony, What?" *International Organization,* Vol. 41, No. 1 (1987), pp. 1–26. For other views discounting the role of the hegemon on the trading system, see John A. C. Conybeare, "Tariff Protection in Developed and Developing Countries: A Cross-Sectional and Longitudinal Analysis," *International Organization,* Vol. 37, No. 3 (1983), pp. 441–63; Sven Grassman, "Long-Term Trends in Openness of National Economies," *Oxford Economic Papers* (New Series), Vol. 32, No. 1 (1980), pp. 123–33; and Timothy J. McKeown, "The Limitations of 'Structural' Theories of Commercial Policy," *International Organization,* Vol. 40, No. 1 (1986), pp. 43–64.

40. Keith Cowling and Roger Sugden, "Strategic Trade Policy Reconsidered: National Rivalry vs. Free Trade vs. International Cooperation," *Kyklos,* Vol. 51, No. 3 (1998), 339–57.

41. T. Baumgartner and T. R. Burns, "The Structuring of International Economic Relations," *International Studies Quarterly,* Vol. 19, No. 2 (1975), pp. 126–59, and Charles P. Kindleberger, *World Economic Primacy: 1500 to 1900* (New York: Oxford University Press, 1996), p. 71.

42. Kent Jones, "Voluntary Export Restraint: Political Economy, History, and the Role of the GATT," *Journal of World Trade,* Vol. 23, No. 3 (1989), pp. 125–40, and James D. Reitzes, "The Impact of Quotas and Tariffs on Strategic R&D Behaviour," *International Economic Review,* Vol. 32, No. 4 (1991), pp. 985–1007.

43. Keith Anderson, "Antidumping Laws in the United States: Use and Welfare Consequences," *Journal of World Trade*, Vol. 27, No. 2 (1993), pp. 99–117; Robert C. Feenstra, "Quality Change under Trade Restraints in Japanese Autos," *Quarterly Journal of Economics*, Vol. 103, No.1 (1998), pp. 131–46; Heinz Hauser, "Foreign Trade Policy and the Function of Rules for Trade Policy-Making," in Detlev Chr. Dicke and Ernst-Ulrich Petersmann (eds.), *Foreign Trade in the Present and a New International Economic Order*, Progress in Undercurrents in Public International Law, Vol. 4, (Fribourg: University Press, 1988), p. 29; John H. Jackson, *The World Trading System: Law and Policy of International Economic Relations* (Cambridge, MA: MIT Press, 1989), pp. 180–81; William H. Kaempfer, Stephen V. Marks, and Thomas D. Willett, "Why Do Large Countries Prefer Quantitative Trade Restrictions," *Kyklos*, Vol. 41, No. 4 (1988), 625–46; Ram Khanna, "Market Sharing under Multi-fibre Arrangement: Consequences of Non-Tariff Barriers in the Textiles Trade," *Journal of World Trade*, Vol. 24, No. 1 (1990), pp. 71–104; Ernst-Ulrich Petersmann, "Grey Area Policy and the Rule of Law," *Journal of World Trade*, Vol. 22, No. 2 (1988), pp. 23–44; and B. Peter Rosendorff, "Voluntary Export Restraints, Antidumping Procedure, and Domestic Politics," *American Economic Review*, Vol. 86, No. 3 (1996), pp. 544–61.

44. Timothy E. Josling, Stefan Tangermann, and T. K. Warley, *Agriculture in the GATT* (Houndmills, Basingstoke: Macmillan, 1996), pp. 11–12.

45. Theodore H. Cohn, "The Changing Role of the United States in the Global Agricultural Trade Regime," in William P. Avery (ed.), *World Agriculture and the GATT* (Boulder, CO: Lynne Rienner, 1993), pp. 17–38, and Josling, Tangermann, and Warley, *Agriculture in the GATT,* chaps. 4 and 5.

46. I. M. Destler, "Protecting Congress or Protecting Trade," *Foreign Policy*, No. 62 (1986), pp. 96–107, and "U.S. Trade Policy-Making in the Eighties," in Alberto Alexina and Geoffrey Carliner (eds.), *Politics and Economics in the Eighties* (Chicago: University of Chicago Press, 1991), pp. 251–81, and Judith Goldstein and Stefanie Ann Lenway, "Interests or Institutions: An Inquiry into Congressional-ITC Relations," *International Studies Quarterly*, Vol. 33, No. 3 (1990), pp. 303–27.

47. Julia Christine Bliss, "The Amendments to Section 301: An Overview and Suggested Strategies for Foreign Response," *Law and Policy in International Business*, Vol. 20, No. 3 (1989), pp. 501–28; Alfred E. Eckes, "Epitaph for the Escape Clause?" in Khosrow Fatemi (ed.), *International Trade and Finance in a Rapidly Changing Environment*, Proceedings of the International Trade and Finance Association, Vol. 1, International Trade and International Banking (Laredo, TX: 1992), pp. 29–44; Gary N. Horlick and Geoffrey D. Oliver, "Antidumping and Countervailing Duty Law Provisions of the Omnibus Trade and Competitiveness Act of 1988," *Journal of World Trade*, Vol. 23, No. 3 (1989), pp. 5–49; and J. David Richardson, "U.S. Trade Policy in the 1980s:

Turns—and Roads not Taken," in Martin Feldstein (ed.), *American Economic Policy in the 1980s* (Chicago: University of Chicago Press, 1994), pp. 627–58.

48. Michael P. Ryan, *Playing by the Rules: American Trade Power and Diplomacy in the Pacific* (Washington, D.C.: Georgetown University Press, 1995).

49. Michael Bailey and David W. Brady, "Heterogeneity and Representation: The Senate and Free Trade," *American Journal of Political Science,* Vol. 42, No. 2 (1998), pp. 524–44; John A. C. Conybeare, "Voting for Protection: An Electoral Model of Tariff Policy," *International Organization,* Vol. 45, No. 1 (1991), pp. 57–81; Cletus C. Coughlin, "Domestic Content Legislation: House Voting and the Economic Theory of Regulation," *Economic Inquiry,* Vol. 23, No. 3 (1985), pp. 437–48; Robert E. Cumby and Theodore H. Moran, "Testing Models of the Trade Policy Process; Antidumping and the 'New Issues'," in Robert C. Feenstra (ed.), *The Effects of U.S. Trade Protection and Promotion Policies* (Chicago: University of Chicago Press, 1997), pp. 161–90; William R. Keech and Kyongsan Pak, "Partisanship, Institutions and Change in American Trade Politics," *Journal of Politics,* Vol. 57, No. 4 (1995), pp. 1130–42; James M. Lutz, "Determinants of Protectionist Attitudes in the U.S. House of Representatives," *International Trade Journal,* Vol. 5, No. 3 (1991), pp. 301–28; John MacArthur and Stephen V. Marks, "Constituent Interests vs. Legislator Ideology: The Role of Political Opportunity Costs," *Economic Inquiry,* Vol. 26, No. 3 (1988), pp. 461–70; and Kenneth A. Wink, C. Don Livingston, and James C. Garand, "Dispositions, Constituencies, and Cross-Pressures: Modeling Roll-Call Voting on the North American Free Trade Agreement in the U.S. House," *Political Research Quarterly,* Vol. 49, No. 4 (1996), pp. 749–70.

50. William R. Cline, "Macroeconomic Influences on Trade Policy," *American Economic Review,* Vol. 79, No. 2 (1989), pp. 319–30, and Julia K. Hughes, "A Retail Industry View of the Multifibre Arrangement: How Congressional Politics Influence International Negotiations," *Law and Policy in International Business,* Vol. 19, No. 1 (1987), pp. 257–61.

51. Don P. Clark and Simonetta Zarrelli, "Non-Tariff Measures and Industrial Nation Imports of GSP-Covered Products," *Southern Economic Journal,* Vol. 59, No. 4 (1992), pp. 284–93.

52. Nipoli Kamdar and Jorge Gonzalez, "Quis, Quid, Ubi, Quibus Auxiliis, Cur, Quo Modo, Quando?: The U.S. House of Representatives Votes on NAFTA and GATT," in Khosrow Fatemi (ed.), *International Business in the New Millennium: Volume II, International Trade and Policy Issues* (Laredo, TX: Texas A&M International University, 1997), pp. 435–49, and Wink et al., "Dispositions, Constituencies, and Cross-Pressures."

53. Carl B. Hamilton, *The Transient Nature of "New" Protectionism,* Seminar Paper No. 425 (Stockholm: Institute for International Economic Studies, 1988), pp. 9–10.

54. Wendy L. Hansen and Thomas J. Prusa, "Cumulation and ITC Decision-Making: The Sum of the Parts Is Greater than the Whole," *Economic Inquiry,*

Vol. 34, No. 4 (1996), pp. 746–69, and John T. White, "A Test of Consistency in the Administration of U.S. Antidumping Laws," *Journal of World Trade*, Vol. 31, No. 4 (1997), pp. 117–28.

55. James M. DeVault, "U.S. Antidumping Administrative Reviews," *International Trade Journal*, Vol. 10, No. 2 (1996), pp. 247–67.

56. James Bovard, *The Fair Trade Fraud* (New York: St. Martin's, 1991), pp. 145–6.

57. Michael P. Ryan, "Court of International Trade Judges, Binational Panelists, and Judicial Review of U.S. Antidumping and Countervailing Duty Policies," *Journal of World Trade*, Vol. 30, No. 6 (1996), pp. 103–20.

58. Jagdish Bhagwati, *Protectionism* (Cambridge, MA: MIT Press, 1988), pp. 48–53; J. M. Finger, "Subsidies and Countervailing Duties," in P. K. M. Tharakan (ed.), *Policy Implications of Antidumping Measures,* Advanced Series in Management, Vol. 14 (Amsterdam: North Holland, 1991), p. 179; Jackson, *The World Trading System,* pp. 271–72; Pietro S. Nivola, *Regulating Unfair Trade* (Washington, D.C.: The Brookings Institution, 1993), p. 72; N. David Palmeter, "Injury Determinations in Antidumping and Countervailing Duty Cases—A Commentary on U.S. Practice," *Journal of World Trade Law,* Vol. 21, No. 1 (1987), pp. 7–45; Stanislaw Soltysinski, "U.S. Antidumping Laws and State-Controlled Economies," *Journal of World Trade Law,* Vol. 15, No. 3 (1981), p. 265; and Jean Waelbroeck, "Exports of Manufactures from Developing Countries to the European Community," in Colin I. Bradford, Jr., and William H. Branson (eds.), *Trade and Structural Change in Pacific Asia* (Chicago: University of Chicago Press, 1987), p. 84.

59. Finger, "Subsidies and Countervailing Duties," pp. 177–79, and Bernard M. Hoekman and Michel M. Kostecki, *The Political Economy of the World Trading System: From GATT to WTO* (Oxford: Oxford University Press, 1995), p. 184.

60. Rambod Behboodi, *Industrial Subsidies and Friction in World Trade: Policy or Trade Politics* (London: Routledge, 1994), and Terry Collins-Williams and Gerry Salembier, "International Disciplines on Subsidies: The GATT, the WTO and the Future Agenda," *Journal of World Trade,* Vol. 30, No. 1 (1996), pp. 5–17.

61. Honma Masayoshi, "Japan's Agricultural Policy and Protection Growth," in Takatoshi Ito and Anne O. Krueger (eds.), *Trade and Protectionism,* National Bureau of Economic Research—East Asia Seminar on Economics, Vol. 2 (Chicago: University of Chicago, 1993), pp. 95–111.

62. Fumio Egaitsu, "Japanese Agricultural Policy: Unfair and Unreasonable?" in William T. Coyle, Dermont Hayes, and Hiroshi Yamauchi (eds.), *Agriculture and Trade in the Pacific: Toward the Twenty-First Century* (Boulder, CO: Westview, 1992), pp. 101–18, and David P. Rapkin and Aurelia George, "Rice Liberalization and Japan's Role in the Uruguay Round: A Two-Level Game Approach," in William P. Avery (ed.), *World Agriculture and the GATT* (Boulder, CO: Lynne Rienner, 1993), pp. 55–94.

63. Peter J. Katzenstein, "Conclusion: Domestic Structures and Strategies of Foreign Economic Policy," *International Organization,* Vol. 31, No. 4 (1977), pp. 879–920; Kozo Yamamura, "Caveat Emptor: The Industrial Policy of Japan," in Paul R. Krugman (ed.), *Strategic Trade Policy and the New International Economics* (Cambridge, MA: MIT Press, 1987), pp. 169–209; and Rogowski, *Commerce and Coalitions.*

64. Ippei Yamazawa, "Japan and Her Asian Neighbours in a Dynamic Perspective," in Colin I. Bradford, Jr., and William H. Branson (eds.), *Trade and Structural Change in Pacific Asia* (Chicago: University of Chicago Press, 1987), p. 102.

65. Syed Javed Maswood, *Japan and Protection: The Growth of Protectionist Sentiment and the Japanese Response* (London: Routledge and Nissan Institute for Japanese Studies, 1989), p. 108.

66. Edward J. Lincoln, *Japan's New Global Role* (Washington, D.C.: The Brookings Institution, 1993), p. 84.

67. Marie Anchordoguy, "The Public Corporation: A Potent Japanese Policy Weapon," *Political Science Quarterly,* Vol. 103, No. 4 (1988–89), pp. 709–24, and "Japanese-American Trade Conflict and Supercomputers," *Political Science Quarterly,* Vol. 109, No. 1 (1994), pp. 35–80; Bela Balassa and Marcus Noland, *Japan in the World Economy* (Washington, D.C.: Institute for International Economics, 1988); Bhagwati, *Protectionism,* p. 45; Timothy A. Deyak, W. Charles Sawyer, and Richard L. Sprinkle, "A Comparison of the Demand for Imports and Exports in Japan and the United States," *Journal of World Trade,* Vol. 27, No. 5 (1993), pp. 63–74; Kenneth A. Froot and David B. Yoffie, "Trading Blocs and the Incentives to Protect: Implications for Japan and East Asia," in Jeffrey A. Frankel and Miles Kahler (eds.), *Regionalism and Rivalry: Japan and the United States* (Chicago: University of Chicago Press, 1993) pp. 125–53; Gilpin, "The Implications of the Changing Trade Regime," p. 163; Mordechai E. Kreinin, "Super-301 and Japan—A Dissenting View," in Mordechai E. Kreinin (ed.), *International Commercial Policy: Issues for the 1990s* (Washington D.C.: Taylor and Francis, 1993), pp. 65–101; Robert Z. Lawrence, "How Open Is Japan?" in Paul Krugman (ed.), *Trade with Japan: Has the Door Opened Wider?* (Chicago: University of Chicago Press, 1991), pp. 9–37; Joseph A. McKinney, "Degree of Access to the Japanese Market: 1979 vs. 1986," *Columbia Journal of World Business,* Vol. 24, No. 2 (1989), pp. 53–59; Maswood, *Japan and Protection,* pp. 99–100; Michael F. Oppenheimer and Donna M. Tuths, *Non-Tariff Barriers: The Effects on Corporate Strategy in High-Technology Sectors* (Boulder CO: Westview, 1987), Sueo Sekiguchi, "Japan: A Plethora of Programs," in Hugh Patrick with Larry Meissner (ed.), *Pacific Basin Industries in Distress: Structural Adjustment and Trade Policy in the Nine Industrialized Economies* (New York: Columbia University Press, 1991), pp. 418–68; and Karel van Wolferen, "The Japan Problem Revisited," *Foreign Affairs,* Vol. 69, No. 4 (1990), pp. 42–55.

68. Richard E. Baldwin and Paul R. Krugman, "Market Access and International Competition: A Simulation Study of 16K Random Access Memories," in Robert C. Feenstra (ed.), *Empirical Methods for International Trade* (Cambridge, MA: MIT Press, 1988), pp. 171–97.

69. Kenneth Flamm, *Mismanaged Trade: Strategic Policy and the Semiconductor Industry* (Washington, D.C.: Brookings Institution, 1996), p. 431.

70. Mitsuo Matsushita, "Comments on Antidumping Law Enforcement in Japan," in John H. Jackson and Edwin A. Vermulst (eds.), *Antidumping Law and Practice: A Comparative Study* (Ann Arbor: University of Michigan Press, 1989), pp. 389–95, and Sekiguchi, "Japan: A Plethora of Programs," p. 463.

71. Balassa and Noland, *Japan in the World Economy*, pp. 55–57.

72. Carl B. Hamilton and Chyngsoo Kim, "Republic of Korea: Rapid Growth in Spite of Protection Abroad," in Carl B. Hamilton (ed.), *Textiles Trade and the Developing Countries: Eliminating the Multi-Fibre Arrangement in the 1990s* (Washington, D.C.: World Bank, 1988, pp. 169–71; Lawrence B. Krause, "The Structure of Trade in Manufactured Goods in the East and Southeast Asian Region," in Colin I. Bradford, Jr., and William H. Branson (eds.), *Trade and Structural Change in Pacific Asia* (Chicago: University of Chicago Press, 1987), pp. 217–18; and Lawrence. "How Open is Japan?," p. 22.

73. Woo, *Race to the Swift*, p. 164.

74. K. C. Fung, "Characteristics of Japanese Industrial Groups and their Potential Impact on U.S.-Japanese Relations," in Robert E. Baldwin (ed.), *Empirical Studies of Commercial Policy* (Chicago: University of Chicago Press, 1991), pp. 137–64. Angelina Helou, "The Nature and Competitiveness of Japan's Keiretsu," *Journal of World Trade*, Vol. 25, No. 3 (1991), pp. 99–131, provides a good summary of the operations of the *keiretsu*.

75. Marcus Noland, "Public Policy, Private Preferences, and the Japanese Trade Pattern," *Review of Economics and Statistics*, Vol. 79, No. 2 (1997), pp. 259–66.

76. Rob Steven, *Japan and the New World Order* (Houndmills, Basingstoke: Macmillan Press, 1996), p. 255.

77. Michael Tracy, *Government and Agriculture in Western Europe, 1880–1988,* 3rd ed. (New York: New York University Press, 1989).

78. Allan E. Buckwell, David R. Harvey, Kenneth J. Thomson, and Kevin A. Parton, *The Costs of the Common Agricultural Policy* (London: Croom Helm, 1982), p. 166.

79. Peter Alexis Gourevitch, "International Trade, Domestic Coalitions and Liberty: Comparative Responses to the Crisis of 1873–1896," *Journal of Interdisciplinary History*, Vol. 8, No. 2 (1977), pp. 281–313; Katzenstein, "Conclusion"; and James M. Lutz, "The United States and Managed Trade: A Minnow Swimming with Piranhas," *World Competition*, Vol. 21, No. 3 (1998), pp. 45–61.

80. Alexander Gerschenkron, *Economic Backwardness in Historical Perspective: A Book of Essays* (Cambridge: Cambridge University Press, 1962).

81. Rogowski, *Commerce and Coalitions,* pp. 163–65.
82. Stephen S. Cohen, "Informed Bewilderment: French Economic Strategy and the Crisis," in Stephen S. Cohen and Peter A. Gourevitch (eds.), *France in the Troubled World Economy* (London: Butterworth Scientific, 1982), pp. 21–48; Hayes, *Making Trade Policy,* chap. 7; Katzenstein, "Conclusion"; Lynn Kreiger Mytelka, "The French Textile Industry: Crisis and Adjustment," in Harold K. Jacobsen and Dusan Sidjanski (eds.), *The Emerging International Economic Order: Dynamic Processes, Constraints and Opportunities* (Beverly Hills, CA: Sage, 1982), pp. 129–66; Oppenheimer and Tuths, *Non-Tariff Barriers;* Rogowski, *Commerce and Coalitions;* and John Zysman, *Political Strategies for Industrial Order: State, Market, and Industry in France* (Berkeley: University of California Press, 1977).
83. Vivien A. Schmidt, *From State to Market? The Transformation of French Business and Government* (Cambridge: Cambridge University Press, 1996), p. 443, and "Loosening the Ties that Bind: The Impact of European Integration on French Government and Its Relationship to Business," *Journal of Common Market Studies,* Vol. 34, No. 2 (1996), pp. 223–54.
84. Paul Krugman, *The Accidental Theorist: And Other Dispatches from the Dismal Science* (New York: Norton, 1998), p. 37.
85. Schmidt, "Loosening the Ties that Bind."
86. Edward A. Kolodziej, *French International Policy under DeGaulle and Pompidou: The Politics of Grandeur* (Ithaca, NY: Cornell University Press, 1974), pp. 313–14.
87. Michael Dolan, "European Restructuring and Import Policies for a Textile Industry in Crisis," *International Organization,* Vol. 37, No. 4 (1983), pp. 583–616; Hayes, *Making Trade Policy;* Jean-Pierre Lehmann, "France, Japan, Europe, and Industrial Competition: The Automobile Case," *International Affairs* (London), Vol. 68, No. 1 (1992), pp. 37–53; and Frank H. Westhoff, Beth V. Yarbrough, and Robert M. Yarbrough, "Preferential Trade Agreements and the GATT: Can Bilateralism and Multilateralism Coexist," *Kyklos,* Vol. 47, No. 4 (1994), pp. 179–95.
88. W. Daniel Garst, "From Factor Endowments to Class Struggle: Pre–World War I Germany and Rogowski's Theory of Trade and Political Cleavage," *Comparative Political Studies,* Vol. 31, No. 1 (1998), pp. 22–44, and Cheryl Schonhardt-Bailey, "Parties and Interests in the 'Marriage of Iron and Rye'," *British Journal of Political Science,* Vol. 28, No. 2 (1998), pp. 291–330.
89. Garst, "From Factor Endowments to Class Struggle."
90. Cf. Albert O. Hirschman, *National Power and the Structure of Foreign Trade* (Berkeley: University of California Press, 1969, originally published 1945).
91. Robert Mark Spaulding, "German Trade Policy in Eastern Europe, 1890–1990: Preconditions for Applying International Trade Leverage," *International Organization,* Vol. 45, No. 3 (1996), pp. 343–68.
92. Katzenstein, "Conclusion"; Krasner, "State Power"; and Andrew Marrison, *British Business and Protection, 1903–1912* (Oxford: Clarendon Press, 1996).

93. Paul A. Brenton and L. Alan Winters, "Voluntary Export Restraints and Rationing: UK Leather Footwear Imports from Eastern Europe," *Journal of International Economics,* Vol. 34, No. 3/4 (1993), pp. 289–308, Hayes, *Making Trade Policy,* chap. 8; and Marrison, *British Business and Protection.*

94. Charles Collyns, *Can Protection Cure Unemployment,* Thames Essay No. 31 (London: Trade Policy Research Centre, 1982); Andrew Kilpatrick and Tony Lawson, "On the Name of Industrial Decline in the U.K.," *Cambridge Journal of Economics,* Vol. 4, No. 1 (1980), pp. 85–102; and Patrick Minford, "The New Cambridge Economic Policy: A Critique of Its Prescriptions," *Government and Opposition,* Vol. 17, No. 1 (1982), pp. 48–60.

95. Markus M. L. Crepaz, "Consensus versus Majoritarian Democracy: Political Institutions and Their Impact on Macroeconomic Performance and Industrial Disputes," *Comparative Political Studies,* Vol. 29, No. 1 (1996), pp. 4–26; Michael Gallagher, Michael Laver, and Peter Mair, *Representative Government in Modern Europe,* 2nd ed. (New York: McGraw-Hill, 1995), pp. 360–64; Peter J. Katzenstein, *Small States in World Markets: Industrial Policy in Europe* (Ithaca, NY: Cornell University Press, 1985); and Lutz, "The United States and Managed Trade."

96. Andre Blais, "The Political Economy of Public Subsidies," *Comparative Political Studies,* Vol. 19, No. 2 (1986), pp. 201–16.

97. Cristina Corado and Jaime de Melo, "An Ex-Ante Model for Estimating the Impact on Trade Flows of a Country's Joining a Customs Union," *Journal of Development Economics,* Vol. 24, No. 1 (1986), pp. 153–66; Mordechai Kreinin, "Static Effect of E.C. Enlargement on Trade Flows in Manufactured Products," *Kyklos,* Vol. 34, No. 1 (1981), pp. 60–71; and Peter Moser, "Preferential Trade Agreements and the GATT: Can Bilateralism and Multilateralism Coexist?" *Kyklos,* Vol. 45, No. 4 (1995), pp. 593–98.

98. Lee Kendall Metcalf, *The Council of Mutual Economic Assistance: The Failure of Reform,* East European Monographs, Boulder (New York: Columbia University Press, 1997), pp. 59–60.

99. Gilpin, "The Implications of the Changing Trade Regime," p. 141.

100. Michael G. Plummer, "Efficiency Effects of the Accession of Spain and Portugal to the EC," *Journal of Common Market Studies,* Vol. 29, No. 3 (1991), pp. 317–25, and L. Alan Winters, "The European Community: A Case of Successful Integration," in Jaime de Melo and Arvind Panagariya (eds.), *New Dimensions in Regional Integration* (Cambridge: Cambridge University Press, 1993), p. 207.

101. Kym Anderson, "Europe 1992 and the Western Pacific Economies," *Economic Journal,* Vol. 101, No. 409 (1991), pp. 1538–52; Michael W. S. Davenport, "The External Policy of the Community and Its Effects upon the Manufactured Exports of the Developing Countries," *Journal of Common Market Studies,* Vol. 29, No. 2 (1990), pp. 181–200; and Rolf J. Langhammer, "Fuelling a New Engine of Growth or Separating Europe from Non-Europe?" *Journal of Common Market Studies,* Vol. 29, No. 2 (1990), pp. 123–35.

102. Steve Peers, "Reform of the European Community's Generalized System of Preferences," *Journal of World Trade,* Vol. 29, No. 6 (1995), pp. 79–96, and L. Alan Winters, "Expanding EC Membership and Association Accords: Recent Experience and Future Prospects," in Kym Anderson and Richard Blackhurst (eds.), *Regional Integration and the Global Trading System* (New York: St. Martin's, 1993), pp. 104–25.

103. Richard Pomfret, *The Economics of Discriminatory International Trade Policies* (Oxford: Basil Blackwell 1988), pp. 4–5.

104. Charles E. Hanrahan Hamilton, "European Integration: Implications for U.S. Food and Agriculture," in Glennon J. Harrison (ed.), *Europe and the United States: Competition and Cooperation in the 1990s,* A Study Submitted to the Subcommittee on International Economic Policy and Trade and the Subcommittee on Europe and the Middle East of the Committee on Foreign Affairs, U.S. House of Representatives (Armonk, NY: M. E. Sharpe, 1994), pp. 229–38.

105. Hamilton, "European Integration," p. 235.

106. Brian Hindley, "Antidumping Actions and the EC: A Wider Perspective," in Meinhard Hilf and Ernst-Ulrich Petersmann (eds.), *National Constitutions and International Economic Law,* Vol. 8 Studies in Transnational Economic Law (Deventer, Netherlands: Kluwer, 1993), pp. 371–90; Robert Z. Lawrence, *Regionalism, Multilateralism, and Deeper Integration* (Washington, D.C.: Brookings Institution, 1995); Norman Scott, "Protectionism in Western Europe," in Dominick Salvatore (ed.), *Protectionism and World Welfare* (Cambridge: Cambridge University Press, 1993), pp. 371–95; Paul Waer and Edwin Vermulst, "EC Anti-Dumping Law and Practice after the Uruguay Round," *Journal of World Trade,* Vol. 28, No. 2 (1994), pp. 5–21; Martin Wolf, "Cooperation or Conflict? The European Union in a Liberal Global Economy," *International Affairs* (London), Vol. 71, No. 2 (1995), 325–37; and George N. Yannopoulos, "The European Community's Common External Commercial Policy: Internal Contradictions and Institutional Weaknesses," *Journal of World Trade Law,* Vol. 19, No. 5 (1985), pp. 451–65.

107. Patrick A. Messerlin, "The Uruguay Negotiations on Antidumping Enforcement: Some Basic Issues," in P. K. M. Tharakan (ed.), *Policy Implications of Antidumping Measures,* Advanced Series in Management, Vol. 14 (Amsterdam: North Holland, 1991), pp. 45–76; Willem Rycken, "Some Specific Issues in the Antidumping Proceedings of the European Communities," in P. K. M. Tharakan (ed.), *Policy Implications of Antidumping Measures,* Advanced Series in Management, Vol. 14 (Amsterdam: North Holland, 1991), pp. 191–218; and P. K. Mathew Tharakan and Birgit Kestens, "Contingent Protection and International Trade: An Analysis of the Antidumping Policy of the European Union," in P. K. M. Tharakan and D. Ven Den Bulcke (eds.), *International Trade, Foreign Direct Investment and the Economic Environment: Essays in Honour of Professor Sylvain Plasschaert* (Houndmills, Basingstoke: Macmillan, 1998), pp. 41–58.

108. Paul Waer and Edwin Vermulst, "EC Anti-Subsidy Law and Practice after the Uruguay Round: A Wolf in Sheep's Clothing," *Journal of World Trade*, Vol. 33, No. 3 (1999), pp. 19–43.

109. Gallagher et al., *Representative Government in Modern Europe*, pp. 133–36; Walter Goldstein, "The EC: Capitalist or *Dirigiste* Regime," in Alan M. Cafruny and Glenda G. Rosenthal (eds.), *The State of the European Community: Volume 2, The Maastricht Debates and Beyond* (Boulder, CO: Lynne Rienner, 1993), pp. 303–19; and Scott, "Protectionism in Western Europe."

110. Winters, "The European Community," p. 210.

111. Hayes, *Making Trade Policy*, p. 86.

112. Katzenstein, *Small States in World Markets*, p. 69. Results from James M. Lutz, "Industrialized Markets for Developing-Country Manufactured Exports: The Good, the Poor, and the Indifferent," *Journal of Developing Areas*, Vol. 31, No. 3 (1997), pp. 367–86, "Relative Import Propensities of Less Developed Countries' Manufactures in Industrialized Countries," in Raul Moncarz (ed.), *International Trade and the New Economic Order* (Oxford: Pergamon, 1995), pp. 221–32, and "To Import or Protect?: Industrialized Countries and Manufactured Products," *Journal of World Trade*, Vol. 28, No. 4 (1994), pp. 123–46, would seem to confirm the fact that Germany has been willing to restrict imports.

113. Sanoussi Bilal, "Political Economy Considerations on the Supply of Trade Protection in Regional Integration Agreements," *Journal of Common Market Studies*, Vol. 36, No. 1 (1998), pp. 1–31.

114. R. M. Conlon, "Transport Costs and Tariff Protection of Australian and Canadian Manufacturing: A Comparative Study," *Canadian Journal of Economics*, Vol. 14, No. 4 (1981), pp. 700–707.

115. Rolf Mirus, Barry Scholnick, and Dean Spinanger, "Front-Loading Protection: Canada's Approach to Phasing Out the Multi-Fiber Arrangement," *International Trade Journal*, Vol. 11, No. 4 (1997), pp. 433–51.

116. Stephen Bell, "Globalisation, Neoliberalism and the Transformation of the Australian State," *Australian Journal of Political Science*, Vol. 32, No. 3 (1997), p. 345.

117. Kym Anderson and Ross Garnaut, "The Political Economy of Manufacturing Protection in Australia," in Christopher Findlay and Ross Garnaut (eds.), *The Political Economy of Manufacturing Protection: Experiences of ASEAN and Australia* (Sydney: Allen and Unwin, 1986), pp. 159–83, and Rogowski, *Commerce and Coalitions*.

118. Kym Anderson, "Australia's Changing Trade Pattern and Growth Performance," in Richard Pomfret (ed.), *Australia's Trade Policies* (Melbourne: Oxford University Press, 1995), pp. 29–52, and Jonathan Pincus, "Evolution and Political Economy of Australian Trade Policies," in Richard Pomfret (ed.), *Australia's Trade Policies* (Melbourne: Oxford University Press, 1995), pp. 53–73.

119. James M. Lutz, "Japanese Imports of Manufactures from East Asia: Is the Glass Half Empty or Hall Full?" *International Trade Journal,* Vol. 7, No. 2 (1992), pp. 151–79.

120. Bell, "The Transformation of the Australian State," p. 360; Bijit Bora and Richard Pomfret, "Policies Affecting Manufacturing," in Richard Pomfret (ed.), *Australia's Trade Policies* (Melbourne: Oxford University Press, 1995), pp. 91–111; and Pincus, "Evolution and Political Economy."

121. Greg Mastel, *Antidumping Laws and the U.S. Economy* (Armonk, NY: M. E. Sharpe, 1998), p. 189, and P. K. M. Tharakan, "Some Facets of Antidumping Policy: Summary of the Contents of the Volume," in P. K. M. Tharakan (ed.), *Policy Implications of Antidumping Measures* (Amsterdam: North Holland, 1991), p. 15.

122. Anthony C. Rayner and Ralph Lattimore, "New Zealand," in Demetris Papageorgiou, Michael Michaely, and Armeane M. Choksi (eds.), *Liberalizing Foreign Trade; Volume 6, The Experience of New Zealand, Spain, and Turkey* (Oxford: Basil Blackwell, 1991), pp. 1–135.

123. Forrest H. Capie, *Tariffs and Growth: Some Illustrations from the World Economy, 1850–1940* (Manchester: Manchester University Press, 1994), p. 91.

124. Rayner and Lattimore, "New Zealand."

125. "New Zealand's Advantage," *Economist,* Vol. 352, No. 8137 (September 18, 1999), p. 47.

126. Robin Broad, John Cavanagh, and Walden Bello, "Development: The Market Is Not Enough," *Foreign Policy,* No. 81 (1990–91), pp. 144–62, and Sunil Kukreja, "The Development Dilemma: NICS and LDCs," in David N. Balaam and Michael Veseth, *Introduction to Political Economy* (Upper Saddle River, NJ: Prentice Hall, 1996), pp. 324–29.

127. Aharoni and Hirsch, "Enhancing Competitive Advantage."

128. Jorge Castro-Bernieri and Paul Anthony Levine, "The Venezuelean Antidumping and Countervailing Duties Regime," *Journal of World Trade,* Vol. 30, No. 1 (1996), pp. 124–41.

129. Brian Hindley, "The Economics of Dumping and Antidumping Action: Is There a Baby in the Bathwater," in P. K. M. Tharakan (ed.), *Policy Implications of Antidumping Measures* (Amsterdam: North Holland, 1991), pp. 25–43.

Chapter 3: Imports of the Industrialized Countries

1. Belgium and Luxembourg formed a complete customs union after World War I; thus, all trade data reflected the combined trade of the two countries. Luxembourg's small size mitigated any problems that might arise from this situation. Similarly, Swiss trade data included that of Liechtenstein, and the

data for France included Monaco, even smaller countries, whose overall influence on total trade data would have been miniscule.

2. Israel, of course, is technically not an European state in a geographic sense, but it clearly had been European in a cultural sense.

3. World Bank, *World Development Report* (Oxford: Oxford University Press, various years—annual publication since 1978), *World Tables, 1976* (Baltimore: Johns Hopkins University Press, 1976), and *World Tables, 1995* (Baltimore: Johns Hopkins University Press, 1995).

4. Purchasing power parity figures would solve the cost of living difficulty, but they have only recently come into common use; therefore, the necessary historical points for data collection and comparisons were unavailable.

5. United Nations Statistical Office, *Yearbook of International Trade Statistics* (New York: United Nations, various years) from 1948 to 1982, continued by Department of International Economic and Social Affairs, Statistical Office, *International Trade Statistics Yearbook* (New York: United Nations, various years) from 1983 on.

6. The international Standard Industrial Classification is different from the Standard Industrial Standard used in the United States for reporting purposes. U.S. trade data, however, have utilized the SITC categories.

7. The World Bank, *World Development Reports* and *World Tables*, for example.

8. Inclusion of SITC 68 could clearly have overstated the level of imports of manufactured goods given the nature of the products involved. To use an extreme example from the export side, Zambia with its copper exports would have been an exporter of manufactured products at the 95 per cent level if this category were included; yet Zambia can hardly have been considered to be a true example of an industrialized country by any other criteria. The level of manufacturing in countries such as Bolivia and Malaysia (tin) and Chile (copper) for at least some periods would also have overstated their levels of industrialization.

9. Elio Londero and Simon Teitel with Hector Ceruini, Rodrigo Parot, and Jorge Remes Lenicov, *Resources, Industrialization and Exports in Latin America: The Primary Input Content of Sustained Exports of Manufactures from Argentina, Colombia, and Venezuela* (New York: St. Martin's, 1998), pp. 26–28. Robert T. Green and James M. Lutz, *The United States and World Trade: Changing Patterns and Dimensions* (New York: Praeger, 1978) used a similarly broad definition but distinguished between technology-intensive and non-technology-intensive products for their analyses (with the additional categories of manufactures such as SITC 68 all being in the latter category).

10. Cf. Young Whan Kihl and James M. Lutz, *World Trade Issues: Regime, Structure, and Policy* (New York: Praeger, 1985), pp. 49–58.

Chapter 4: Overall Import Levels of the Industrialized Countries

1. Bela Balassa, "Intra-Industry Trade among Exporters of Manufactured Goods," in David Greenaway and P. K. M. Tharakan (eds.), *Imperfect Competition and International Trade: The Policy Aspects of Intra-Industry Trade* (Sussex: Wheatsheaf, 1986), pp. 108–28; Barry Bosworth, Susan M. Collins, and Yu-chin Chen, "Accounting for Differences in Economic Growth," *Brookings Discussion Papers in International Economics,* No. 115 (October 1995), p. 40; James Harrigan, "Openness to Trade in Manufactures in the OECD," *Journal of International Economics,* Vol. 40, Nos. 1/2 (1996), pp. 23–39; Stephen D. Krasner, "State Power and the Structure of International Trade," *World Politics,* Vol. 28, No. 3 (1976), pp. 317–43; and Edward D. Mansfield and Marc L. Busch, "The Political Economy of Nontariff Barriers: A Cross National Analysis," *International Organization,* Vol. 44, No. 4 (1995), pp. 723–749.

2. Michael Michaely, Demetris Papageorgiou, and Armeane M. Choksi, *Liberalizing Foreign Trade: Volume 7, Lessons of Experience in the Developing World* (Cambridge, MA: Basil Blackwell, 1991), pp. 118–19.

3. There was another statistical consequence of using multiple regression with adjusted R^2s as opposed to using a composite size measure. Using two independent variables instead of one reduced the adjusted value; thus, the adjusted values penalized the inclusion of additional variables and made significant results somewhat less likely. In some respects, it was a more conservative approach to use both variables separately in the statistical analysis since higher values were required to achieve acceptable levels of statistical significance.

4. An alternate series of regression equations with the years for EC membership set at a maximum of twenty years—to reflect the leveling out of potential import increases—yielded similar results for the equations; therefore, this explanation was not supported.

5. Guillermo de la Dehesa, Jose Juan Ruiz, and Angel Torres, "Spain," in Demetris Papageorgiou, Michael Michaely, and Armeane M. Choksi (eds.), *Liberalizing Foreign Trade: Volume 6, The Experience of New Zealand, Spain, and Turkey* (Oxford: Basil Blackwell, 1991), pp. 173, 252–57.

6. Nadav Halevi and Joseph Baruh, "Israel," in Demetris Papageorgiou, Michael Michaely, and Armeane M. Choksi (eds.), *Liberalizing Foreign Trade: Volume 3, The Experience of Israel and Yugoslavia* (Oxford: Basil Blackwell, 1991), p. 152.

7. John T. Rourke, *International Politics on the World Stage,* 7th ed. (Guilford, CT: Dushkin/McGraw-Hill, 1999), p. 402.

8. Jaime de Melo and David Tarr, "Welfare Costs of U.S. Quotas in Textiles, Steel and Autos," *Review of Economics and Statistics,* Vol. 72, No. 3 (1990), pp. 489–97.

Chapter 5: Imports of Manufactured Goods (and Raw Materials Too)

1. David P. Calleo and Benjamin M. Rowland, *America and the World Political Economy: Atlantic Dreams and National Realities* (Bloomington: Indiana University Press, 1973), pp. 122–23; H. Peter Gray, "Free International Economic Policy in a World of Schumpeter Goods," *International Trade Journal,* Vol. 12, No. 3 (1998), pp. 323–44; James M. Lutz, "Trade in Manufactures among Industrialized States," *International Journal of Management,* Vol. 4, No. 3 (1987), pp. 403–15; and Wilbur F. Monroe, *International Trade Policy in Transition* (Lexington, MA: Lexington Books, 1975), p. 29.

2. Paul Krugman, *EFTA and 1992,* Occasional Paper No. 23, European Free Trade Association (Geneva: EFTA, June 1988), p. 7.

3. Harald Sander, "Deep Integration, Shallow Regionalism, and Strategic Openness: Three Notes on Economic Integration in East Asia," in Franz Peter Land and Renate Ohr (eds.), *International Economic Integration,* Studies in Contemporary Economics (Heidelberg: Physica-Verlag, 1997), p. 226.

4. Jose de la Torre, *Clothing-Industry Adjustment in Developed Countries* (New York: St. Martin's, 1986), and Brian Toyne, Jeffrey S. Arpan, Andy H. Barnett, David A. Ricks, and Terence A. Shimp, "The International Competitiveness of the U.S. Textile Mill Products Industry: Corporate Strategies for the Future," *Journal of International Business Studies,* Vol. 15, No. 3 (1984), pp. 145–65.

5. Bela Balassa, "Industrial Prospects and Policies in the Developed Countries," in Fritz Machlup, Gerhard Fels, and Huburtus Muller-Groeling (eds.), *Reflections on a Troubled World Economy: Essays in Honor of Herbert Giersch* (New York: St. Martin's, 1983), pp. 271–72; Michael J. Gilligan, "Lobbying as a Private Good with Intra-Industry Trade," *International Studies Quarterly,* Vol. 41, No. 3 (1997), p. 471; Akransanee Narongchai, "Industrialization of ASEAN and Structural Adjustment in the Pacific," in Roger Benjamin and Robert T. Kudrle (eds.), *The Industrial Future of the Pacific Basin* (Boulder, CO: Westview, 1984), pp. 59–78; and Jan E. Kolm, "Regional and National Consequences of Globalizing Industries of the Pacific Rim," in Janet H. Muroyama and H. Guyford Stever (eds.), *Globalization of Technology: International Perspectives* (Washington, D.C.: National Academy Press, 1988), pp. 106–40.

6. Kang Rae Cho, "The Role of Product-Specific Factors in Intra-Firm Trade of U.S. Manufacturing Multinational Corporations," *Journal of International Business Studies,* Vol. 21, No. 2 (1990), pp. 319–30; Brigitte Levy, "Globalization and Regionalization: Main Issues in International Trade Patterns," in Khosrow Fatemi (ed.), *International Trade in the 21st Century* (Kidlington, Oxford: Pergamon, 1997), p. 70; Charles Lipson, "The Transformation of Trade: The Sources and Effects of Regime Change," *International Organization,* Vol. 36, No. 2 (1982), p. 445; Charles-Albert Michalet, "From International Trade to World Economy: A New Paradigm," in Harry Makler, Alberto Martinelli,

and Neil Smelser (eds.), *The New International Economy,* Sage Studies in International Sociology, 26 (Beverly Hills, CA: Sage, 1982), pp. 40–44; and David B. Yoffie, "The Newly Industrializing Countries and the Political Economy of Protectionism," *International Studies Quarterly,* Vol. 25, No. 4 (1981), pp. 569–99.

7. Gilligan, "Lobbying as a Private Good."

8. Richard J. Grant, Maria C. Papdakis, and J. David Richardson, "Global Trade Flows: Old Structures, New Issues, Empirical Evidence," in C. Fred Bergsten and Marcus Noland (eds.) *Pacific Dynamism and the International Economic System* (Washington, D.C.: Institute for International Economics, 1993), pp. 17–63.

9. Kishore Gawande and Wendy L. Hansen, "Retaliation, Bargaining, and the Pursuit of 'Free and Fair' Trade," *International Organization,* Vol. 53, No. 1 (1999), pp. 117–59.

10. Barry Bracewell-Milnes, *Eastern and Western European Economic Integration* (New York: St. Martin's, 1976), p. 116; Lutz, "Trade in Manufactures among Industrialized States"; and F.V. Meyer, *International Trade Policy* (New York: St. Martin's, 1978), p. 180.

11. David Greenaway and Robert C. Hine, "Intra-Industry Specialization, Trade Expansion, and Adjustment in the European Economic Space," *Journal of Common Market Studies,* Vol. 29, No. 6 (1991), p. 610.

12. Bela Balassa, "Intra-Industry Trade among Exporters of Manufactured Goods," in David Greenaway and P. K. M. Tharakan (eds.), *Imperfect Competition and International Trade: The Policy Aspects of Intra-Industry Trade* (Sussex: Wheatsheaf, 1986), pp. 108–28.

13. Balassa, "Industrial Prospects and Policies," p. 268; Carl J. Dahlman, "Structural Change and Trade in the East Asian Newly Industrial Economies and Emerging Industrial Economies," in Randall B. Purcell (ed.), *The Newly Industrializing Countries in the World Economy: Challenges for U.S. Policy* (Boulder, CO: Lynne Rienner, 1989), pp. 51–94; and J. M. Finger, "Trade and Domestic Effects of the Offshore Assembly Provision in the U.S. Tariff," *American Economic Review,* Vol. 66, No. 4 (1976), pp. 598–611.

14. Simon Holmes, "Anti-Circumvention under the European Union's New Anti-Dumping Rules," *Journal of World Trade,* Vol. 29, No. 3 (1995), pp. 161–80, and Edwin Vermulst and Paul Waer, "European Community Rules of Origin as Commercial Policy Instruments," *Journal of World Trade,* Vol. 24, No. 3 (1990), pp. 55–99.

15. Gilligan, "Lobbying as a Private Good."

16. Patrick A. Messerlin and Stephan Becuwe, "Intra-Industry Trade in the Long Run: The French Case," in David Greenaway and P. K. M. Tharakan (eds.), *Imperfect Competition and International Trade: The Policy Aspects of Intra-Industry Trade* (Sussex: Wheatsheaf, 1986), pp. 191–215.

17. James Harrigan, "Openness to Trade in Manufactures in the OECD," *Journal of International Economics,* Vol. 40, No. 1/2 (1996), pp. 23–39, and Edward J.

Lincoln, *Japan's New Global Role* (Washington, D.C.: Brookings Institution, 1993), pp. 82–88.

18. Lincoln, *Japan's New Global Role*, pp. 84, 280–81.

19. There was a possibility that some German manufactures that previously had been exported elsewhere had been diverted to the former East Germany to upgrade factories or to supply consumer goods in this region of the unified country.

20. Oli Havrylyshyn, "Yugoslavia," in Demetris Papageorgiou, Michael Michaely, and Armeane M. Choski (eds.), *Liberalizing Foreign Trade: Volume 3, The Experience of Israel and Yugoslavia* (Oxford: Basil Blackwell, 1991), p. 343.

21. Kozo Yamamura, "The Deliberate Emergence of a Free Trader: The Japanese Political Economy in Transition," in Craig Garby and Mary Brown Bullock (eds.), *Japan: A New Kind of Superpower* (Washington, D.C.: Woodrow Wilson Center Press, 1994), pp. 35–52.

22. Gary R. Saxonhouse, "The Micro- and Macroeconomics of Foreign Sales to Japan," in William R. Cline (ed.), *Trade Policy in the 1980s* (Washington, D.C.: Institute for International Economics, 1983), pp. 259–304. As Hideo Kanemitsu, "Comment," in Cline (ed.), *Trade Policy in the 1980s* (Washington, D.C.: Institute for International Economics, 1983), pp. 313–18, notes, the study had one obvious shortcoming in that it did not include intermediate goods. Mitchell Kellman and Daniel Landau, "The Nature of Japan's Comparative Advantage, 1965–80," *World Development*, Vol. 12, No. 4 (1984), pp. 433–38, argue, however, that the product life cycle theory explained most of Japanese trade patterns, not factor endowments.

23. Ryutaro Komiya and Motoshige Itoh, "Japan's International Trade and Trade Policy," in Taskashi Inoguchi and Daniel I. Okimoto (eds.), *The Political Economy of Japan: Volume 2, The Changing International Context* (Stanford: Stanford University Press, 1988), pp. 173–224; Gary R. Saxonhouse, "The Micro- and Macroeconomics of Foreign Sales to Japan," and "Comparative Advantage, Structural Adaptation, and Japanese Performance," in Inoguchi and Okimoto (eds.), *The Political Economy of Japan: Volume 2, The Changing International Context* (Stanford: Stanford University Press, 1988), pp. 138–70; and Gary R. Saxonhouse and Robert M. Stern, "An Analytic Survey of Formal and Informal Barriers to International Trade and Investment in the United States, Canada, and Japan," in Robert M. Stern (ed.), *Trade and Investment Relations among the United States, Canada, and Japan* (Chicago: University of Chicago Press, 1988), pp. 293–353.

24. Marcus Noland, "Chasing Phantoms: The Political Economy of USTR," *International Organization*, Vol. 51, No. 3 (1997), pp. 365–87.

25. The lumber industry is a case in point. Domestic producers have received many forms of protection, especially against competitors in Canada. Subtle protection continued even after the conclusion of the Canadian-United States free trade agreement. Cf. Gilbert Cagne, "The Canada–US *Softwood*

Lumber Dispute: An Assessment after 15 Years," *Journal of World Trade,* Vol. 33, No. 1 (1999), pp. 67–86, and R. Quentin Grafton, Robert W. Lynch, and Harry W. Nelson, "British Columbia's Stumpage System's Economic and Trade Policy Implications," *Canadian Public Policy,* Vol. 24, Sup. 2 (1998), pp. 541–50.

26. Barry P. Bosworth and Robert Z. Lawrence, "America's Global Role: From Dominance to Interdependence," in John D. Steinbruner (ed.), *Restructuring American Foreign Policy* (Washington D.C.: Brookings Institution, 1989), pp. 12–47, and James M. Lutz, "The United States and Managed Trade: A Minnow Swimming with Piranhas," *World Competition,* Vol. 21, No. 3 (1998), pp. 45–61.

27. Forrest H. Capie, *Tariffs and Growth: Some Illustrations from the World Economy, 1850 - 1940* (Manchester: Manchester University Press, 1994), p. 41.

28. Anthony C. Rayner and Ralph Lattimore, "New Zealand," in Demetris Papageorgiou, Michael Michaely, and Armeane M. Choski (eds.), *Liberalizing Foreign Trade: Volume 6, The Experience of New Zealand, Spain, and Turkey* (Oxford: Basil Blackwell, 1991), p. 106.

Chapter 6: Manufactured Exports from the Developing World

1. J. Michael Finger and Sam Laird, "Protection in Developed and Developing Countries—An Overview," *Journal of World Trade,* Vol. 21, No. 6 (1987), pp. 9–23; Helen Hughes, "The Prospects of ASEAN Countries in Industrialized Country Markets," in Ross Garnaut (ed.), *ASEAN in a Changing Pacific and World Economy* (Canberra: Australian National University Press, 1980), pp. 347–63; Deepak Lal, "Trade Blocs and Multilateral Free Trade," *Journal of Common Market Studies,* Vol. 31, No. 3 (1993), pp. 349–58; and Edwin Vermulst and Paul Waer, "The Calculation of Injury Margins in EC Anti-Dumping Proceedings," *Journal of World Trade,* Vol. 25, No. 6 (1991), pp. 5–42.

2. Don P. Clark, "Nontariff Measures and Developing Country Exports," *Journal of Developing Areas,* Vol. 27, No. 2 (1993), p. 169.

3. Stephany Griffith-Jones, "Economic Integration in Europe: Implications for Developing Countries," in Diana Tussie and David Glover (eds.), *The Developing Countries in World Trade: Policies and Bargaining Strategies* (Boulder, CO: Lynne Reinner, 1993), p. 35.

4. Clark, "Nontariff Measures," pp. 163–72.

5. Cf. Chong-Hyun Nam, "Protectionist U.S. Trade Policy and Korean Exports," in Takatoshi Ito and Anne O. Krueger (eds.), *Trade and Protectionism,* National Bureau of Economic Research—East Asia Seminar on Economics, Vol. 2 (Chicago: University of Chicago Press, 1993), pp. 183–218.

6. Marcus Noland, "Chasing Phantoms: The Political Economy of USTR," *International Organization,* Vol. 51, No. 3 (1997), pp. 365–87.

7. Lars Anell and Birgitta Nygren, *The Developing Countries and the World Economic Order* (London: Frances Pinter, 1980), pp. 60–61; Emmanuel Opoku Awuku, "How Do the Results of the Uruguay Round Affect the North-South Trade," *Journal of World Trade*, Vol. 28, No. 2 (1994), pp. 75–93; Jagdish Bhagwati, *Free Trade, "Fairness" and the New Protectionism: Reflections on an Agenda for the World Trade Organisation*, IEA Occasional Paper 96 (London: Institute of Economic Affairs for the Wincott Foundation, 1995), pp. 31–32; Robert S. Browne, "How Can Africa Prosper?" *World Policy Journal*, Vol. 11, No. 3 (1994), pp. 29–39; Alan V. Deardorff and Robert M. Stern, "The Structure of Tariff Protection: Effects of Foreign Tariffs and Existing NTBs," *Review of Economics and Statistics*, Vol. 67, No. 4 (1985), pp. 539–48; Stephan Haggard and Chung-In Moon, "The South Korean State in the International Economy: Liberal, Dependent, or Mercantile," in John Gerard Ruggie (ed.), *The Antinomies of Interdependence: National Welfare and the International Division of Labor* (New York: Columbia University Press, 1983), pp. 162–63; Bernard M. Hoekman and Michel M. Kostecki, *The Political Economy of the World Trading System: From GATT to WTO* (Oxford: Oxford University Press, 1995), p. 3; Tigani Ibrahim, "Developing Countries and the Tokyo Round," *Journal of World Trade Law*, Vol. 12, No. 1 (1978), pp. 1–26; Charles Lipson, "The Transformation of Trade: The Sources and Effects of Regime Change," *International Organization*, Vol. 36, No. 2 (1982), p. 420; and Erich Scherzer, "Consequences of European Integration for Developing Countries," in Marjan Svetlicic and H. W. Singer (eds.), *The World Economy: Challenges of Globalization and Regionalization* (Houndmills, Basingstoke: Macmillan, 1996), pp. 229–46.

8. Browne, "How Can Africa Prosper?"; Hoekman and Kostecki, *The Political Economy of the World Trading System*, Chap. 4; and A. J. Yeats, "Effective Tariff Protection in the United States, The European Economic Community and Japan," *Quarterly Review of Economics and Business*, Vol. 14, No. 2 (1974), pp. 41–50.

9. James Bovard, *The Fair Trade Fraud* (New York: St. Martin's, 1991), p. 8.

10. Jong-Wha Lee and Phillip Swagel, "Trade Barriers and Trade Flows across Countries and Industries," *Review of Economics and Statistics*, Vol. 79, No. 3 (1997), pp. 372–82.

11. Juan A. de Castro, "Protectionist Pressures in the 1990s and the Coherence of North-South Trade Policies," in Jean-Marc Fontaine (ed.), *Foreign Trade Reforms and Development Strategy* (London: Routledge, 1992), pp. 165–98; David Glover, "Bypassing Barriers: Lessons from the Asian NICs," in Diana Tussie and David Glover (eds.), *The Developing Countries in World Trade: Policies and Bargaining Strategies* (Boulder, CO: Lynne Reinner, 1993), pp. 171–78; Griffith-Jones, "Economic Integration in Europe"; G. K. Helleiner, "Protectionism and the Developing Countries," in Dominick Salvatore (ed.), *Protectionism and World Welfare* (Cambridge: Cambridge University Press, 1993), pp.

396–418; and L. Alan Winters, "The European Community: A Case of Successful Integration," in Jaime de Melo and Arvind Panagariya (eds.), *New Dimensions in Regional Integration* (Cambridge: Cambridge University Press, 1993), pp. 202–28.

12. Bela Balassa and Marcus Noland, "Prospects of Trade and Regional Cooperation of the Industrialized Economies of East Asia," in Shu-Chin Yang (ed.), *Manufactured Exports of East Asian Industrializing Economies: Possible Regional Cooperation* (Armonk, NY: M. E. Sharpe, 1994), pp. 237–60; Riccardo Faini, Jaime de Melo, and Wendy Takacs, "A Primer on the MFA Maze," in Giorgio Navaretti, Riccardo Faini, and Aubrey Silberston (eds.), *Beyond the Multifibre Arrangement: Third World Competition and Restructuring Europe's Textile Industry* (Paris: Organisation of Economic Co-Operation and Development, 1995), pp. 27–44; Loretta Lundy, "The GATT Safeguards Debacle and the Canadian Textiles and Clothing Policy: A Proposal for an Equitable Approach to North-South Relations," *Journal of World Trade*, Vol. 22, No. 6 (1988), pp. 71–94; and Yongzheng Yang, "The Impact of the MFA Phasing Out on World Clothing and Textile Markets," *Journal of Development Studies*, Vol. 30, No. 4 (1994), pp. 892–915.

13. Alberto Brugnoli and Laura Permini, "The Restrictiveness of the MFA: Evidence on Eastern European Exports to the EU," in Meine Pieter van Dijk and Sandro Sideri (eds.), *Multilateralism versus Regionalism: Trade Issues after the Uruguay Round* (London: Frank Cass, 1996), p. 177.

14. Balassa and Noland, "Prospects of Trade and Regional Cooperation," p. 247; Vincent Cable, "Adjusting to Textile and Clothing Quotas: A Summary of Some Commonwealth Countries' Experiences as a Pointer to the Future," in Carl B. Hamilton (ed.), *Textiles Trade and the Developing Countries: Eliminating the Multi-Fibre Arrangement in the 1990s* (Washington, D.C.: World Bank, 1990), pp. 103–35; Judith M. Dean, "The Effects of the U.S. MFA on Small Exporters," *Review of Economics and Statistics*, Vol. 72, No. 1 (1990), pp. 63–69; Sara U. Douglas, "The Textile Industry in Malaysia: Coping with Protectionism," *Asian Survey*, Vol. 29, No. 4 (1989), pp. 416–38; Refik Erzan, Junichi Goto, and Paula Holmes, "Effects of the Multi-Fibre Arrangement on Developing Countries' Trade: An Empirical Investigation," in Carl B. Hamilton (ed.), *Textiles Trade and the Developing Countries: Eliminating the Multi-Fibre Arrangement in the 1990s* (Washington, D.C.: World Bank, 1990), pp. 63–102; Riccardo Faini, "Demand and Supply Factors in Textile Trade," in Giorgio Navaretti, Riccardo Faini, and Aubrey Silberston (eds.), *Beyond the Multifibre Arrangement: Third World Competition and Restructuring Europe's Textile Industry* (Paris: Organisation for Economic Co-Operation and Development, 1995), pp. 45–60; Richard C. Kearney, "Mauritius and the NIC Model Redux: Or, How Many Cases Make a Model?" *Journal of Developing Areas*, Vol. 24, No. 2 (1990), pp. 195–216; Sri Ram Khanna, *International Trade in Textiles: MFA Quotas and a Developing Exporting Country* (New Delhi: Sage, 1991); Rajiv

Kumar and Sri Ram Khanna, "India, the Multi-Fibre Arrangement and the Uruguay Round," in Carl B. Hamilton (ed.), *Textiles Trade and the Developing Countries: Eliminating the Multi-Fibre Arrangement in the 1990s* (Washington, D.C.: World Bank, 1990), pp. 182–212; Dean Spinanger, "The Spillover of Export Capabilities in the Textile and Clothing Industry: The Case of Hong Kong," in Giorgio Navaretti, Riccardo Faini, and Aubrey Silberston (eds.), *Beyond the Multifibre Arrangement: Third World Competition and Restructuring Europe's Textile Industry* (Paris: Organisation for Economic Co-Operation and Development, 1995), pp. 237–50; Irene Trela and John Whalley, "Global Effects of Developed Country Trade Restrictions on Textiles and Apparel," *Economic Journal,* Vol. 100, No. 403 (1990), pp. 1190–1205.

15. Maarteen Smerts, "Main Features of the Uruguay Round Agreement on Textiles and Clothing, and Implications for the Trading System," *Journal of World Trade,* Vol. 29, No. 5 (1995), pp. 97–109.

16. Sanjay Bagchi, "The Integration of the Textile Trade into GATT," *Journal of World Trade,* Vol. 28, No. 6 (1994), pp. 31–42; Rolf Mirus, Barry Scholnick, and Dean Spinanger, "Front-Loading Protection: Canada's Approach to Phasing Out the Multi-Fiber Arrangement," *International Trade Journal,* Vol. 11, No. 4 (1997), pp. 433–51; and Martin Wolf, "How to Cut the Textile Knot: Alternative Paths to Liberalization of the MFA," in Carl B. Hamilton (ed.), *Textiles Trade and the Developing Countries: Eliminating the Multi-Fibre Arrangement in the 1990s* (Washington, D.C.: World Bank, 1990), pp. 215–37.

17. William R. Cline, *Exports of Manufactures from Developing Countries: Performance and Prospects for Market Access* (Washington, D.C.: Brookings Institution, 1984); James M. Lutz and Young Whan Kihl, "The NICs, Shifting Comparative Advantage, and the Product Life Cycle," *Journal of World Trade,* Vol. 24, No. 1 (1990), pp. 113–34; and V. A. Muscatelli, A. A. Stevenson, and C. Montagna, "Intra-NIE Competition in Exports of Manufactures," *Journal of International Economics,* Vol. 37, No. 1/2 (1994), pp. 29–47.

18. *Yearbook of International Trade Statistics,* various years.

19. Faini, de Melo, and Takacs, "A Primer on the MFA Maze."

20. Cristina Corado and Joao Ferreira Gomes, "Adjusting to Trade Liberalisation: The Case of Portugal," in Giorgio Navaretti, Riccardo Faini, and Aubrey Silberston (eds.), *Beyond the Multifibre Arrangement: Third World Competition and Restructuring Europe's Textile Industry* (Paris: Organisation for Economic Co-Operation and Development, 1995), pp. 61–76; Juergen Donges and Klaus-Werner Schatz, "The Iberian Countries in the EEC—Risks and Chances for Their Manufacturing Industries," in George N. Yannopoulos (ed.), *European Integration and the Iberian Economies* (New York: St. Martin's, 1989), pp. 254–306; Armindo da Silva, "The Portuguese Experience of European Integration—A Quantitative Assessment of the Effects of EFTA and EEC Tariff Preferences," in George N. Yannopoulos (ed.), *European Integration and the Iberian Economies* (New York: St. Martin's, 1989), pp. 87–143; and

George N.Yannopoulos, "The Effects of Tariff Preferences in Export Expansion, Export Diversification and Investment Diversification: A Comparative Analysis of the Iberian and Other Mediterranean Economies," in George N. Yannopoulos (ed.), *European Integration and the Iberian Economies* (New York: St. Martin's, 1989), pp. 66–86.

21. Brugnoli and Permini, "The Restrictiveness of the MFA," p. 177.

22. Kumar and Khanna, "India, the Multi-Fibre Arrangement, and the Uruguay Round," and Ganeshan Wignaraja, *Trade Liberalization in Sri Lanka: Exports, Technology and Industrial Policy* (London: Macmillan, 1998).

23. Jose de la Torre, "Public Intervention Strategies in the European Clothing Industries," *Journal of World Trade Law,* Vol. 15, No. 2 (1981), pp. 124–48.

24. Lynn Krieger Mytelka, "The French Textile Industry: Crisis and Adjustment," in Harold K. Jacobson and Dusan Sidjanski (eds.), *The Emerging International Economic Order: Dynamic Processes, Constraints and Opportunities* (Beverly Hills, CA: Sage, 1982), pp. 129–66.

25. Cf. Oli Havrylyshyn, "Yugoslavia," in Demetris Papgeorgiou, Michael Michaely, and Armeane M. Choski (eds.), *Liberalizing Foreign Trade: Volume 3, The Experience of Israel and Yugoslavia* (Oxford: Basil Blackwell, 1991), p. 261.

26. I. M. Destler, *American Trade Politics,* 2nd ed. (Washington, D.C.: Institute for International Economics with the Twentieth Century Fund, 1992), p. 191.

27. Paul A. Brenton and L. Alan Winters, "Voluntary Export Restraints and Rationing: UK Leather Footwear Imports from East Europe," *Journal of International Economics,* Vol. 34, No. 3/4 (1993), pp. 289–308.

28. Given the potential timing of economic downturns, economic problems might not be immediately obvious in terms of GNP per capita figures, or there might have been a lag time before economic problems were apparent in import levels.

29. Cf. Lutz and Kihl, "The NICs, Shifting Comparative Advantage, and the Product Life Cycle."

30. The higher rank in 1982 might have been due to inclusion of some items in the new SITC category that should have been placed elsewhere.

31. Jette Steen Knudsen, "Integrating Western and Eastern European Markets: Changing Trade Preferences in Traditional Manufacturing Sectors in the European Union," *Comparative Political Studies,* Vol. 31, No. 2 (1998), pp. 188–216.

32. Rob Steven, *Japan and the New World Order* (Houndmills, Basingstoke: Macmillan, 1996), p. 197.

33. David B. Yoffie, *Power and Protectionism: Strategies of the Newly Industrializing Countries* (New York: Columbia University Press, 1983), argued years ago that the U.S. efforts were ineffective.

34. Brugnoli and Permini, "The Restrictiveness of the MFA," pp. 177–205.

35. Giorgio Barba Navaretti, "Trade Policy and Foreign Investments: An Analytical Framework," in Giorgio Navaretti, Riccardo Faini, and Aubrey Silber-

ston (eds.), *Beyond the Multifibre Arrangement: Third World Competition and Restructuring Europe's Textile Industry* (Paris: Organisation for Economic Co-Operation and Development, 1995), pp. 121–44.

Chapter 7: Imports and Domestic Production of Selected Manufactured Products

1. The data was contained in United Nations Statistical Office, *Growth of World Industry* (New York: United Nations, various years to 1973), continued by the *Yearbook of Industrial Statistics* (New York: United Nations, various years from 1974–1981), and then continued by the *Industrial Statistics Yearbook* (New York: United Nations, various years).

2. Each country utilized its own definitions as to which factories produced textiles or clothing, with some variation among countries in terms of classifications of these activities or others. In some countries, very small establishments were excluded from the tabulations.

3. World Bank, *World Tables 1976* (Baltimore: Johns Hopkins University Press, 1976), *World Tables 1995* (Baltimore: Johns Hopkins University Press, 1995) and *World Development Reports* (Oxford: Oxford University Press, various years).

4. Again, there were national differences in allocating materials to different sectors, but the general volumes of activity could be compared across nations.

5. The extreme decentralization of the Swiss federal system would seem to have mitigated against the collection of comprehensive national statistics since individual cantons would have had to collect the necessary data.

6. Automotive output would appear to have been a sensitive area for some countries, especially since the missing data include some of the major producers. Such industries have received subsidies and other forms of government support, including protection.

7. The figures for 1960 were based on imports, total GNP, and the percentage of GNP devoted to manufacturing sectors as of 1960. The percentage distribution of production to the categories used varied, based on data for 1958, 1960, or 1961. It was assumed that there had been no major changes between the other years and 1960 when the other years were used. For later years, in a few cases 1969 instead of 1970 or 1987 instead of 1988 was used to calculate the industry percentages in order to increase the number of countries in the data set.

8. The data sources were invariably a number of years behind in terms of publishing the data. Thus, the 1988 yearbook was effectively in print about five years after the fact.

9. Mark Mason, "Elements of Consensus: Europe's Response to the Japanese Auto Challenge," *Journal of Common Market Studies,* Vol. 32, No. 4 (1994), pp. 433–53.

10. The adjusted R^2s are somewhat lower when per capita domestic production is included, since there is one additional variable in the equation.

11. Loukas Tsoukalis and Robert Strauss, "Crisis and Adjustment in European Steel: Beyond Laisser-Faire," *Journal of Common Market Studies*, Vol. 23, No. 3 (1985), pp. 207–28, and Stephen Woolcock, "Iron and Steel," in Susan Strange and Roger Tooze (eds.), *The International Politics of Surplus Capacity* (London: Allen and Unwin, 1981), pp. 69–79.

12. Charles P. Kindleberger, *World Economic Primacy: 1500 to 1990* (New York: Oxford University Press, 1996), p. 197.

13. Stephen Woolcock, "Iron and Steel," in Louis Turner and Neil McMullen (eds.), *The Newly Industrializing Countries: Trade and Adjustment* (London: Allen and Unwin, 1982), pp. 94–117.

14. Stephen Woolcock, "The International Politics of Trade and Protection in the Steel Industry," in John Pinder (ed.), *National Industrial Strategies and the World Economy* (Totowa, NJ: Allanheld Osmun, 1982), pp. 53–84.

15. Kent Albert Jones, *Politics versus Economics in World Steel Trade* (Winchester, MA: Allen and Unwin, 1986), and Jonathan Haughton and Balu Swaminathan, "The Employment and Welfare Effects of Quantitative Restrictions on Steel Imports into the United States," *Journal of World Trade*, Vol. 26, No. 2 (1992), pp. 95–118.

16. Rather than indicating the presence of intra-industry activity, the figures for 1970 could also have indicated that Japan was undergoing a transition during which it was still importing some steel products as the domestic sector was getting started. It was probably more likely in 1970, however, that Japanese steel production included only some types of steel and that local industries had not yet moved to the point of manufacturing the full spectrum of steel products, thus necessitating continued imports of some items.

17. Neil McMullen and Laura L. Megna, "Automobiles," in Louis Turner and Neil McMullen (eds.), *The Newly Industrializing Countries: Trade and Adjustment* (London: George Allen and Unwin, 1982), pp. 69–93, and James P. Womack and Daniel T. Jones, "European Automotive Policy: Past, Present, and Future," in Glennon J. Harrison (ed.), *Europe and the United States: Competition and Cooperation in the 1990s,* A Study Submitted to the Subcommittee on International Economic Policy and Trade and the Subcommittee on Europe and the Middle East of the Committee on Foreign Affairs, U.S. House of Representatives (Armonk, NY: M. E. Sharpe, 1994), pp. 193–213.

18. Cf. James M. Lutz, "Determinants of Protectionist Attitudes in the U.S. House of Representatives," *International Trade Journal,* Vol. 5, No. 3 (1991), pp. 301–28, and Deborah L. Swenson, "Explaining Domestic Content: Evidence from Japanese and U.S. Automobile Production in the United States," in Robert C. Feenstra (ed.), *The Effects of U.S. Trade Protection and Promotion Policies* (Chicago: University of Chicago Press, 1997), pp. 33–53.

19. James Levinsohn, "Carwars: Trying to Make Sense of U.S.-Japan Trade Frictions in the Automobile and Automobile Parts Markets," in Robert C. Feenstra (ed.), *The Effects of U.S. Trade Protection and Promotion Policies* (Chicago: University of Chicago Press, 1997), pp. 11–32.

20. Pietro Nivola, *Regulating Unfair Trade* (Washington, D.C.: Brookings Institution, 1993), p. 30.

21. Mason, "Elements of Consensus."

22. Mason, "Elements of Consensus."

23. Susan Strange, "The Management of Surplus Capacity: Or How Does Theory Stand Up to Protectionism 1970s Style?" *International Organization*, Vol. 33, No. 3 (1979), pp. 303–34.

Chapter 8: Import Levels of the Developing Countries

1. Ernest H. Preeg, *From Here to Free Trade: Essays in Post–Uruguay Round Trade Strategy* (Washington, D.C., and Chicago: Center of Strategic and International Studies and University of Chicago Press, 1998), p. 115.

2. Eliezer B. Ayal and Georgios Karras, "Components of Economic Freedom and Growth: An Empirical Study," *Journal of Developing Areas,* Vol. 32, No. 3 (1998), pp. 327–38; Sebastian Edwards, "Openness, Productivity and Growth: What Do We Really Know?" *Economic Journal,* Vol. 108, No. 447 (1998), pp. 383–98, and "Trade Orientation, Distortions, and Growth in Developing Countries," *Journal of Development Economics,* Vol. 39, No. 1 (1992), pp. 31–58; Jeffrey A. Frankel and David Romer, "Does Trade Cause Growth," *American Economic Review,* Vol. 89, No. 3 (1999), pp. 379–99; David Greenaway, Wyn Morgan, and Peter Wright, "Trade Reform, Adjustment and Growth: What Does the Evidence Tell Us," *Economic Journal,* Vol. 108, No. 450 (1998), pp. 1547–61; Ioannis N. Kessides, "Formal Testing of Hypotheses," in Michael Michaely, Demetris Papageorgiou, and Armeane M. Choski, *Liberalizing Foreign Trade: Volume 7, Lessons of Experience in the Developing World* (Cambridge, MA: Basil Blackwell, 1991), p. 306; Anne O. Krueger, "Why Trade Liberalisation Is Good for Growth," *Economic Journal,* Vol. 108, No. 450 (1998), pp. 1513–22; Gerald M. Meier, "Trade Policy, Development, and the New Political Economy," in Ronald W. Jones and Anne O. Krueger (eds.), *The Political Economy of International Trade: Essays in Honor of Robert E. Baldwin* (Cambridge, MA: Basil Blackwell, 1990), pp. 179–96; Michael Michaely, Demetris Papageorgiou, and Armeane M. Choski, *Liberalizing Foreign Trade: Volume 7, Lessons of Experience in the Developing World* (Cambridge, MA: Basil Blackwell, 1991); Diego Puga and Anthony J. Venables, "Agglomeration and Economic Development: Import Substitution vs. Trade Liberalisation," *Economic Journal,* Vol. 109, No. 455 (1999), pp. 292–311; and Joseph E. Stiglitz and Lyn Squire,

"International Development: Is It Possible?" *Foreign Policy,* No. 110 (1998), pp. 138–51.

3. Anita Doraisami, "Export Growth and Economic Growth: A Reexamination of Some Time-Series Evidence of the Malaysian Experience," *Journal of Developing Areas,* Vol. 30, No. 2 (1996), pp. 223–30.

4. Subrata Ghatak and Uktu Utkulu, "Trade Liberalisation and Economic Development: The Asian Experience—Turkey, Malaysia and India," in V. N. Balasubramanyam and D. Greenaway (ed.), *Trade and Development: Essays in Honour of Jagdish Bhagwati* (London: Macmillan, 1996), pp. 81–116; Michaely, Papageorgiou, and Choski, *Liberalizing Foreign Trade;* and Mauricio Mesquita Moreira and Paulo Guilherme Correa, "A First Look at the Impacts of Trade Liberalization on Brazilian Manufacturing Industry," *World Development,* Vol. 26, No. 10 (1998), pp. 1859–74.

5. Xin Xie, "Contagion through Interactive Production and Dynamic Effects of Trade," *International Economic Review,* Vol. 40, No. 1 (1999), pp. 165–86.

6. Enrico Colombatto, "An Analysis of Exports and Growth in the LDCs," *Kyklos,* Vol. 43, No. 4 (1990): 579–97; Bruce E. Moon, "Exports, Outward-Oriented Development and Economic Growth," *Political Research Quarterly,* Vol. 61, No. 1 (1998), pp. 7–36; and Abhijit Sen, "On Economic Openness and Industrialization," in Deepak Nayyar (ed.), *Trade and Industrialization* (Delhi: Oxford University Press, 1997), pp. 88–168. Paul Krugman, "Cycles of Conventional Wisdom on Economic Development," *International Affairs* (London), Vol. 71, No. 4 (1995), pp. 717–32, argues that conventional wisdom on the value of free trade and privatization is unlikely to be very relevant given that Japan and South Korea, for example, grew with restricted trade and a great deal of government involvement.

7. Barry Bosworth, Susan M. Collins, and Yu-chin Chen, "Accounting for Differences in Economic Growth," *Brookings Discussion Papers in International Economics,* No. 115 (1995), and Krugman, "Cycles of Conventional Wisdom."

8. Santo Dodaro, "Comparative Advantage, Trade and Growth: Export-Led Growth Revisited," *World Development,* Vol. 19, No. 9 (1991), pp. 1153–65.

9. Sebastian Edwards, "Trade Policy, Growth, and Income Distribution," *American Economic Review,* Vol. 87, No. 2 (1997), pp. 205–10; Vincent Mahler, David K. Jesuit, and Douglas D. Roscoe, "Explaining the Impact of Trade and Investment on Income Inequality," *Comparative Political Studies,* Vol. 32, No. 3 (1999), pp. 363–95, and Stiglitz and Squire, "International Development," p. 104.

10. Michaely, Papageorgiou, and Choski, *Liberalizing Foreign Trade,* p. 112.

11. Cf. Manuel Castells and Laura D'Andrea Tyson, "High Technology and the Changing International Division of Production: Implications for the U.S. Economy," in Randall B. Purcell (ed.), *The Newly Industrializing Countries in the World Economy: Challenges for U.S. Policy* (Boulder, CO: Lynne Rienner, 1989), p. 21.

12. Cf. Folker Frobel, Jurgen Heinrichs, and Otto Kreye, *The New International Division of Labour: Structural Unemployment in Industrialised Countries and Industrialisation in Developing Countries,* trans. Pete Burgess (Cambridge: Cambridge University Press, 1980), and Johan Galtung, "A Structural Theory of Imperialism," *Journal of Peace Research,* Vol. 8, No. 2 (1971), pp. 81–118.

13. Michaely, Papageorgiou, and Choski, *Liberalizing Foreign Trade,* p. 101.

14. Jose Antonio Ocampo and Lance Taylor, "Trade Liberalisation in Developing Economies: Modest Benefits but Problems with Productivity Growth, Macro Prices, and Income Distribution," *Economic Journal,* Vol. 108, No. 450 (1998), pp. 1523–46.

15. David Kaplan and Raphael Kaplinsky, "Trade and Industrial Policy on an Uneven Playing Field: The Case of the Deciduous Fruit Canning Industry in South Africa," *World Development,* Vol. 27, No. 10 (1999), pp. 1787–801, and Stephen Redding, "Dynamic Comparative Advantage and the Welfare Effects of Trade," *Oxford Economic Papers,* Vol. 51, No. 1 (1999), pp. 15–39.

16. Barkey, Henri J., "State Autonomy and the Crisis of Import Substitution," *Comparative Political Studies,* Vol. 22, No. 3 (1989), 291–314; Jorge Garcia Garcia, "Colombia," in Demetris Papageorgiou, Michael Michaely, and Armeane M. Choski (eds.), *Liberalizing Foreign Trade: Volume 4, The Experience of Brazil, Colombia, and Peru* (London: Basil Blackwell, 1991), p. 257; Anne O. Krueger, "Asymmetries in Policy between Exportables and Import-Competing Goods," in Ronald W. Jones and Anne O. Krueger (eds.), *The Political Economy of International Trade: Essays in Honor of Robert E. Baldwin* (Cambridge, MA: Basil Blackwell, 1990); Hector E. Schamis, "Distributional Coalitions and the Politics of Economic Reform in Latin America," *World Politics,* Vol. 51, No. 2 (1999), pp. 236–68; and Norma A. Tan, "The Structure of and Causes of Manufacturing Sector Protection in the Philippines," in Christopher Findlay and Ross Garnaut (eds.), *The Political Economy of Manufacturing Protection: Experiences of ASEAN and Australia* (Sydney: Allen and Unwin, 1986), pp. 48–76.

17. Dominick Salvatore, "International Trade Politics, Industrialization, and Economic Development," in Khosrow Fatemi (ed.), *International Trade in the 21st Century* (Kidlington, Oxford: Pergamon, 1997), pp. 249–68.

18. John Waterbury, "The Long Gestation and Brief Triumph of Import Substituting Industrialization," *World Development,* Vol. 27, No. 2 (1999), pp. 323–41.

19. Donald V. Coes, "Brazil," in Demetris Papageorgiou, Michael Michaely, and Armeane M. Choski (eds.), *Liberalizing Foreign Trade: Volume 4, The Experience of Brazil, Colombia, and Peru* (London: Basil Blackwell, 1991), p. 40, and Sergio de la Cuerda and Dominique Hachette, "Chile," in Demetris Papageorgiou, Michael Michaely, and Armeane M. Choski (eds.), *Liberalizing Foreign Trade: Volume 1, The Experience of Argentina, Chile, and Uruguay* (London: Basil Blackwell, 1991), p. 181.

20. Stiglitz and Squire, "International Development," p. 144, and Vinod Thomas and Yan Wang, "Distortions, Interventions, and Productivity Growth: Is East Asia Different?" *Economic Development and Cultural Change*, Vol. 44, No. 2 (1996), pp. 265–88.

21. Jagdish Bhagwati, *India in Transition: Freeing the Economy* (Oxford: Clarendon Press, 1993); David B. H. Denoon, "Cycles in Indian Economic Liberalization, 1966–1996," *Comparative Politics*, Vol. 31, No. 1 (1998), pp. 43–60; Ashok V. Desai, "The Politics of India's Trade Policy," in Henry R. Nau (ed.), *Domestic Trade Policy and the Uruguay Round* (New York: Columbia University Press, 1989), pp. 91–110; and Rajiv Kumar, "The Walk Away from Leadership: India," in Diana Tussie and David Glover (eds.), *The Developing Countries in World Trade: Policies and Bargaining Strategies* (Boulder, CO: Lynne Reinner, 1993), pp. 155–69.

22. Forrest H. Capie, *Tariffs and Growth: Some Illustrations from the World Economy, 1850–1940* (Manchester: Manchester University Press, 1994), p. 3. Paul Kennedy, *The Rise and Fall of Great Powers: Economic Change and Military Conflict from 1500 to 2000* (New York: Random House, 1987), pp. 222–23) provides a historical example of such negative effects when he argues that the high protection utilized in France in the late nineteenth century limited the ability of the French economy to keep up with economic advances made by the other Great Powers, especially Germany.

23. Bee-Yan Aw, "Singapore," in Demetris Papageorgiou, Michael Michaely, and Armeane M. Choski (eds.), *Liberalizing Foreign Trade: Volume 2, The Experience of Korea, the Philippines and Singapore* (London: Basil Blackwell, 1991), pp. 403–404; Tain-Jy Chen and Chi-ming Hou, "The Political Economy of Trade Protection in the Republic of China on Taiwan," in Takatoshi Ito and Anne O. Krueger (eds.), *Trade and Protectionism*, National Bureau of Economic Research—East Asia Seminar on Economics, Vol. 2 (Chicago: University of Chicago Press, 1993), pp. 339–55; Bruce Cumings, "The Origins and Development of the Northeast Asian Political Economy: Industrial Sectors, Product Cycles, and Political Consequences," *International Organization*, Vol. 38, No. 1 (1984), pp. 25–26; Richard R. Nelson and Howard Pack, "The Asian Miracle and Modern Growth Theory," *Economic Journal*, Vol. 109, No. 457 (1999), pp. 416–36; and Robert Wade, "Managing Trade: Taiwan and South Korea as Challengers to Economics and Political Science," *Comparative Politics*, Vol. 25, No. 2 (1993), pp. 147–67.

24. Wan-Wen Chu, "Import Substitution and Export-Led Growth: A Study of Taiwan's Petrochemical Industry," *World Development*, Vol. 22, No. 5 (1994), pp. 781–94; David Lim, "Explaining the Growth Performances of Asian Developing Economies," *Economic Development and Cultural Change*, Vol. 42, No. 4 (1994), pp. 829–44; and Stiglitz and Squire, "International Development," p. 147.

25. Aw, "Singapore," p. 317.

26. Taiwan has technically been considered a province of the People's Republic of China by the UN since China was admitted to the UN; consequently, no separate and comparable data are available for Taiwan from UN sources.

27. "New Zealand's Advantage," *Economist,* Vol. 352, No. 8137 (September 18, 1999), p. 47.

28. Regression equations were undertaken using the square root of GNP per capita on the assumption that states with lower wealth figures would have understated wealth levels due to the greater amount of subsistence activity present. Equations with the modified wealth variable had either equal or lower explanatory values; hence, the unmodified values were used.

29. Given the range of population sizes, the square root of population was also used as an alternative independent variable. The explanatory value of the equations was either the same or less with this variable, so the unmodified population was retained, as was the case with GNP per capita figures.

30. Victor Bulmer-Thomas, "The Central American Common Market: From Closed to Open Regionalism," *World Development,* Vol. 26, No. 2 (1998), pp. 313–22; Shelton A. Nicholls, "Measuring Trade Creation and Trade Diversion in the Central American Common Market: A Hicksian Alternative," *World Development,* Vol. 26, No. 2 (1998), pp. 323–35; and Ennio Rodriquez, "The Multiple Tracks of a Small Open Economy," in Diana Tussie and David Glover (eds.), *The Developing Countries in World Trade: Policies and Bargaining Strategies* (Boulder, CO: Lynne Rienner, 1993), pp. 99–117.

31. Mark M. Pitt, "Indonesia," in Demetris Papageorgiou, Michael Michaely, and Armeane M. Choski (eds.), *Liberalizing Foreign Trade: Volume 5, The Experience of Indonesia, Pakistan, and Sri Lanka* (London: Basil Blackwell, 1991), p. 186.

32. Michael T. Rock, "Reassessing the Effectiveness of Industrial Policy in Indonesia: Can the Neoliberals Be Wrong?" *World Development,* Vol. 27, No. 4 (1999), pp. 691–704.

33. Judith M. Dean, Seema Desai, and James Riedel, *Trade Policy Reform in Developing Countries since 1985: A Review of the Evidence,* World Bank Discussion Paper 267 (Washington, D.C.: World Bank, 1994).

34. Stephen Guisinger and Gerald Scully, "Pakistan," in Demetris Papageorgiou, Michael Michaely, and Armeane M. Choski (eds.), *Liberalizing Foreign Trade: Volume 5, The Experience of Indonesia, Pakistan, and Sri Lanka* (London: Basil Blackwell, 1991), p. 205.

35. Andrew G. Cuthbertson and Premachandra Athukorala, "Sri Lanka," in Demetris Papageorgiou, Michael Michaely, and Armeane M. Choski (eds.), *Liberalizing Foreign Trade: Volume 5, The Experience of Indonesia, Pakistan, and Sri Lanka* (London: Basil Blackwell, 1991), p. 327.

36. Cuthbertson and Athukorala, "Sri Lanka," p. 302.

37. Deepak Lal and Sarath Rajapatirana, *Impediments to Trade Liberalization in Sri Lanka,* Thames Essay No. 51 (Gower: Aldershot, 1989), N. M. C. Navaratne, "Who Bears the Incidence of Import Protection? Evidence from Sri Lanka,"

World Development, Vol. 9, No. 10 (1991), pp. 1409–19; and S. Rajapatirana, "Foreign Trade and Economic Development: Sri Lanka's Experience," *World Development,* Vol. 16, No. 10 (1988), pp. 1143–57.

38. Richard C. Kearney, "Mauritius and the NIC Model Redux: Or, How Many Cases Make a Model?" *Journal of Developing Areas,* Vol. 24, No. 2 (1990), pp. 195–216.

39. Cf. Dean, Desai, and Riedel, *Trade Policy Reform.*

40. Lodewijk Berlage and Sophie Vandermeulen, "Have Imports Constrained Economic Growth in Sub-Saharan Africa," in P. K. M. Tharakan and D. Ven Den Bulcke (eds.), *International Trade, Foreign Direct Investment, and the Economic Environment: Essays in Honour of Professor Sylvain Passchaert* (Houndmills, Basingstoke: Macmillan, 1998), pp. 11–29.

41. Chris Milner, "Trade Regime Bias and the Response to Trade Liberalisation in Sub-Saharan Africa," *Kyklos,* Vol. 51, No. 2 (1998), pp. 219–36.

42. Tercan Baysan and Charles Blitzer, "Turkey," in Demetris Papageorgiou, Michael Michaely, and Armeane M. Choski (eds.), *Liberalizing Foreign Trade: Volume 6, The Experience of New Zealand, Spain, and Turkey* (London: Basil Blackwell, 1991), p. 289.

43. Andrew Elek, Hal Hill, and Steven R. Tabor, "Liberalization and Diversification in a Small Island Economy: Fiji since the 1987 Coups," *World Development,* Vol. 21, No. 5 (1993), pp. 749–69.

44. T. Ademola Oyejide, *Tariff Policy and Industrialization in Nigeria* (Ibadan: Ibadan University Press, 1975), p. 74.

45. Kwang Suk Kim, "Korea," in Demetris Papageorgiou, Michael Michaely, and Armeane M. Choski (eds.), *Liberalizing Foreign Trade: Volume 2, The Experience of Korea, the Philippines and Singapore* (London: Basil Blackwell, 1991), pp. 11, 44.

46. Richard Grabowski, "Import Substitution, Export Promotion and the State in Economic Development," *Journal of Developing Areas,* Vol. 28, No. 4 (1994), pp. 535–54.

47. Narongchai Akrasanee and Juanjai Ajanant, "Manufacturing Industry Protection in Thailand: Issues and Empirical Studies," in Christopher Findlay and Ross Garnaut (eds.), *Protection: Experiences of ASEAN and Australia* (Sydney: Allen and Unwin, 1986), pp. 77–98; Supote Chunanuntathum, Somsak Tambunlertchai, and Atchana Wattananukit, "Thailand," in Sheila Page, *Trade, Finance and Developing Countries: Strategies and Constraints in the 1990s* (New York: Harvester, 1990), pp. 56–90; and Geoffrey Shepherd and Florian Alburo, "The Philippines," in Demetris Papageorgiou, Michael Michaely, and Armeane M. Choski (eds.), *Liberalizing Foreign Trade: Volume 2, The Experience of Korea, the Philippines and Singapore* (London: Basil Blackwell, 1991), pp. 133–308.

48. Helen Hughes, "Has There Been a Miracle in the Developing Economies of East Asia," in Lauge Stetting, Knud Erik Svendsen, and Ebbe Yndgaard (eds.),

Global Change and Transformation: Economic Essays in Honor of Karsten Laursen, Copenhagen Studies in Economics and Management 1 (Copenhagen: Handelshojskolens Forlag, 1993), pp. 143–63.

49. Domingo Cavallo and Joaquin Cottani, "Argentina," in Demetris Papageorgiou, Michael Michaely, and Armeane M. Choski (eds.), *Liberalizing Foreign Trade: Volume 1, The Experience of Argentina, Chile, and Uruguay* (London: Basil Blackwell, 1991), p. 134; Edgardo Favaro and Pablo T. Spiller, "Uruguay," in Demetris Papageorgiou, Michael Michaely, and Armeane M. Choski (eds.), *Liberalizing Foreign Trade: Volume 1, The Experience of Argentina, Chile, and Uruguay* (London: Basil Blackwell, 1991), p. 330; and Michaely, Papageorgiou, and Choski, *Liberalizing Foreign Trade,* p. 39.

50. Cavallo and Cottani, "Argentina," p. 72.

51. Coes, "Brazil."

52. Regis Bonelli, "Growth and Productivity in Brazilian Industries: Impacts of Trade Orientation," *Journal of Development Economics,* Vol. 39, No. 1 (1992), pp. 85–109, and Moreira and Correa, "A First Look at the Impacts of Trade Liberalization."

53. Michaely, Papageorgiou, and Choski, *Liberalizing Foreign Trade,* p. 39.

54. Garcia, "Colombia," p. 171.

55. Cuthbertson and Athukorala, "Sri Lanka," p. 333.

56. Ganeshan Wignaraja, *Trade Liberalization in Sri Lanka: Exports, Technology and Industrial Policy* (London: Macmillan, 1998).

57. Saman Kelegama and Fritz Foley, "Impediments to Promoting Backward Linkages from the Garment Industry in Sri Lanka," *World Development,* Vol. 27, No. 8 (1999), pp. 1445–60.

58. Kelegama and Foley, "Impediments to Promoting Backward Linkages."

59. Cf., for example, Cavallo and Cottani, "Argentina."

60. Denoon, "Cycles in Indian Economic Liberalization." Sanjaya Lall, "India's Manufactured Exports: Comparative Structure and Prospects," *World Development,* Vol. 27, No. 10 (1999), pp. 1769–86, argues that more than liberalization would be necessary for effective growth. India may in fact be suffering from the persistent effects of past protectionist policies.

61. Vittorio Corbo, "Trade Reform and Uniform Import Tariffs: The Chilean Experience," *American Economic Review,* Vol. 87, No. 2 (1997), pp. 73–77; de la Cuarda and Hachette, "Chile"; Eva A. Paus, "Economic Growth through Neo-Liberal Restructuring? Insights from the Chilean Experience," *Journal of Developing Areas,* Vol. 29, No. 1 (1994), pp. 31–55; and Eduardo Silva, "Capitalist Coalitions, the State, and Neoliberal Economic Restructuring: Chile, 1973–88," *World Politics,* Vol. 45, No. 4 (1993), pp. 526–59.

62. Barkey, "State Autonomy," and Baysan and Blitzer, "Turkey."

63. Baysan and Blitzer, "Turkey," p. 391; Anne O. Krueger and Okan H. Aktan, *Swimming against the Tide: Turkish Trade Reform in the 1980s* (San Francisco: Institute for Contemporary Studies Press, 1992); James Levinsohn, "Testing the

Imports-as-Market-Discipline Hypothesis," *Journal of International Economics,* Vol. 35, No. 1/2 (1993), pp. 1–22; and Nurhan Yenturk-Coban, "Industrialization Strategies, Foreign Trade Regimes and Structural Change in Turkey 1980–8," in Jean-Marc Fontaine (ed.), *Foreign Trade Reforms and Development Strategy* (London: Routledge, 1992), pp. 274–89.

64. John Weiss, "Trade Policy Reform and Performance in Manufacturing: Mexico 1975–88," *Journal of Development Studies,* Vol. 29, No. 1 (1992), pp. 1–23.

65. Sanjaya Lall, "Imperfect Markets and Fallible Governments: The Role of the State in Industrial Development," in Deepak Nayyar (ed.), *Trade and Industrialization* (Dehli: Oxford University Press, 1997), pp. 43–87.

66. Sen, "On Economic Openness and Industrialization."

67. Dani Rodrik, "Conceptual Issues in the Design of Trade Policy for Industrialization," *World Development,* Vol. 20, No. 3 (1992), pp. 309–20.

68. Dodaro, "Comparative Advantage, Trade and Growth."

Chapter 9: Conclusions

1. Daniel Gros, "A Note on the Optimal Tariff Retaliation and the Welfare Loss from Tariff Wars in a Framework with Intra-Industry Trade," *Journal of International Economics,* Vol. 23, No. 3/4 (1987), pp. 356–67; Paul Krugman, "Market Access and Competition in High Technology Industries: A Simulation Exercise," in Henry Kierskowski (ed.), *Protection and Competition in International Trade: Essays in Honor of W. M. Corden* (Oxford: Basil Blackwell, 1987), pp. 128–42; Kelvin Lancaster, "The 'Product Variety' Case for Protection," *Journal of International Economics,* Vol. 31, No. 1/2 (1991), pp. 1–26; and Ramana Polavarapu and Ashish Vaidya, "Optimal Trade Policy with Quality-Differentiated Goods," *International Trade Journal,* Vol. 10, No. 3 (1996), pp. 379–406.

2. It is perhaps appropriate that *dirigiste* and *dirigisme,* terms that refer to government attempts at economic management (or strategic trade policy), have been borrowed from the French into English.

3. Vivien A. Schmidt, *From State to Market? The Transformation of French Business and Government* (Cambridge: Cambridge University Press, 1996), p. 442.

4. Michael Gallagher, Michael Laver, and Peter Mair, *Representative Government in Modern Europe,* 2nd ed. (New York: McGraw-Hill, 1995), p. 361, and Jurg Steiner, *European Democracies,* 3rd ed. (White Plains, NY: Longman, 1995), p. 156.

5. Flanders, of course, has historically been one of the areas of Europe to benefit from trade. Early periodic fairs were held in the area, Flemish artisans were in demand throughout Europe, and trade flowed through the area.

6. Recall the lack of data availability for industrial activity for Switzerland at the national level in chapter 7.

7. Kozo Yamamura, "The Deliberate Emergence of a Free Trader: The Japanese Political Economy in Transition," in Craig Garby and Mary Brown Bullock (eds.), *Japan: A New Kind of Superpower* (Washington, D.C.: Woodrow Wilson Center Press, 1994), pp. 32–52.

8. Robert Scollay, "Australia–New Zealand Closer Economic Relations Agreement," in Bijit Bora and Christopher Findlay (eds.) *Regional Integration and the Asia Pacific* (Melbourne: Oxford University Press, 1996, pp. 184–96).

9. The effects of NAFTA on Mexico and Canada, of course, will be larger because they are smaller economies in comparison to that of the United States.

10. Peter Svensson, "Strategic Trade Policy and Endogenous R&D-Subsidies: An Empirical Study," *Kyklos*, Vol. 51, No. 2 (1998), pp. 259–75.

11. Robert H. Bates, Philip Brock, and Jill Tiefenthaler, "Risk and Trade Regimes: Another Exploration," *International Organization*, Vol. 45, No. 1 (1991), and Dani Rodrik, "Why Do More Open Economies have Bigger Governments," *Journal of Political Economy*, Vol. 106, No. 5 (1998), pp. 997–1032.

12. Alex Mourmouras, "Infant Governments and the Fiscal Role of Tariffs, Inflation, and Reserve Requirements: A Welfare Analysis," *Journal of International Economics*, Vol. 31, No. 3/4 (1991), pp. 271–90.

13. Bates et al., "Risk and Trade Regimes."

14. James M. Lutz, "Japanese Imports of Manufactures from East Asia: Is the Glass Half Empty or Half Full?" *International Trade Journal*, Vol. 7, No. 2 (1992), pp. 151–79. For future analyses of trade patterns, it would probably be justified to include Singapore with the industrialized countries.

15. Bernard M Hoekman and Michel M. Kostecki, *The Political Economy of the World Trading System: From GATT to WTO* (Oxford: Oxford University Press, 1995), p. 11.

16. Leonard J. Schoppa, *Bargaining with Japan: What American Pressure Can and Cannot Do* (New York: Columbia University Press, 1997), pp. 315–16.

17. Hoekman and Kostecki, *The Political Economy of the World Trading System*, p. 3, and James M. Lutz, "GATT Reform or Regime Maintenance: Differing Solutions to World Trade Problems," *Journal of World Trade*, Vol. 25, No. 2 (1991), pp. 107–22.

18. Brian McDonald, *The World Trading System: The Uruguay Round and Beyond* (New York: St. Martin's, 1998), p. 31, and Enrico Sassoon, "Objectives and Results of the Uruguay Round," in Riccardo Faini and Enzo Grilli (eds.), *Multilateralism and Regionalism after the Uruguay Round* (Houndmills, Basingstoke: Macmillan, 1997), pp. 1–51.

19. Hoekman and Kostecki, *The Political Economy of the World Trading System*, pp. 183–84.

20. Hoekman and Kostecki, *The Political Economy of the World Trading System*, p. 271.

21. McDonald, *The World Trading System*, p. 93.

22. Robert E. Baldwin, "Imposing Multilateral Discipline on Administered Protection," in Anne O. Krueger with Chonira Aturupane (ed.), *The WTO as an International Organization* (Chicago: University of Chicago Press, 1998), pp. 297–327. Such collusion might even explain why countervailing duties have not prevent the continuing use of subsidies. Cf. Larry D. Qui, "Why Can't Countervailing Duties Deter Export Subsidization?" *Journal of International Economics,* Vol. 39, No. 3/4 (1995), pp. 249–72, for a discussion of the failure of such measures.

23. Terry Collins-Williams and Gerry Salembier, "International Disciplines on Subsidies: The GATT, the WTO and the Future Agenda," *Journal of World Trade,* Vol. 30, No. 1 (1996), pp. 5–17.

24. Baldwin, "Imposing Multilateral Discipline"; McDonald, *The World Trading System,* p. 31; and David Palmeter, "A Commentary on the WTO Anti-Dumping Code," *Journal of World Trade,* Vol. 30, No. 4 (1996), pp. 43–70.

Bibliography

Aharoni, Yair, and Seev Hirsch, "Enhancing Competitive Advantage in Technology-Intensive Industries," in John H. Dunning and Khalil A. Hamdani (eds.), *The New Globalism and Developing Countries* (Tokyo: United Nations University Press, 1997), pp. 260–302.

Akrasanee, Narongchai, and Juanjai Ajanant, "Manufacturing Industry Protection in Thailand: Issues and Empirical Studies," in Christopher Findlay and Ross Garnaut (eds.), *The Political Economy of Manufacturing Protection: Experiences of ASEAN and Australia* (Sydney: Allen and Unwin, 1986), pp. 77–98.

Anchordoguy, Marie, "The Public Corporation: A Potent Japanese Policy Weapon," *Political Science Quarterly*, Vol. 103, No. 4 (1988–89), pp. 709–24.

———, "Japanese-American Trade Conflict and Supercomputers," *Political Science Quarterly*, Vol. 109, No. 1 (1994), pp. 35–80.

Anderson, Keith, "Antidumping Laws in the United States: Use and Welfare Consequences," *Journal of World Trade*, Vol. 27, No. 2 (1993), pp. 99–117.

Anderson, Kym, "Australia's Changing Trade Pattern and Growth Performance," in Richard Pomfret (ed.), *Australia's Trade Policies* (Melbourne: Oxford University Press, 1995), pp. 29–52.

———, "Europe 1992 and the Western Pacific Economies," *Economic Journal*, Vol. 101, No. 409 (1991), pp. 1538–52.

Anderson, Kym and Ross Garnaut, "The Political Economy of Manufacturing Protection in Australia," in Christopher Findlay and Ross Garnaut (eds.), *The Political Economy of Manufacturing Protection: Experiences of ASEAN and Australia* (Sydney: Allen and Unwin, 1986), pp. 159–83.

Anderson, Kym, and Hege Norheim, "History, Geography and Regional Economic Integration," in Kym Anderson and Richard Blackhurst (eds.), *Regional Integration and the Global Trading System* (New York: St. Martin's, 1993), pp. 19–51.

Anell, Lars, and Birgitta Nygren, *The Developing Countries and the World Economic Order* (London: Francis Pinter, 1982).

Aw, Bee-Yan, "Singapore," in Demetris Papageorgiou, Michael Michaely, and Armeane M. Choksi (eds.), *Liberalizing Foreign Trade: Volume 2, The Experience of Korea, the Philippines, and Singapore* (Oxford: Basil Blackwell, 1991), pp. 309–428.

Awuku, Emmanuel Opoku, "How Do the Results of the Uruguay Round Affect the North-South Trade," *Journal of World Trade,* Vol. 28, No. 2 (1994), pp. 75–93.

Ayal, Eliezer B., and Georgios Karras, "Components of Economic Freedom and Growth: An Empirical Study," *Journal of Developing Areas,* Vol. 32, No. 3 (1998), pp. 327–38.

Bagchi, Sanjay, "The Integration of the Textile Trade into GATT," *Journal of World Trade,* Vol. 28, No. 6 (1994), pp. 31–42.

Bailey, Michael, and David W. Brady, "Heterogeneity and Representation: The Senate and Free Trade," *American Journal of Political Science,* Vol. 42, No. 2 (1998), pp. 524–44.

Balassa, Bela, "Industrial Prospects and Policies in the Developed Countries," in Fritz Machlup, Gerhard Fels, and Huburtus Muller-Groeling (eds.), *Reflections on a Troubled World Economy: Essays in Honor of Herbert Giersch* (New York: St. Martin's, 1983), pp. 257–78.

———, "Intra-Industry Trade among Exporters of Manufactured Goods," in David Greenaway and P. K. M. Tharakan (eds.), *Imperfect Competition and International Trade: The Policy Aspects of Intra-Industry Trade* (Sussex: Wheatsheaf, 1986), pp. 108–28.

Balassa, Bela, and Marcus Noland, *Japan in the World Economy* (Washington, D.C.: Institute for International Economics, 1988).

———, "Prospects of Trade and Regional Cooperation of the Industrialized Economies of East Asia," in Shu-Chin Yang (ed.), *Manufactured Exports of East Asian Industrializing Economies: Possible Regional Cooperation* (Armonk, NY: M. E. Sharpe, 1994), pp. 237–60.

Baldwin, Richard E., and Paul R. Krugman, "Market Access and International Competition: A Simulation Study of 16K Random Access Memories," in Robert C. Feenstra (ed.), *Empirical Methods for International Trade* (Cambridge, MA: MIT Press, 1988), pp. 171–97.

Baldwin, Robert E., "Imposing Multilateral Discipline on Administered Protection," in Anne O. Krueger with Chonira Aturupane (ed.), *The WTO as an International Organization* (Chicago: University of Chicago Press, 1998), pp. 297–327.

Barkey, Henri J., "State Autonomy and the Crisis of Import Substitution," *Comparative Political Studies,* Vol. 22, No. 3 (1989), pp. 291–314.

Bates, Robert H., Philip Brock, and Jill Tiefenthaler, "Risk and Trade Regimes: Another Exploration," *International Organization,* Vol. 45, No. 1 (1991), pp. 1–18.

Baumgartner, T., and T. R. Burns, "The Structuring of International Economic Relations," *International Studies Quarterly,* Vol. 19, No. 2 (1975), pp. 126–59.

Baumol, William J., and Ralph E. Gomory, "Inefficient and Locally Stable Trade Equilibria under Scale Economies: Comparative Advantage Revisited," *Kyklos,* Vol. 49, No. 4 (1996): 509–40.

Baysan, Tercan, and Charles Blitzer, "Turkey," in Demetris Papageorgiou, Michael Michaely, and Armeane M. Choksi (eds.), *Liberalizing Foreign Trade: Volume 6, The*

Experience of New Zealand, Spain, and Turkey (Oxford: Basil Blackwell, 1991), pp. 263–405.

Behoodi, Rambod, *Industrial Subsidies and Friction in World Trade: Trade Policy or Trade Politics* (London: Routledge, 1994).

Bell, Stephen, "Globalisation, Neoliberalism and the Transformation of the Australian State," *Australian Journal of Political Science,* Vol. 32, No. 3 (1997), pp. 345–67.

Bergsten, C. Fred, "Globalizing Free Trade," *Foreign Affairs,* Vol. 75, No. 3 (1996), pp. 105–20.

Berlage, Lodewijk, and Sophie Vandermeulen, "Have Imports Constrained Economic Growth in Sub-Saharan Africa," in P. K. M. Tharakan and D. Ven Den Bulcke (eds.), *International Trade, Foreign Direct Investment, and the Economic Environment: Essays in Honour of Professor Sylvain Passchaert* (Houndmills, Basingstoke: Macmillan, 1998), pp. 11–29.

Bhagwati, Jagdish, *Free Trade, "Fairness" and the New Protectionism: Reflections on an Agenda for the World Trade Organisation,* IEA Occasional Paper 96 (London: Institute of Economic Affairs for the Wincott Foundation, 1995).

———, *India In Transition: Freeing the Economy* (Oxford: Clarendon Press, 1993).

———, *Protectionism* (Cambridge, MA: MIT Press, 1988).

Bilal, Sanoussi, "Political Economy Considerations on the Supply of Trade Protection in Regional Integration Agreements," *Journal of Common Market Studies,* Vol. 36, No. 1 (1998), pp. 1–31.

Blais, Andre, "The Political Economy of Subsidies," *Comparative Political Studies,* Vol. 19, No. 2 (1986), pp. 201–16.

Bliss, Julia Christine, "The Amendments to Section 301: An Overview and Suggested Strategies for Foreign Response," *Law and Policy in International Business,* Vol. 20, No. 3 (1989), pp. 501–28.

Bonelli, Regis, "Growth and Productivity in Brazilian Industries: Impacts of Trade Orientation," *Journal of Development Economics,* Vol. 39, No. 1 (1992), pp. 85–109.

Bora, Bijit, and Richard Pomfret, "Policies Affecting Manufacturing," in Richard Pomfret (ed.), *Australia's Trade Policies* (Melbourne: Oxford University Press, 1995), pp. 91–111.

Bosworth, Barry, Susan M. Collins, and Yu-chin Chen, "Accounting for Differences in Economic Growth," *Brookings Discussion Papers in International Economics,* No. 115 (Washington, D.C.: Brookings Institution, October 1995).

Bosworth, Barry P., and Robert Z. Lawrence, "America's Global Role: From Dominance to Interdependence," in John D. Steinbruner (ed.), *Restructuring American Foreign Policy* (Washington, D.C.: Brookings Institution, 1989), pp. 12–47.

Bovard, James, *The Fair Trade Fraud* (New York: St. Martin's, 1991).

Bracewell-Milnes, Barry, *Eastern and Western European Economic Integration* (New York: St. Martin's, 1976).

Brander, James A., "Rationales for Strategic Trade and Industrial Policy," in Paul R. Krugman (ed.), *Strategic Trade Policy and the New International Economics* (Cambridge, MA: MIT, 1987), pp. 23–46.

Brecher, Richard A., and Ehsan U. Choudhri, "The Factor Content of Consumption in Canada and the United States: A Two-Country Test of the Heckscher-Ohlin-Vanek Model," in Robert C. Feenstra (ed.), *Empirical Methods for International Trade* (Cambridge, MA: MIT Press, 1988), pp. 5–17.

Brenton, Paul A., and L. Alan Winters, "Voluntary Export Restraints and Rationing: UK Leather Footwear Imports from Eastern Europe," *Journal of International Economics,* Vol. 34, No. 3/4 (1993), pp. 289–308.

Broad, Robin, John Cavanagh, and Walden Bello, "Development: The Market is Not Enough," *Foreign Policy,* No. 81 (1990–91), pp. 144–62.

Browne, Robert S., "How Can Africa Prosper," *World Policy Journal,* Vol. 11, No. 3 (1994), pp. 29–39.

Brugnoli, Alberto, and Laura Permini, "The Restrictiveness of the MFA: Evidence on Eastern European Exports to the EU," in Meine Pieter van Dijk and Sandro Sideri (eds.), *Multilateralism versus Regionalism: Trade Issues after the Uruguay Round* (London: Frank Cass, 1996), pp. 177–205.

Buckwell, Allan E., David R. Harvey, Kenneth J. Thomson, and Kevin A. Parton, *The Costs of the Common Agricultural Policy* (London: Croom Helm, 1982).

Bulmer-Thomas, Victor, "The Central American Common Market: From Closed to Open Regionalism," *World Development,* Vol. 26, No. 2 (1998), pp. 313–22.

Cable, Vincent, "Adjusting to Textile and Clothing Quotas: A Summary of Some Commonwealth Countries' Experiences as a Pointer to the Future," in Carl B. Hamilton (ed.), *Textiles Trade in the Developing Countries: Eliminating the Multi-Fibre Arrangement in the 1990s* (Washington, D.C.: World Bank, 1990), pp. 103–35.

Cagne, Gilbert, "The Canada-US Softwood Lumber Dispute: An Assessment after 15 Years," *Journal of World Trade,* Vol. 33, No. 1 (1999), pp. 6–86.

Calleo, David P., and Benjamin M. Rowland, *America and the World Political Economy: Atlantic Dreams and National Realities* (Bloomington: Indiana University Press, 1973).

Capie, Forrest, *Tariffs and Growth: Some Illustrations from the World Economy, 1850–1940* (Manchester: Manchester University Press, 1994).

Castells, Manuel, and Laura D'Andrea Tyson, "High Technology and the Changing International Division of Production: Implications for the U.S. Economy," in Randal B. Purcell (ed.), *The Newly Industrializing Countries in the World Economy: Challenges for U.S. Policy* (Boulder, CO: Lynne Rienner, 1989), pp. 13–50.

Castro-Bernieri, Jorge, and Paul Anthony Levine, "The Venezuelan Antidumping and Countervailing Duties Regime," *Journal of World Trade,* Vol. 30, No. 1 (1996), pp. 124–41.

Cavallo, Domingo, and Joaquin Cottani, "Argentina," in Demetris Papageorgiou, Michael Michaely, and Armeane M. Choksi (eds.), *Liberalizing Foreign Trade: Vol-*

ume 1, *The Experience of Argentina, Chile, and Uruguay* (Oxford: Basil Blackwell, 1991), pp. 1–167.

Chau, Nancy H., "Dynamic Stability and International Trade under Uncertainty," *Economica,* Vol. 65, No. 259 (1998), pp. 381–99.

Chen, Tain-Jy, and Chi-ming Hou, "The Political Economy of Trade Protection in the Republic of China on Taiwan," in Takatoshi Ito and Anne O. Krueger (eds.), *Trade and Protectionism,* National Bureau of Economic Research—East Asia Seminar on Economics, Vol. 2 (Chicago: University of Chicago, 1993), pp. 339–55.

Cho, Kang Rae, "The Role of Product-Specific Factors in Intra-Firm Trade of U.S. Manufacturing Multinational Corporations," *Journal of International Business Studies,* Vol. 21, No. 2 (1990), pp. 319–30.

Chu, Wan-Wen, "Import Substitution and Export-Led Growth: A Study of Taiwan's Petrochemical Industry," *World Development,* Vol. 22, No. 5 (1994), pp. 781–94.

Chunanuntathum, Supote, Somsak Tambunlertchai, and Atchana Wattananukit, "Thailand," in Sheila Page, *Trade, Finance and Developing Countries: Strategies and Constraints in the 1990s* (New York: Harvester, 1990), pp. 56–90.

Clark, Don P., "Determinants of Intraindustry Trade between the United States and Industrial Nations," *International Trade Journal,* Vol. 12, No. 3 (1998), pp. 345–62.

———, "Nontariff Measures and Developing Country Exports," *Journal of Developing Areas,* Vol. 27, No. 2 (1993), pp. 163–72.

Clark, Don P., and Simonetta Zarrelli, "Non-Tariff Measures and Industrial Nation Imports of GSP-Covered Products," *Southern Economic Journal,* Vol. 59, No. 4 (1992), pp. 284–93.

Cline, William R., *Exports of Manufactures from Developing Countries: Performance and Prospects for Market Access* (Washington, D.C.: Brookings Institution, 1984).

———, "Macroeconomic Influences on Trade Policy," *American Economic Review,* Vol. 79, No. 2 (1989), pp. 319–30.

Coes, Donald V., "Brazil," in Demetris Papageorgiou, Michael Michaely, and Armeane M. Choksi (eds.), *Liberalizing Foreign Trade: Volume 4, The Experience of Brazil, Colombia, and Peru* (Oxford: Basil Blackwell, 1991), pp. 1–141.

Cohen, Stephen S., "Informed Bewilderment: French Economic Strategy and the Crisis," in Stephen S. Cohen and Peter A. Gourevitch (eds.), *France in the Troubled World Economy* (London: Butterworth Scientific, 1982), pp. 21–48.

Cohn, Theodore H., "The Changing Role of the United States in the Global Agricultural Trade Regime," in William P. Avery, *World Agriculture and the GATT* (Boulder, CO: Lynne Rienner, 1993), pp. 17–38.

Collins-Williams, Terry, and Gerry Salembier, "International Disciplines on Subsidies: The GATT, the WTO and the Future Agenda," *Journal of World Trade,* Vol. 30, No. 1 (1996), pp. 5–17.

Collyns, Charles, *Can Protection Cure Unemployment,* Thames Essay No. 31 (London: Trade Policy Research Centre, 1982).

Colombatto, Enrico, "An Analysis of Exports and Growth in the LDCs," *Kyklos,* Vol. 43, No. 4 (1990), pp. 579–97.

Conlon, R. M., "Transport Costs and Tariff Protection of Australian and Canadian Manufacturing: A Comparative Study," *Canadian Journal of Economics,* Vol. 14, No. 4 (1981), pp. 700–707.

Conybeare, John A. C., "Tariff Protection in Developed and Developing Countries: A Cross-Sectional and Longitudinal Analysis," *International Organization,* Vol. 37, No. 3 (1983), pp. 441–63.

———, "Voting for Protection: An Electoral Model of Tariff Policy," *International Organization,* Vol. 45, No. 1 (1991), pp. 57–81.

Corado, Cristina, and Jaime de Melo, "An Ex-Ante Model for Estimating the Impact on Trade Flows of a Country's Joining a Customs Union," *Journal of Development Economics,* Vol. 24, No. 1 (1986), pp. 153–66.

Corado, Cristina, and Joao Ferreira Gomes, "Adjusting to Trade Liberalisation: The Case of Portugal," in Giorgio Navaretti, Riccardo Faini, and Aubrey Silberston (eds.), *Beyond the Multifibre Arrangement: Third World Competition and Restructuring Europe's Textile Industry* (Paris: Organisation of Economic Co-Operation and Development, 1993), pp. 61–76.

Corbo, Vittorio, "Trade Reform and Uniform Import Tariffs: The Chilean Experience," *American Economic Review,* Vol. 87, No. 2 (1997), pp. 73–77.

Coughlin, Cletus C., "Domestic Content Legislation: House Voting and the Economic Theory of Regulation," *Economic Inquiry,* Vol. 23, No. 3 (1985), pp. 437–48.

Cowling, Keith, and Roger Sugden, "Strategic Trade Policy Reconsidered: National Rivalry vs. Free Trade vs. International Cooperation," *Kyklos,* Vol. 51, No. 3 (1998), 339–57.

Crepaz, Markus M. L., "Consensus versus Majoritarian Democracy: Political Institutions and Their Impact on Macroeconomic Performance and Industrial Disputes," *Comparative Political Studies,* Vol. 29, No. 1 (1996), pp. 4–26.

Cumby, Robert E., and Theodore H. Moran, "Testing Models of the Trade Policy Process: Antidumping and the 'New Issues'," in Robert C. Feenstra (ed.), *The Effects of U.S. Trade Protection and Promotion Policies* (Chicago: University of Chicago Press, 1997), pp. 161–90.

Cumings, Bruce, "The Origins and Development of the Northeast Asian Political Economy: Industrial Sectors, Product Cycles, and Political Consequences," *International Organization,* Vol. 38, No. 1 (1984), pp. 1–40.

Cuthbertson, Andrew G., and Premachandra Athukorala, "Sri Lanka," in Demetris Papageorgiou, Michael Michaely, and Armeane M. Choksi (eds.), *Liberalizing Foreign Trade: Volume 5, The Experience of Indonesia, Pakistan, and Sri Lanka* (London: Basil Blackwell, 1991), pp. 283–416.

Dahlman, Carl J., "Structural Change and Trade in the East Asian Newly Industrial Economies and Emerging Industrial Economies," in Randall B. Purcell (ed.),

The Newly Industrializing Countries in the World Economy: Challenges for U.S. Policy (Boulder, CO: Lynne Rienner, 1989), pp. 51–94.

Dasgupta, Partha, and Joseph Stiglitz, "Learning-By-Doing, Market Structure and Industrial and Trade Policies," *Oxford Economic Papers,* New Series, Vol. 40, No. 2 (1988), pp. 246–68.

da Silva, Armindo, "The Portuguese Experience of European Integration—A Quantitative Assessment of the Effects of EFTA and EEC Tariff Preferences," in George N. Yannopoulos (ed.), *European Integration and the Iberian Economies* (New York: St. Martin's, 1989), pp. 87–143.

Davenport, Michael W. S., "The External Policy of the Community and Its Effects upon the Manufactured Exports of the Developing Countries," *Journal of Common Market Studies,* Vol. 29, No. 2 (1990), pp. 181–200.

Davis, Donald R., "Critical Evidence on Comparative Advantage: North-North Tread in a Multilateral World," *Journal of Political Economy,* Vol. 105, No. 5 (1997), pp. 1051–60.

Dean, Judith M., "The Effects of the U.S. MFA on Small Exporters," *Review of Economics and Statistics,* Vol. 72, No. 1 (1990), pp. 63–69.

Dean, Judith, Seema Desai, and James Riedel, *Trade Policy Regimes in Developing Countries since 1985: A Review of the Evidence,* World Bank Discussion Paper 267 (Washington, D.C.: World Bank, 1994).

Deardorff, Alan V., and Robert M. Stern, "The Structure of Tariff Protection: Effects of Foreign Tariffs and Existing NTBs," *Review of Economics and Statistics,* Vol. 67, No. 4 (1985), pp. 539–48.

de Castro, Juan, "Protectionist Pressures in the 1990s and the Coherence of North-South Trade Policies," in Jean-Marc Fontaine (ed.), *Foreign Trade Reforms and Development Strategy* (London: Routledge, 1992), pp. 165–98.

de la Cuadra, Sergio, and Dominique Hachette, "Chile," in Demetris Papageorgiou, Michael Michaely, and Armeane M. Choksi (eds.), *Liberalizing Foreign Trade: Volume 1, The Experience of Argentina, Chile, and Uruguay* (Oxford: Basil Blackwell, 1991), pp. 169–319.

de la Dehesa, Guillermo, Jose Juan Ruiz, and Angel Torres, "Spain," in in Demetris Papageorgiou, Michael Michaely, and Armeane M. Choksi (eds.), *Liberalizing Foreign Trade: Volume 6, The Experience of New Zealand, Spain, and Turkey* (Oxford: Basil Blackwell, 1991), pp. 137–262.

de la Torre, Jose, *Clothing-Industry Adjustment in Developed Countries* (New York: St. Martin's, 1986).

———, "Public Intervention Strategies in the European Clothing Industries," *Journal of World Trade Law,* Vol. 15, No. 2 (March/April 1981), pp. 124–48.

de Melo, Jaime, and David Tarr, "Welfare Costs of U.S. Quotas in Textiles, Steel and Autos," *Review of Economics and Statistics,* Vol. 72, No. 3 (1990), pp. 489–97.

Denoon, David B. H., "Cycles in Indian Economic Liberalization, 1966–1996," *Comparative Politics,* Vol. 31, No. 1 (1998), pp. 43–60.

Department of International Economic and Social Affairs, Statistical Office, *International Trade Statistics Yearbook* (New York: United Nations, various years).

Desai, Ashok V., "The Politics of India's Trade Policy," in Henry R. Nau (ed.), *Domestic Trade Policy and the Uruguay Round* (New York: Columbia University Press, 1989), pp. 91–110.

Destler, I. M., *American Trade Politics,* 2nd ed. (Washington, D.C.: Institute for International Economics with the Twentieth Century Fund, 1992).

———, "Protecting Congress or Protecting Trade," *Foreign Policy,* No. 62 (1986), pp. 96–107.

———, "U.S. Trade Policy-Making in the Eighties," in Alberto Alexina and Geoffrey Carliner (eds.), *Politics and Economics in the Eighties* (Chicago: University of Chicago Press, 1991), pp. 251–81.

DeVault, James M., "U.S. Antidumping Administrative Reviews," *International Trade Journal,* Vol. 10, No. 2 (1996), pp. 247–67.

Deyak, Timothy A., W. Charles Sawyer, and Richard L. Sprinkle, "A Comparison of the Demand for Imports and Exports in Japan and the United States," *Journal of World Trade,* Vol. 27, No. 5 (1993), pp. 63–74.

Dodaro, Santo, "Comparative Advantage, Trade and Growth: Export-Led Growth Revisited," *World Development,* Vol. 19, No. 9 (1991), pp. 1153–65.

Dolan, Michael, "European Restructuring and Import Policies for a Textile Industry in Crisis," *International Organization,* Vol. 37, No. 4 (1983), pp. 583–616.

Donges, Juergen B., and Klaus-Werner Schatz, "The Iberian Countries in the EEC—Risks and Chances for Their Manufacturing Industries," in George N. Yannopoulos (ed.), *European Integration and the Iberian Economies* (New York: St. Martin's, 1989), pp. 254–306.

Doraisami, Anita, "Export Growth and Economic Growth: A Reexamination of Some Time-Series Evidence of the Malaysian Experience," *Journal of Developing Areas,* Vol. 30, No. 2 (1996), pp. 223–30.

Douglas, Sara U., "The Textile Industry in Malaysia: Coping with Protectionism," *Asian Survey,* Vol. 29, No. 4 (1989), pp. 416–38.

Dunning, John H., *Multinational Enterprises and the Global Economy* (Reading, MA: Addison Wesley, 1993).

———, "The Theory of International Production," *International Trade Journal,* Vol. 3, No. 1 (1988), pp. 21–66.

———, "Towards an Eclectic Theory of International Production: Some Empirical Tests," *Journal of International Business Studies,* Vol. 11, No. 1 (1980), pp. 9–31.

———, "What's Wrong—and Right—with Trade Theory," *International Trade Journal,* Vol. 9, No. 2 (1995), pp. 163–202.

Eckes, Alfred E., "Epitaph for the Escape Clause?" in Khosrow Fatemi (ed.), *International Trade and Finance in a Rapidly Changing Environment,* Proceedings of the International Trade and Finance Association, Vol. 1, International Trade and International Banking (Laredo, TX: 1992), pp. 29–44.

Edwards, Sebastian, "Openness, Productivity and Growth: What Do We Really Know?" *Economic Journal,* Vol. 108, No. 447 (1998), pp. 383–98.

———, "Trade Orientation, Distortions, and Growth in Developing Countries," *Journal of Development Economics,* Vol. 39, No. 1 (1992), pp. 31–58.

———, "Trade Policy, Growth, and Income Distribution," *American Economic Review,* Vol. 87, No. 2 (1997), pp. 205–10.

Egaitsu, Fumio, "Japanese Agricultural Policy: Unfair and Unreasonable?" in William T. Coyle, Dermont Hayes, and Hiroshi Yamauchi (eds.), *Agriculture and Trade in the Pacific: Toward the Twenty-First Century* (Boulder, CO: Westview, 1992), pp. 101–88.

Elek, Andrew, Hal Hill, and Steven R. Tabor, "Liberalization and Diversification in a Small Island Economy: Fiji since the 1987 Coups," *World Development,* Vol. 21, No. 5 (1993), pp. 749–69.

Erzan, Refik, Junichi Goto, and Paula Holmes, "Effects of the Multi-Fibre Arrangement on Developing Countries' Trade: An Empirical Investigation," in Carl B. Hamilton (ed.), *Textiles Trade and the Developing Countries: Eliminating the Multi-Fibre Arrangement in the 1990s* (Washington, D.C.: World Bank, 1990), pp. 63–102.

Faini, Riccardo, "Demand and Supply Factors in Textile Trade," in Giorgio Navaretti, Riccardo Faini, and Aubrey Silberston (eds.), *Beyond the Multifibre Arrangement: Third World Competition and Restructuring Europe's Textile Industry* (Paris: Organisation of Economic Co-Operation and Development, 1993), pp. 45–60.

Faini, Riccardo, Jaime de Melo, and Wendy Takacs, "A Primer on the MFA Maze," in Giorgio Navaretti, Riccardo Faini, and Aubrey Silberston (eds.), *Beyond the Multifibre Arrangement: Third World Competition and Restructuring Europe's Textile Industry* (Paris: Organisation of Economic Co-Operation and Development, 1993), pp. 27–44.

Fatemi, Khosrow, "International Trade in the 21st Century," in Khosrow Fatemi (ed.), *International Trade in the 21st Century* (Kidlington, Oxford: Pergamon, 1997), pp. 3–12.

Favaro, Edgardo, and Pablo T. Spiller, "Uruguay," in Demetris Papageorgiou, Michael Michaely, and Armeane M. Choksi (eds.), *Liberalizing Foreign Trade: Volume 1, The Experience of Argentina, Chile, and Uruguay* (Oxford: Basil Blackwell, 1991), pp. 321–406.

Feenstra, Robert C., "Quality Change under Trade Restraints in Japanese Autos," *Quarterly Journal of Economics,* Vol. 103, No. 1 (1988), pp. 131–46.

Finger, J. M. "Subsidies and Countervailing Duties," in P. K. M. Tharakan (ed.), *Policy Implications of Antidumping Measures,* Advanced Series in Management, Vol. 14 (Amsterdam: North Holland, 1991), pp. 175–89.

———, "Trade and Domestic Effects of the Offshore Assembly Provision in the U.S. Tariff," *American Economic Review,* Vol. 66, No. 4 (1976), pp. 598–611.

Finger, J. Michael, and Sam Laird, "Protection in Developed and Developing Countries—An Overview," *Journal of World Trade,* Vol. 21, No. 4 (1987), pp. 9–23.

Flamm, Kenneth, *Mismanaged Trade? Strategic Policy and the Semiconductor Industry* (Washington, D.C.: Brookings Institution, 1996).

Frankel, Jeffrey A., and David Romer, "Does Trade Cause Growth," *American Economic Review,* Vol. 89, No. 3 (1999), pp. 379–99.

Frankel, Jeffrey A., Ernesto Stein, and Shang-Jin Wei, "Regional Trading Arrangements: Natural or Supernatural?" *American Economic Review,* Vol. 86, No. 2 (1996), pp. 52–56.

Frobel, Folker, Jurgen Heinrichs, and Otto Kreye, *The New International Division of Labour: Structural Unemployment in Industrialized Countries and Industrialisation in Developing Countries,* trans. Pete Burgess (Cambridge: Cambridge University Press, 1980).

Froot, Kenneth A., and David B. Yoffie, "Trading Blocs and the Incentives to Protect: Implications for Japan and East Asia," in Jeffrey A. Frankel and Miles Kahler (eds.), *Regionalism and Rivalry: Japan and the United States in Pacific Asia* (Chicago: University of Chicago Press, 1993), pp. 125–53.

Fung, K. C., "Characteristics of Japanese Industrial Groups and their Potential Impact on U.S.-Japanese Relations," in Robert E. Baldwin (ed.), *Empirical Studies of Commercial Policy* (Chicago: University of Chicago Press, 1991), pp. 137–64.

Gallagher, Michael, Michael Laver, and Peter Mair, *Representative Government in Modern Europe,* 2nd ed. (New York: McGraw-Hill, 1995).

Galtung, Johan, "A Structural Theory of Imperialism," *Journal of Peace Research,* Vol. 8, No. 2 (1971), pp. 81–118.

Garcia, Jorge Garcia, "Colombia," in Demetris Papageorgiou, Michael Michaely, and Armeane M. Choksi (eds.), *Liberalizing Foreign Trade: Volume 4, The Experience of Brazil, Colombia, and Peru* (Oxford: Basil Blackwell, 1991), pp. 143–270.

Garst, W. Daniel, "From Factor Endowments to Class Struggle: Pre–World War I Germany and Rogowski's Theory of Trade and Political Cleavage," *Comparative Political Studies,* Vol. 31, No. 1 (1998), pp. 22–44.

Gawande, Kishore, and Wendy L. Hansen, "Retaliation, Bargaining, and the Pursuit of 'Free and Fair' Trade," *International Organization,* Vol. 53, No. 1 (1999), pp. 117–59.

Gerschenkron, Alexander, *Economic Backwardness in Historical Perspective: A Book of Essays* (Cambridge: Cambridge University Press, 1962).

Ghatak, Subrata, and Uktu Utkulu, "Trade Liberalisation and Economic Development: The Asian Experience—Turkey, Malaysia and India," in V. N. Balasubramanyam and D. Greenaway (eds.), *Trade and Development: Essays in Honour of Jagdish Bhagwati* (London: Macmillan, 1996), pp. 81–116.

Gilligan, Michael J., "Lobbying as a Private Good with Intra-Industry Trade," *International Studies Quarterly,* Vol. 41, No. 3 (1997), pp. 455–74.

Gilpin, Robert C., "The Implications of the Changing Trade Regime for U.S.-Japanese Relations," in Taskashi Inoguichi and Daniel I. Okimoto (eds.), *The Po-*

litical Economy of Japan: Volume 2, The Changing International Context (Stanford: Stanford University Press, 1988), pp. 138–70.

Glover, David, "Bypassing Barriers: Lessons from the Asian NICs," in Diana Tussie and David Glover (eds.), *The Developing Countries in World Trade: Policies and Bargaining Strategies* (Boulder, CO: Lynne Reinner, 1993), pp. 171–8.

Goldstein, Judith, and Stefanie Ann Lenway, "Interests or Institutions: An Inquiry into Congressional-ITC Relations," *International Studies Quarterly,* Vol. 33, No. 3 (1990), pp. 303–27.

Goldstein, Walter "The EC: Capitalist or *Dirigiste* Regime," in Alan M. Cafruny and Glenda G. Rosenthal (eds.), *The State of the European Community: Volume 2, The Maastricht Debates and Beyond* (Boulder, CO: Lynne Rienner, 1993), pp. 303–19.

Gomes, Leonard, *Foreign Trade and the National Economy: Mercantilist and Classical Perspectives* (New York: St. Martin's, 1987).

Gourevitch, Peter Alexis, "International Trade, Domestic Coalitions and Liberty: Comparative Responses to the Crisis of 1873–1896," *Journal of Interdisciplinary History,* Vol. 8, No. 2 (1977), pp. 281–313.

Grabowski, Richard, "Import Substitution, Export Promotion and the State in Economic Development," *Journal of Developing Areas,* Vol. 28, No. 4 (1994), pp. 535–54.

Grafton, R. Quentin, Robert W. Lynch, and Harry W. Nelson, "British Columbia's Stumpage System's Economic and Trade Policy Implications," *Canadian Public Policy,* Vol. 24, Sup. 2 (1998), pp. 541–50.

Grant, Richard J., Maria C. Papdakis, and J. David Richardson, "Global Trade Flows: Old Structures, New Issues, Empirical Evidence," in C. Fred Bergsten and Marcus Noland (eds.), *Pacific Dynamism and the International Economic System* (Washington, D.C.: Institute for International Economics. 1993), pp. 17–63.

Grassman, Sven, "Long-Term Trends in Openness of National Economies," *Oxford Economic Papers,* New Series, Vol. 32, No. 1 (1980), pp. 123–33.

Gray, H. Peter, "Free International Economic Policy in a World of Schumpeter Goods," *International Trade Journal,* Vol. 12, No. 3 (1998), pp. 323–44.

Green, Robert T., and James M. Lutz, *The United States and World Trade: Changing Patterns and Dimensions* (New York: Praeger, 1978).

Greenaway, David, and Robert C. Hine, "Intra-Industry Specialization, Trade Expansion, and Adjustment in the European Economic Space," *Journal of Common Market Studies,* Vol. 29, No. 6 (1991), pp. 603–22.

Greenaway, David, Wyn Morgan, and Peter Wright, "Trade Reform, Adjustment and Growth: What Does the Evidence Tell Us?" *Economic Journal,* Vol. 108, No. 450 (1998), pp. 1547–61.

Griffith-Jones, Stephany, "Economic Integration in Europe: Implications for Developing Countries," in Diana Tussie and David Glover (eds.), *The Developing Countries in World Trade: Policies and Bargaining Strategies* (Boulder, CO: Lynne Reinner, 1993), pp. 33–49.

Gros, Daniel, "A Note on the Optimal Tariff, Retaliation and the Welfare Loss from Tariff Wars in a Framework with Intra-Industry Trade," *Journal of International Economics,* Vol. 23, No. 3/4 (1987), pp. 357–67.

Guisinger, Stephen, and Gerald Scully, "Pakistan," in Demetris Papageorgiou, Michael Michaely, and Armeane M. Choksi (eds.), *Liberalizing Foreign Trade: Volume 5, The Experience of Indonesia, Pakistan, and Sri Lanka* (London: Basil Blackwell, 1991), pp. 197–282.

Haberler, Gotfried, "Strategic Trade Policy and the New International Economics," in Ronald W. Jones and Anne O. Krueger (eds.), *The Political Economy of International Trade: Essays in Honor of Robert E. Baldwin* (Cambridge, MA: Basil Blackwell, 1990), pp. 25–39.

Haggard, Stephan, and Chung-In Moon, "The South Korean State in the International Economy: Liberal, Dependent, or Mercantile?" in John Gerard Ruggie (ed.), *The Antinomies of Interdependence: National Welfare and the International Division of Labor* (New York: Columbia University Press, 1983), pp. 130–89.

Halevi, Nadav, and Joseph Baruh, "Israel," in Demetris Papageorgiou, Michael Michaely, and Armeane M. Choksi (eds.), *Liberalizing Foreign Trade: Volume 3, The Experience of Israel and Yugoslavia* (Oxford: Basil Blackwell, 1991), pp. 1–156.

Hamilton, Carl B., *The Transient Nature of "New" Protectionism,* Seminar Paper No. 425 (Stockholm: Institute for International Economic Studies, 1988).

Hamilton, Carl B., and Chyngsoo Kim, "Republic of Korea: Rapid Growth in Spite of Protection Abroad," in Carl B. Hamilton (ed.), *Textiles Trade and the Developing Countries: Eliminating the Multi-Fibre Arrangement in the 1990s* (Washington, D.C.: World Bank, 1988), pp. 159–181.

Hamilton, Charles E. Hanrahan, "European Integration: Implications for U.S. Food and Agriculture," in Glennon J. Harrison (ed.), *Europe and the United States: Competition and Cooperation in the 1990s,* A Study Submitted to the Subcommittee on International Economic Policy and Trade and the Subcommittee on Europe and the Middle East of the Committee on Foreign Affairs, U.S. House of Representatives (Armonk, NY: M. E. Sharpe, 1994), pp. 229–38.

Hansen, Wendy L., and Thomas J. Prusa, "Cumulation and ITC Decision-Making: The Sum of the Parts Is Greater than the Whole," *Economic Inquiry,* Vol. 34, No. 4 (1996), pp. 746–69.

Harrigan, James, "Factor Endowments and the International Location of Production: Econometric Evidence for the OECD, 1970–1985," *Journal of International Economics,* Vol. 39, No. 1/2 (1995), pp. 123–41.

————, "Openness to Trade in Manufactures in the OECD," *Journal of International Economics,* Vol. 40, No. 1/2 (1996), pp. 23–39.

Haughton, Jonathan, and Balu Swaminathan, "The Employment and Welfare Effects of Quantitative Restrictions on Steel Imports into the United States," *Journal of World Trade,* Vol. 26, No. (1992), pp. 95–118.

Hauser, Heinz, "Foreign Trade Policy and the Function of Rules for Trade Policy-Making," in Detlev Chr. Dicke and Ernst-Ulrich Petersmann (eds.), *Foreign*

Trade in the Present and a New International Economic Order, Progress in Undercurrents in Public International Law, Vol. 4, (Fribourg: University Press, 1988), pp. 18–38.

Havrylyshyn, Oli, "Yugoslavia," in Demetris Papageorgiou, Michael Michaely, and Armeane M. Choksi (eds.), *Liberalizing Foreign Trade: Volume 3, The Experience of Israel and Yugoslavia* (Oxford: Basil Blackwell, 1991), pp. 157–354.

Hayes, J. P., *Making Trade Policy in the European Community* (Houndmills, Basingstoke: Macmillan for the Trade Policy Research Centre, University of Reading, 1993).

Helleiner, G. K., "Protectionism and the Developing Countries," in Dominick Salvatore (ed.), *Protectionism and World Welfare* (Cambridge: Cambridge University Press, 1993), pp. 396–418.

Helou, Angelina, "The Nature and Competitiveness of Japan's *Keiretsu,*" *Journal of World Trade,* Vol. 25, No. 3 (1991), pp. 99–131.

Helpman, Elhanen, and Paul R. Krugman, *Market Structure and Foreign Trade: Increasing Returns, Imperfect Competition, and the International Economy* (Cambridge: MIT Press, 1985).

Hindley, Brian, "Antidumping Actions and the EC: A Wider Perspective," in Meinhard Hilf and Ernst-Ulrich Petersmann (eds.), *National Constitutions and International Economic Law,* Vol. 8, Studies in Transnational Economic Law (Deventer, Netherlands: Kluwer, 1993), pp. 371–90.

———, "The Economics of Dumping and Antidumping Action: Is There a Baby in the Bathwater," in P. K. M. Tharakan (ed.), *Policy Implications of Antidumping Measures,* Advanced Series in Management, Vol. 14 (Amsterdam: North Holland, 1991), pp. 25–43.

Hirschman, Albert O., *National Power and the Structure of Foreign Trade* (Berkeley: University of California Press, 1969, originally published 1945).

Hoekman, Bernard M., and Michel M. Kostecki, *The Political Economy of the World Trading System: From GATT to WTO* (Oxford: Oxford University Press, 1995).

Holmes, Simon, "Anti-Circumvention under the European Union's New Anti-Dumping Rules," *Journal of World Trade,* Vol. 29, No. 3 (1995), pp. 161–80.

Horlick, Gary N., and Geoffrey D. Oliver, "Antidumping and Countervailing Duty Law Provisions of the Omnibus Trade and Competitiveness Act of 1988," *Journal of World Trade,* Vol. 23, No. 3 (1989), pp. 5–49.

Hughes, Helen, "Has There Been a Miracle in the Developing Economies of East Asia," in Lauge Stetting, Knud Erik Svendsen, and Ebbe Yndgaard (eds.), *Global Change and Transformation: Economic Essays in Honor of Karsten Laursen,* Copenhagen Studies in Economics and Management 1 (Copenhagen: Handelshojskolens Forlag, 1993), pp. 143–63.

———, "The Prospects of ASEAN Countries in Industrialized Country Markets," in Ross Garnaut (ed.), *ASEAN in a Changing Pacific and World Economy* (Canberra: Australian National University Press, 1980), pp. 347–63.

Hughes, Julia K., "A Retail Industry View of the Multifibre Arrangement: How Congressional Politics Influence International Negotiations," *Law and Policy in International Business,* Vol. 19, No. 1 (1987), pp. 257–61.

Ibrahim, Tigani, "Developing Countries and the Tokyo Round," *Journal of World Trade Law,* Vol. 12, No. 1 (1978), pp. 1–26.

Jackson, John H., *The World Trading System: Law and Policy of International Economic Relations* (Cambridge, MA: MIT Press, 1989).

Jones, Kent Albert, *Politics versus Economics in World Steel Trade* (Winchester, MA: Allen and Unwin, 1986).

Jones, Kent, "Voluntary Export Restraint: Political Economy, History, and The Role of the GATT," *Journal of World Trade,* Vol. 23, No. 3 (1989), pp. 125–40.

Josling, Timothy E., Stefan Tangermann, and T. K. Warley, *Agriculture in the GATT* (Houndmills, Basingstoke: Macmillan, 1996).

Kaempfer, William H., Stephen V. Marks, and Thomas D. Willett, "Why Do Large Countries Prefer Quantitative Trade Restrictions," *Kyklos,* Vol. 41, No. 4 (1988), 625–46.

Kamdar, Nipoli, and Jorge Gonzalez, "Quis, Quid, Ubi, Quibus Auxiliis, Cur, Quo Modo, Quando?: The U.S. House of Representatives Votes on NAFTA and GATT," in Khosrow Fatemi (ed.), *International Business in the New Millennium: Volume II, International Trade and Policy Issues* (Laredo, TX: Texas A&M International University, 1997), pp. 435–49.

Kanemitsu, Hideo, "Comment," in William R. Cline (ed.), *Trade Policy in the 1980s* (Washington, D.C.: Institute for International Economics, 1983), pp. 313–18.

Kaplan, David, and Raphael Kaplinsky, "Trade and Industrial Policy on an Uneven Playing Field: The Case of the Deciduous Fruit Canning Industry in South Africa," *World Development,* Vol. 27, No. 10 (1999), pp. 1787–1801.

Katzenstein, Peter J., "Conclusion: Domestic Structures and Strategies of Foreign Economic Policy," *International Organization,* Vol. 31, No. 4 (1977), pp. 879–920.

———, "Japan, Switzerland of the Far East?" in Taskashi Inoguichi and Daniel I. Okimoto (eds.), *The Political Economy of Japan: Volume 2, The Changing International Context* (Stanford: Stanford University Press, 1988), pp. 275–304.

———, *Small States in World Markets: Industrial Policy in Europe* (Ithaca, NY: Cornell University Press, 1985).

Kearney, Richard C., "Mauritius and the NIC Model Redux: Or, How Many Cases Make a Model?" *Journal of Developing Areas,* Vol. 24, No. 2 (1990), pp. 195–216.

Keech, William R., and Kyongsan Pak, "Partisanship, Institutions and Change in American Trade Politics," *Journal of Politics,* Vol. 57, No. 4 (1995), pp. 1130–42.

Kelegama, Saman, and Fritz Foley, "Impediments to Promoting Backward Linkages from the Garment Industry in Sri Lanka," *World Development,* Vol. 27, No. 8 (1999), pp. 1445–60.

Kellman, Mitchell, and Daniel Landau, "The Nature of Japan's Comparative Advantage, 1965–80," *World Development,* Vol. 12, No. 4 (1984), pp. 433–38.

Kennedy, Paul, *The Rise and Fall of the Great Powers: Economic Change and Military Conflict from 1500 to 2000* (New York: Random House, 1987).

Keohane, Robert O., "The Theory of Hegemonic Stability and Changes in International Economic Regimes, 1967–1977," in Ole R. Holsti, Randolph M. Siverson, and Alexander L. George (eds.), *Change in the International System* (Boulder, CO: Westview Press, 1980), pp. 131–62.

Kessides, Ioannis N., "Formal Testing of Hypotheses," in Michael Michaely, Demetris Papageorgiou, and Armeane M. Choski, *Liberalizing Foreign Trade: Volume 7, Lessons of Experience in the Developing World* (Cambridge, MA: Basil Blackwell, 1991), pp. 302–17.

Khanna, Ram, "Market Sharing under Multifibre Arrangement: Consequences of Non-Tariff Barriers in the Textiles Trade," *Journal of World Trade,* Vol. 24, No. 1 (1990), pp. 71–104.

Khanna, Sri Ram, *International Trade in Textiles: MFA Quotas and a Developing Exporting Country* (New Delhi: Sage, 1991).

Kihl, Young Whan, and James M. Lutz, *World Trade Issues: Regime, Structure, and Policy* (New York: Praeger, 1985).

Kilpatrick, Andrew and Tony Lawson, "On the Name of Industrial Decline in the U.K.," *Cambridge Journal of Economics,* Vol. 4, No. 1 (1980), pp. 85–102.

Kim, Kwang Suk, "Korea," in Demetris Papageorgiou, Michael Michaely, and Armeane M. Choksi (eds.), *Liberalizing Foreign Trade: Volume 2, The Experience of Korea, the Philippines, and Singapore* (Oxford: Basil Blackwell, 1991), pp. 1–131.

Kindleberger, Charles P., *World Economic Primacy: 1500 to 1990* (New York: Oxford University Press, 1996).

Klein, L. R., and Pingfan Hong, "'Fortress Europe' and Retaliatory Economic Warfare," in Dominick Salvatore (ed.), *Protectionism and World Welfare* (Cambridge: Cambridge University Press, 1993), pp. 99–127.

Knudsen, Jette Steen, "Integrating Western and Eastern European Markets: Changing Trade Preferences in Traditional Manufacturing Sectors in the European Union," *Comparative Political Studies,* Vol. 31, No. 2 (1998), pp. 188–216.

Kolm, Jan E., "Regional and National Consequences of Globalizing Industries of the Pacific Rim," in Janet H. Muroyama and H. Guyford Stever (eds.), *Globalization of Technology: International Perspectives* (Washington, D.C.: National Academy Press, 1988), pp. 106–40.

Kolodziej, Edward A., *French International Policy under DeGaulle and Pompidou: The Politics of Grandeur* (Ithaca, NY: Cornell University Press, 1974).

Komiya, Rutaro, and Motoshige Itoh, "Japan's International Trade and Trade Policy," in Taskashi Inoguchi and Daniel I. Okimoto (eds.), *The Political Economy of Japan: Volume 2, the Changing International Context* (Stanford: Stanford University Press, 1988), pp. 173–224.

Krasner, Stephen D., "American Policy and Global Economic Stability," in William P. Avery and David P. Rapkin (eds.), *America in a Changing World Economy* (New York: Longman, 1982), pp. 29–48.

————, "State Power and the Structure of International Trade," *World Politics,* Vol. 28, No. 3 (1976), pp. 317–43.

Krause, Lawrence B., "The Structure of Trade in Manufactured Goods in the East and Southeast Asian Region," in Colin I. Bradford, Jr., and William H. Branson (eds.), *Trade and Structural Change in Pacific Asia* (Chicago: University of Chicago Press, 1987), pp. 205–25.

Kreinin, Mordechai, "Static Effect of E.C. Enlargement on Trade Flows in Manufactured Products," *Kyklos,* Vol. 34, No. 1 (1981), pp. 60–71.

Kreinin, Mordechai E., "Super–301 and Japan—A Dissenting View," in Mordechai E. Kreinin (ed.), *International Commercial Policy: Issues for the 1990s* (Washington D.C.: Taylor and Francis, 1993), pp. 65–101.

Krishna, Pravin, "Regionalism and Multilateralism: A Political Economy Approach," *Quarterly Journal of Economics,* Vol. 113, No. 1 (1998), pp. 227–51.

Krueger, Anne O., "Asymmetries in Policy between Exportables and Import-Competing Goods," in Ronald W. Jones and Anne O. Krueger (eds.), *The Political Economy of International Trade: Essays in Honor of Robert E. Baldwin* (Cambridge, MA: Basil Blackwell, 1990), pp. 161–78.

————, "Why Trade Liberalisation Is Good for Growth," *Economic Journal,* Vol. 108, No. 450 (1998), pp. 1513–22.

Krueger, Anne O., and Okan H. Aktan, *Swimming against the Tide: Turkish Trade Reform in the 1980s* (San Francisco: Institute for Contemporary Studies Press, 1992).

Krugman, Paul, *The Accidental Theorist: And Other Dispatches from the Dismal Science* (New York: Norton, 1998).

————, "Cycles of Conventional Wisdom on Economic Development," *International Affairs* (London), Vol. 71, No. 4 (1995), pp. 717–32.

————, *EFTA and 1992,* Occasional Paper No. 23, European Free Trade Association (Geneva: EFTA, June 1988).

————, "Import Protection as Export Promotion: International Competition in the Presence of Oligopoly and Economics [*sic*] of Scale," in Henryk Kierzkowski (ed.), *Monopolistic Competition and International Trade* (Oxford: Clarendon Press, 1984), pp. 180–93.

————, "Market Access and Competition in High Technology Industries: A Simulation Exercise," in Henryk Kierzkowski (ed.), *Protection and Competition: Essays in Honor of W. M. Corden* (Oxford: Basil Blackwell, 1987), pp. 128–42.

Kukreja, Sunil, "The Development Dilemma: NICs and LDCs," in David N. Balaam and Michael Veseth, *Introduction to Political Economy* (Upper Saddle River, NJ: Prentice Hall, 1996), pp. 311–37.

Kumar, Rajiv, "The Walk Away from Leadership: India," in Diana Tussie and David Glover (eds.), *The Developing Countries in World Trade: Policies and Bargaining Strategies* (Boulder, CO: Lynne Reinner, 1993), pp. 155–69.

Kumar, Rajiv, and Sri Ram Khanna, "India, the Multi-Fibre Arrangement and the Uruguay Round," in Carl B. Hamilton (ed.), *Textiles Trade and Developing Countries: Eliminating the Multi-Fibre Arrangement in the 1990s* (Washington, D.C.: World Bank, 1990), pp. 182–212.

Lake, David A., "International Economic Structure and American Foreign Economic Policy, 1887–1934," *World Politics,* Vol. 35, No. 4 (1983), pp. 517–43.

Lal, Deepak, "Trade Blocs and Multilateral Free Trade," *Journal of Common Market Studies,* Vol. 31, No. 3 (1993), pp. 349–58.

Lal, Deepak, and Sarath Rajapatirana, *Impediments to Trade Liberalization in Sri Lanka,* Thames Essay No. 51 (Gower: Aldershot, 1989).

Lall, Sanjaya, "Imperfect Markets and Fallible Governments: The Role of the State in Industrial Development," in Deepak Nayyar (ed.), *Trade and Industrialization* (Dehli: Oxford University Press, 1997), pp. 43–87.

———, "India's Manufactured Exports: Comparative Structure and Prospects," *World Development,* Vol. 27, No. 10 (1990), pp. 1769–86.

Lancaster, Kelvin, "The 'Product Variety' Case for Protection," *Journal of International Economics,* Vol. 31, No. 1/2 (1991), pp. 1–26.

Langhammer, Rolf J., "Fuelling a New Engine of Growth or Separating Europe from Non-Europe?" *Journal of Common Market Studies,* Vol. 29, No. 2 (1990), pp. 123–35.

Lawrence, Robert Z., "How Open Is Japan?" in Paul Krugman (ed.), *Trade with Japan: Has the Door Opened Wider?* (Chicago: University of Chicago Press, 1991), pp. 9–37.

———, *Regionalism, Multilateralism, and Deeper Integration* (Washington, D.C.: Brookings Institution, 1995).

Lazer, David, "The Free Trade Epidemic of the 1860s and Other Outbreaks of Economic Discrimination," *World Politics,* Vol. 51, No. 4 (1999), pp. 447–83.

Leamer, Edward R., "Factor-Supply Differences as a Source of Comparative Advantage," *American Economic Review,* Vol. 83, No. 2 (1993), pp. 436–39.

Lee, Jong-Wha, and Phillip Swagel, "Trade Barriers and Trade Flows Across Countries and Industries," *Review of Economics and Statistics,* Vol. 79, No. 3 (1997), pp. 372–82.

Lehmann, Jean-Pierre, "France, Japan, Europe, and Industrial Competition: The Automobile Case," *International Affairs* (London), Vol. 68, No. 1 (1992), pp. 37–53.

Levinsohn, James, "Carwars: Trying to Make Sense of U.S. Trade Frictions in the Automobile and Automobile Parts Markets," in Robert C. Feenstra (ed.), *The Effects of U.S. Trade Protection and Promotion Policies* (Chicago: University of Chicago Press, 1997), pp. 11–32.

———, "Testing the Imports-as-Market-Discipline Hypothesis," *Journal of International Economics,* Vol. 35, No. 1/2 (1993), pp. 1–22.

Levy, Brigitte, "Globalization and Regionalization: Main Issues in International Trade Patterns," in Khosrow Fatemi (ed.), *International Trade in the 21st Century* (Kidlington, Oxford: Pergamon, 1997), pp. 59–74.

Lim, David, "Explaining the Growth Performances of Asian Developing Economies," *Economic Development and Cultural Change,* Vol. 42, No. 4 (1994), pp. 829–44.

Lincoln, Edward J., *Japan's New Global Role* (Washington, D.C.: Brookings Institution, 1993).

Lipson, Charles, "The Transformation of Trade: The Sources and Effects of Regime Change," *International Organization,* Vol. 36, No. 2 (1982), pp. 417–55.

Londero, Elio, and Simon Teitel with Hector Ceruini, Rodrigo Parot, and Remes Lenicov, *Resources, Industrialization and Exports in Latin America: The Primary Input Content of Sustained Exports of Manufactures from Argentina, Colombia and Venezuela* (New York: St. Martin's, 1998).

Lundy, Loretta, "The GATT Safeguards Debacle and the Canadian Textiles and Clothing Policy: A Proposal for an Equitable Approach to North-South Relations," *Journal of World Trade,* Vol. 22, No. 6 (1988), 71–94.

Lutz, James M., "Determinants of Protectionist Attitudes in the U.S. House of Representatives," *International Trade Journal,* Vol. 5, No. 3 (1991), pp. 301–28.

————, "GATT Reform or Regime Maintenance: Differing Solutions to World Trade Problems," *Journal of World Trade,* Vol. 25, No. 2 (1991), pp. 107–22.

————, "Industrialized Markets for Developing-Country Manufactured Exports: The Good, the Poor, and the Indifferent," *Journal of Developing Areas,* Vol. 31, No. 3 (1997), pp. 367–86.

————, "Japanese Imports of Manufactures from East Asia: Is the Glass Half Empty or Hall Full?" *International Trade Journal,* Vol. 7, No. 2 (1992), pp. 151–79.

————, "Relative Import Propensities of Less Developed Countries' Manufactures in Industrialized Countries," in Raul Moncarz (ed.), *International Trade and the New Economic Order* (Oxford: Pergamon, 1995), pp. 221–32.

————, "To Import or Protect?: Industrialized Countries and Manufactured Products," *Journal of World Trade,* Vol. 28, No. 4 (1994), pp. 123–46.

————, "Trade in Manufactures among Industrialized States," *International Journal of Management,* Vol. 4, No. 3 (1987), pp. 403–15.

————, "The United States and Managed Trade: A Minnow Swimming with Piranhas," *World Competition,* Vol. 21, No. 3 (1998), pp. 45–61.

Lutz, James M., and Young Whan Kihl, "The NICs, Shifting Comparative Advantage, and the Product Life Cycle," *Journal of World Trade,* Vol. 24, No. 1 (1990), pp. 113–34.

MacArthur, John and Stephen V. Marks, "Constituent Interests vs. Legislator Ideology: The Role of Political Opportunity Costs," *Economic Inquiry,* Vol. 26, No. 3 (1988), pp. 461–70.

McDonald, Brian, *The World Trading System: The Uruguay Round and Beyond* (New York: St. Martin's, 1998).

McKeown, Timothy J., "The Limitations of 'Structural' Theories of Commercial Policy," *International Organization,* Vol. 40, No. 1 (1986), pp. 43–64.

McKinney, Joseph A., "Degree of Access to the Japanese Market: 1979 vs. 1986," *Columbia Journal of World Business,* Vol. 24, No. 2 (1989), pp. 53–9.

McMullen, Neil, and Laura L. Megna, "Automobiles," in Louis Turner and Neil McMullen (eds.), *The Newly Industrializing Countries: Trade and Adjustment* (London: Allen and Unwin, 1982), pp.

Mahler, Vincent, David K. Jesuit, and Douglas D. Roscoe, "Explaining the Impact of Trade and Investment on Income Inequality," *Comparative Political Studies,* Vol. 32, No. 3 (1999), pp. 363–95.

Mansfield, Edward D., and Rachel Bronson, "Alliances, Preferential Trading Arrangements, and International Trade," *American Political Science Review,* Vol. 91, No. 1 (1997), pp. 94–107.

Mansfield, Edward D., and Marc L. Busch, "The Political Economy of Nontariff Barriers: A Cross National Analysis," *International Organization,* Vol. 44, No.4 (1995), pp. 723–49.

Mardas, Dimitri, "Intra-Industry Trade in Manufactured Products between the European Economic Community and the Eastern European Countries," *Journal of World Trade,* Vol. 26, No. 5 (1992), pp. 5–23.

Markusen, James R., "Comment," in Robert M. Stern (ed.), *Trade and Investment Relations among the United States, Japan, and Canada* (Chicago: University of Chicago Press, 1989), pp. 353–59.

Marrison, Andrew, *British Business and Protection, 1903–1912* (Oxford: Clarendon Press, 1996).

Masayoshi, Honma, "Japan's Agricultural Policy and Protection Growth," in Takatoshi Ito and Anne O. Krueger (eds.), *Trade and Protectionism,* National Bureau of Economic Research—East Asia Seminar on Economics, Vol. 2 (Chicago: University of Chicago, 1993), pp. 95–111.

Mason, Mark, "Elements of Consensus: Europe's Response to the Japanese Auto Challenge," *Journal of Common Market Studies,* Vol. 32, No. 4 (1994), pp. 433–53.

Mastel, Greg, *Antidumping Laws and the U.S. Economy* (Armonk, NY: M. E. Sharpe, 1998).

Maswood, Syed Javed, *Japan and Protection: The Growth of Protectionist Sentiment and the Japanese Response* (London: Routledge and Nissan Institute for Japanese Studies, 1989).

Matsushita, Mitsuo, "Comments on Antidumping Law Enforcement in Japan," in John H. Jackson and Edwin A. Vermulst (eds.), *Antidumping Law and Practice: A Comparative Study* (Ann Arbor: University of Michigan Press, 1989), pp. 389–95.

Meier, Gerald M., "Trade Policy, Development, and the New Political Economy," in Ronald W. Jones and Anne O. Krueger (eds.), *The Political Economy of International Trade: Essays in Honor of Robert E. Baldwin* (Cambridge, MA: Basil Blackwell, 1990), pp. 179–96.

Messerlin, Patrick A., "The Uruguay Negotiations on Antidumping Enforcement: Some Basic Issues," in P. K. M. Tharakan (ed.), *Policy Implications of Antidumping Measures,* Advanced Series in Management, Vol. 14 (Amsterdam: North Holland, 1991), pp. 45–76.

Messerlin, Patrick A., and Stephan Becuwe, "Intra-Industry Trade in the Long Run: The French Case," in David Greenaway and P. K. M. Tharakan (eds.) *Imperfect Competition and International Trade: The Policy Aspects of Intra-Industry Trade* (Sussex: Wheatsheaf, 1986), pp. 191–215.

Metcalf, Lee Kendall, *The Council of Mutual Economic Assistance: The Failure of Reform,* East European Monographs, Boulder (New York: Columbia University Press, 1997).

Meyer, F.V., *International Trade Policy* (New York: St. Martin's, 1978).

Michaely, Michael, Demetris Papageorgiou, and Armeane M. Choksi, *Liberalizing Foreign Trade: Volume 7, Lessons of Experience in the Developing World* (Cambridge, MA: Basil Blackwell, 1991).

Michalet, Charles-Albert, "From International Trade to World Economy: A New Paradigm," in Harry Makler, Alberto Martinelli, and Neil Smelser (eds.), *The New International Economy,* Sage Studies in International Sociology, 26 (Beverly Hills, CA: Sage, 1982), pp. 37–58.

Milner, Chris, "Trade Regime Bias and the Response to Trade Liberalisation in Sub-Saharan Africa," *Kyklos,* Vol. 51, No. 2 (1998), pp. 219–36.

Milner, Helen, "Industries, Governments, and Regional Trade Blocs," in Edward D. Mansfield and Helen V. Milner (eds.), *The Political Economy of Regionalism* (New York: Columbia University Press, 1997), pp. 77–106.

Minford, Patrick, "The New Cambridge Economic Policy: A Critique of Its Prescriptions," *Government and Opposition,* Vol. 17, No. 1 (1982), pp. 48–60.

Mirus, Rolf, Barry Scholnick, and Dean Spinanger, "Front-Loading Protection: Canada's Approach to Phasing Out the Multi-Fiber Arrangement," *International Trade Journal,* Vol. 11, No. 4 (1997), pp. 433–51.

Monroe, Wilbur F., *International Trade Policy in Transition* (Lexington, MA: Lexington Books, 1975).

Moon, Bruce E., "Exports, Outward-Oriented Development and Economic Growth," *Political Research Quarterly,* Vol. 51, No. 1 (1998), pp. 7–36.

Moreira, Mauricio Mesquita, and Paulo Guilherme Correa, "A First Look at the Impacts of Trade Liberalization on Brazilian Manufacturing Industry," *World Development,* Vol. 26, No. 10 (1998), pp. 1859–74.

Moser, Peter, "Preferential Trade Agreements and the GATT: Can Bilateralism and Multilateralism Coexist?" *Kyklos,* Vol. 45, No. 4 (1995), pp. 593–98.

Mourmouras, Alex, "Infant Governments and the Fiscal Role of Tariffs, Inflation, and Reserve Requirements: A Welfare Analysis," *Journal of International Economics,* Vol. 31, No. 3/4 (1991), pp. 271–90.

Muscatelli, V. A., A. A. Stevenson, and C. Montagna, "Intra-NIE Competition in Exports of Manufactures," *Journal of International Economics,* Vol. 37, No. 1/2 (1994), pp. 29–47.

Mytelka, Lynn Kreiger, "The French Textile Industry: Crisis and Adjustment," in Harold K. Jacobsen and Dusan Sidjanski (eds.), *The Emerging International Economic Order: Dynamic Processes, Constraints and Opportunities* (Beverly Hills, CA: Sage, 1982), pp. 129–66.

Nam, Chong-Hyun, "Protectionist U.S. Trade Policy and Korean Exports," in Takatoshi Ito and Anne O. Krueger (eds.), *Trade and Protectionism,* National Bureau of Economic Research—East Asia Seminar on Economics, Vol. 2 (Chicago: University of Chicago Press, 1993), pp. 183–218.

Narongchai, Akransanee, "Industrialization of ASEAN and Structural Adjustment in the Pacific," in Roger Benjamin and Robert T. Kudrle (eds.), *The Industrial Future of the Pacific Basin* (Boulder, CO: Westview. 1984), 59–78.

Navaratne, N. M. C., "Who Bears the Incidence of Import Protection? Evidence from Sri Lanka," *World Development,* Vol. 9, No. 10 (1991), pp. 1409–19.

Navaretti, Giorgio Barba, "Trade Policy and Foreign Investments: An Analytical Framework," in Giorgio Navaretti, Riccardo Faini, and Aubrey Silberston (eds.), *Beyond the Multifibre Arrangement: Third World Competition and Restructuring Europe's Textile Industry* (Paris: Organisation of Economic Co-Operation and Development, 1993), pp. 121–44.

Nelson, Richard R., and Howard Pack, "The Asian Miracle and Modern Growth Theory," *Economic Journal,* Vol. 109, No. 457 (1999), pp. 416–36.

Neven, Damien J., and Lars-Hendrik Roller, "The Structure and Determinants of East-West Trade: A Preliminary Analysis of the Manufacturing Sector," in L. Alan Winters and Anthony J. Venables (eds.), *European Integration: Trade and Industry* (Cambridge: Cambridge University Press, 1991), pp. 96–119.

"New Zealand's Advantage," *Economist,* Vol. 352, No. 8137 (September 18, 1999), p. 47.

Nicholls, Shelton A., "Measuring Trade Creation and Trade Diversion in the Central American Common Market: A Hicksian Alternative," *World Development,* Vol. 26, No. 2 (1998), pp. 323–35.

Nivola, Pietro S., *Regulating Unfair Trade* (Washington, D.C.: Brookings Institution, 1993).

Noland, Marcus, "Chasing Phantoms: The Political Economy of USTR," *International Organization,* Vol. 51, No. 3 (1997), pp. 365–87.

———, "Has Asian Export Performance Been Unique," *Journal of International Economics,* Vol. 43, No. 1/2 (1997), pp. 79–101.

———, "Public Policy, Private Preferences, and the Japanese Trade Pattern," *Review of Economics and Statistics,* Vol. 79, No. 2 (1997), pp. 259–66.

Ocampo, Jose Antonio, and Lance Taylor, "Trade Liberalization in Developing Economies: Modest Benefits but Problems with Productivity Growth, Macro Prices, and Income Distribution," *Economic Journal,* Vol. 108, No. 450 (1998), pp. 1523–46.

Oppenheimer, Michael F., and Donna M. Tuths, *Non-Tariff Barriers: The Effects on Corporate Strategy in High-Technology Sectors* (Boulder CO: Westview, 1987).

Oyejide, T. Ademola, *Tariff Policy and Industrialization in Nigeria* (Ibadan: Ibadan University Press, 1975).

Palmeter, David, "A Commentary on the WTO Anti-Dumping Code," *Journal of World Trade,* Vol. 30, No. 4 (1996), pp. 43–64

———, "Rules of Origin in Customs Unions and Free Trade Areas," in Kym Anderson and Richard Blackhurst (eds.), *Regional Integration and the Global Trading System* (New York: St. Martin's, 1993), pp. 326–43.

Palmeter, N. David, "Injury Determinations in Antidumping and Countervailing Duty Cases—A Commentary on U.S. Practice," *Journal of World Trade Law,* Vol. 21, No. 1 (1987), pp. 7–45.

Paus, Eva A., "Economic Growth through Neoliberal Restructuring? Insights from the Chilean Experience," *Journal of Developing Areas,* Vol. 29, No. 1 (1994), pp. 31–55.

Peers, Steve, "Reform of the European Community's Generalized System of Preferences," *Journal of World Trade,* Vol. 29, No. 6 (1995), p. 79–96.

Petersmann, Ernst-Ulrich, "Grey Area Policy and the Rule of Law," *Journal of World Trade,* Vol. 22, No. 2 (1988), pp. 23–44.

Petri, Peter A., "Market Structure, Comparative Advantage, and Japanese Trade Under the Strong Yen," in Paul Krugman (ed.), *Trade with Japan: Has the Door Opened Wider?* (Chicago: University of Chicago Press, 1991), pp. 51–82.

Pincus, Jonathan, "Evolution and Political Economy of Australian Trade Policies," in Richard Pomfret (ed.), *Australia's Trade Policies* (Melbourne: Oxford University Press, 1995), pp. 53–73.

Pincus, Jonathan J., *Pressure Groups and Politics in Antebellum Tariffs* (New York: Columbia University Press, 1977).

Pitt, Mark M., "Indonesia," in Demetris Papageorgiou, Michael Michaely, and Armeane M. Choksi (eds.), *Liberalizing Foreign Trade: Volume 5, The Experience of Indonesia, Pakistan, and Sri Lanka* (London: Basil Blackwell, 1991), pp. 1–196.

Plummer, Michael G., "Efficiency Effects of the Accession of Spain and Portugal to the EC," *Journal of Common Market Studies,* Vol. 29, No. 3 (1991), pp. 317–25.

Polavarapu, Ramana, and Ashish Vaidya, "Optimal Trade Policy with Quality-Differentiated Goods," *International Trade Journal,* Vol. 10, No. 3 (1996), pp. 379–406.

Pomfret, Richard, *The Economics of Discriminatory International Trade Policies* (Oxford: Basil Blackwell, 1988).

Preeg, Ernest H., *From Here to Free Trade: Essays in Post–Uruguay Round Trade Strategy* (Washington, D.C., and Chicago: Center of Strategic and International Studies and University of Chicago Press, 1998).

Puga, Diego, and Anthony J. Venables, "Agglomeration and Economic Development: Import Substitution vs. Trade Liberalisation," *Economic Journal,* Vol. 109, No. 455 (1999), pp. 292–311.

Qiu, Larry D., "Why Can't Countervailing Duties Deter Export Subsidization?" *Journal of International Economics,* Vol. 39, No. 3/4 (1995), pp. 249–72.

Rajapatirana, S., "Foreign Trade and Economic Development: Sri Lanka's Experience," *World Development,* Vol. 16, No. 10 (1988), pp. 1143–57.

Ramazani, Reza M., and Keith E. Maskus, "A Test of the Factor Endowments Model of Trade in a Rapidly Industrializing Country: The Case of Korea," *Review of Economics and Statistics,* Vol. 75, No. 3 (1993), pp. 568–72.

Rapkin, David P., and Aurelia George, "Rice Liberalization and Japan's Role in the Uruguay Round: A Two-Level Game Approach," in William P. Avery (ed.), *World Agriculture and the GATT* (Boulder, CO: Lynne Reinner, 1993), pp. 55–94.

Rayner, Anthony C., and Ralph Lattimore, "New Zealand," in Demtetris Papageorgiou, Michael Michaely, and Armeane M. Choksi (eds.), *Liberalizing Foreign Trade: Volume 6, The Experience of New Zealand, Spain, and Turkey* (Oxford: Basil Blackwell, 1991), pp. 1–135.

Redding, Stephen, "Dynamic Comparative Advantage and the Welfare Effects of Trade," *Oxford Economic Papers,* Vol. 51, No. 1 (1999), pp. 15–39.

Reitzes, James D., "The Impact of Quotas and Tariffs on Strategic R&D Behaviour," *International Economic Review,* Vol. 32, No. 4 (1991), pp. 985–1007.

Richardson, J. David, "U.S. Trade Policy in the 1980s: Turns—and Roads Not Taken," in Martin Feldstein (ed.), *American Economic Policy in the 1980s* (Chicago: University of Chicago Press, 1994), pp. 627–58.

Rock, Michael T., "Reassessing the Effectiveness of Industrial Policy in Indonesia: Can the Neoliberals Be Wrong?" *World Development,* Vol. 27, No. 4 (1999), pp. 691–704.

Rodriguez, Ennio, "The Multiple Tracks of a Small Open Economy: Costa Rica," in Diana Tussie and David Glover (eds.), *The Developing Countries in World Trade: Policies and Bargaining Strategies* (Boulder, CO: Lynne Reinner, 1993), pp. 99–117.

Rodrik, Dani, "Conceptual Issues in the Design of Trade Policy for Industrialization," *World Development,* Vol. 20, No. 3 (1992), pp. 309–20.

———, "Why Do More Open Economies Have Bigger Governments?" *Journal of Political Economy,* Vol. 106, No. 5 (1998), pp. 997–1032.

Rogowski, Ronald, *Commerce and Coalitions: How Trade Affects Domestic Political Alignments* (Princeton: Princeton University Press, 1989).

Rosendorff, B. Peter, "Voluntary Export Restraints, Antidumping Procedure, and Domestic Politics," *American Economic Review,* Vol. 86, No. 3 (1996), pp. 544–61.

Ruigrok, Winfried, "Paradigm Crisis in International Trade Theory," *Journal of World Trade,* Vol. 25, No. 1 (1991), pp. 77–89.

Ryan, Michael P., "Court of International Trade Judges, Binational Panelists, and Judicial Review of U.S. Antidumping and Countervailing Duty Policies," *Journal of World Trade,* Vol. 30, No. 6 (1996), pp. 103–20.

———, *Playing by the Rules: American Trade Power and Diplomacy in the Pacific* (Washington, D.C.: Georgetown University Press, 1995).

Rycken, Willem, "Some Specific Issues in the Antidumping Proceedings of the European Communities," in P. K. M. Tharakan (ed.), *Policy Implications of Antidumping Measures,* Advanced Series in Management, Vol. 14 (Amsterdam: North Holland, 1991), pp. 191–218.

Salvatore, Dominick, "International Trade Policies, Industrialization, and Economic Development," in Khosrow Fatemi (ed.), *International Trade in the 21st Century* (Kidlington, Oxford: Pergamon, 1997), pp. 249–68.

Sander, Harald, "Deep Integration, Shallow Regionalism, and Strategic Openness: Three Notes on Economic Integration in East Asia," in Franz Peter Land and Renate Ohr (eds.), *International Economic Integration,* Studies in Contemporary Economics (Heidelberg: Physica-Verlag, 1997), pp. 211–44.

Sassoon, Enrico, "Objectives and Results of the Uruguay Round," in Riccardo Faini and Enzo Grilli (eds.), *Multilateralism and Regionalism after the Uruguay Round* (Houndmills, Basingstoke: Macmillan, 1997), pp. 1–51.

Saxonhouse, Gary R., "Comparative Advantage, Structural Adaptation, and Japanese Performance," in Taskashi Inoguchi and Daniel I. Okimoto (eds.), *The Po-*

litical Economy of Japan: Volume 2, The Changing International Context (Stanford: Stanford University Press, 1988), pp. 138–70.

————, "The Micro- and Macroeconomics of Foreign Sales to Japan," in William R. Cline (ed.), *Trade Policy in the 1980s* (Washington, D.C.: Institute for International Economics, 1983), pp. 259–304.

Saxonhouse, Gary R., and Robert M. Stern, "An Analytic Survey of Formal and Informal Barriers to International Trade and Investment in the United States, Japan, and Canada," in Robert M. Stern (ed.), *Trade and Investment Relations among the United States, Japan, and Canada* (Chicago: University of Chicago Press, 1989), pp. 293–353.

Schamis, Hector E., "Distributional Coalitions and the Politics of Economic Reform in Latin America," *World Politics,* Vol. 51, No. 2 (1999), pp. 236–68.

Scherzer, Erich, "Consequences of European Integration for Developing Countries," in Marjan Svetlicic and H. W. Singer (eds.) *The World Economy: Challenges of Globalization and Regionalization* (Houndmills, Basingstoke: Macmillan, 1996), pp. 229–46.

Schmidt, Vivien A., *From State to Market: The Transformation of French Business and Government* (Cambridge: Cambridge University Press, 1996).

————, "Loosening the Ties that Bind: The Impact of European Integration on French Government and Its Relationship to Business," *Journal of Common Market Studies,* Vol. 34, No. 2 (1996), pp. 223–54.

Schonhardt-Bailey, Cheryl, "Parties and Interests in the 'Marriage of Iron and Rye'," *British Journal of Political Science,* Vol. 28, No. 2 (1998), pp. 291–330.

Schoppa, Leonard J., *Bargaining with Japan: What American Pressure Can and Cannot Do* (New York: Columbia University Press, 1997).

Scollay, Robert, "Australia-New Zealand Closer Economic Relations Agreement," in Bijit Bora and Christopher Findlay (eds.), *Regional Integration and the Asia Pacific* (Melbourne: Oxford University Press, 1996), pp. 184–96.

Scott, Norman, "Protectionism in Western Europe," in Dominick Salvatore (ed.), *Protectionism and World Welfare* (Cambridge: Cambridge University Press, 1993), pp. 371–95.

Sekiguchi, Sueo, "Japan: A Plethora of Programs," in Hugh Patrick with Larry Meissner (ed.), *Pacific Basin Industries in Distress: Structural Adjustment and Trade Policy in the Nine Industrialized Economies* (New York: Columbia University Press, 1991), pp. 418–68.

Sen, Abhijit, "On Economic Openness and Industrialization," in Deepak Nayyar (ed.), *Trade and Industrialization* (Dehli: Oxford University Press, 1997), pp. 88–168.

Shepherd, Geoffrey, and Florian Alburo, "Singapore," in Demetris Papageorgiou, Michael Michaely, and Armeane M. Choksi (eds.), *Liberalizing Foreign Trade: Volume 2, The Experience of Korea, the Philippines, and Singapore* (Oxford: Basil Blackwell, 1991), pp. 133–308.

Silva, Eduardo, "Capitalist Coalitions, the State and Neoliberal Economic Restructuring: Chile, 1973–88," *World Politics,* Vol. 45, No. 4 (1993), pp. 526–59.

Smerts, Maarteen, "Main Features of the Uruguay Round Agreement on Textiles and Clothing, and Implications for the Trading System," *Journal of World Trade*, Vol. 29, No. 5 (1995), pp. 97–109.

Soltysinski, Stanislaw, "U.S. Antidumping Laws and State-Controlled Economies," *Journal of World Trade Law*, Vol. 15, No. 3 (1981), pp. 251–65.

Spaulding, Robert Mark, "German Trade Policy in Eastern Europe, 1890–1990: Preconditions for Applying International Trade Leverage," *International Organization*, Vol. 45, No. 3 (1996), pp. 343–68.

Spinanger, Dean, "The Spillover of Export Capabilities in the Textile and Clothing Industry: The Case of Hong Kong," in Giorgio Navaretti, Riccardo Faini, and Aubrey Silberston (eds.), *Beyond the Multifibre Arrangement: Third World Competition and Restructuring Europe's Textile Industry* (Paris: Organisation of Economic Co-Operation and Development, 1993), pp. 237–50.

Steiner, Jurg, *European Democracies,* 3rd ed. (White Plains, NY: Longman, 1995).

Steven, Rob, *Japan and the New World Order* (Houndmills, Basingstoke: Macmillan, 1996).

Stiglitz, Joseph E., and Lyn Squire, "International Development: Is It Possible?" *Foreign Policy,* No. 110 (1998), pp. 138–51.

Strange, Susan, "The Management of Surplus Capacity: Or How Does Theory Stand Up to Protectionism 1970s Style?" *International Organization,* Vol. 33, No. 3 (1979), pp. 303–34.

Svensson, Peter, "Strategic Trade Policy and Endogenous R&D-Subsidies: An Empirical Study," *Kyklos,* Vol. 51, No. 2 (1998), pp. 259–75.

Swenson, Deborah L., "Explaining Domestic Content: Evidence from Japanese and U.S. Automobile Production in the United States," in Robert C. Feenstra (ed.), *The Effects of U.S. Trade Protection and Promotion Policies* (Chicago: University of Chicago Press, 1997), pp. 33–53.

Syropoulos, Constantinos, "Customs Unions and Comparative Advantage," *Oxford Economic Papers,* Vol. 51, No. 2 (1999), pp. 239–66.

Tan, Norma A., "The Structure of and Causes of Manufacturing Sector Protection in the Philippines," in Christopher Findlay and Ross Garnaut (eds.), *The Political Economy of Manufacturing Protection: Experiences of ASEAN and Australia* (Sydney: Allen and Unwin, 1986), pp. 48–76.

Tharakan, P. K. M. "Some Facets of Antidumping Policy: Summary of the Contents of the Volume," in P. K. M. Tharakan (ed.), *Policy Implications of Antidumping Measures* (Amsterdam: North Holland, 1991), pp. 1–23.

Tharakan, P. K. Mathew, and Birgit Kerstens, "Contingent Protection and International Trade: An Analysis of the Antidumping Policy of the European Union," in P. K. M. Tharakan and D. Ven Den Bulcke (eds.), *International Trade, Foreign Direct Investment and the Economic Environment: Essays in Honour of Professor Sylvain Plasschaert* (Houndmills, Basingstoke: Macmillan, 1998), pp. 41–58.

Thomas, Vinod, and Yan Wang, "Distortions, Interventions, and Productivity Growth: Is East Asia Different?" *Economic Development and Cultural Change,* Vol. 44, No. 2 (1996), pp. 265–88.

Thompson, Henry, "Do Tariffs Protect Specific Factors," *Canadian Journal of Economics,* Vol. 22, No. 2 (1989), pp. 406–12.

Tolliday, Steven, "Competition and Maturity in the British Steel Industry, 1870–1914," in Etsuo Abe and Yoshitaka Suzuki (eds.), *Changing Patterns of International Rivalry: Some Lessons from the Steel Industry* (Tokyo: University of Tokyo Press, 1990), pp. 20–72.

Toyne, Brian, Jeffrey S. Arpan, Andy H. Barnett, David A. Ricks, and Terrence A. Shimp, "The International Competitiveness of the U.S. Textile Mill Products Industry: Corporate Strategies for the Future," *Journal of International Business Studies,* Vol. 15, No. 3 (1990), pp. 145–65.

Tracy, Michael, *Government and Agriculture in Western Europe, 1880–1988,* 3rd ed. (New York: New York University Press, 1989).

Trefler, Daniel, "The Case of the Missing Trade and Other Mysteries," *American Economic Review,* Vol. 85, No. 4 (1995), pp. 1029–46.

Trela, Irene, and John Whalley, "Global Effects of Developed Country Trade Restrictions on Textiles and Apparel," *Economic Journal,* Vol. 100, No. 403 (1990), pp. 1190–1205.

Tsoukalis, Loukas, and Robert Strauss, "Crisis and Adjustment in European Steel: Beyond Laisser-Faire," *Journal of Common Market Studies,* Vol. 23, No. 3 (1985), pp. 207–28.

United Nations Statistical Office, *Growth of World Industry* (New York: United Nations, various years).

———, *Industrial Statistics Yearbook* (New York: United Nations, various years).

———, *Yearbook of Industrial Statistics* (New York: United Nations, various years).

———, *Yearbook of International Trade Statistics* (New York: United Nations, various years).

van Wolferen, Karel, "The Japan Problem Revisited," *Foreign Affairs,* Vol. 69, No. 4 (1990), pp. 42–55.

Vermulst, Edwin, and Paul Waer, "The Calculation of Injury Margins in EC Anti-Dumping Proceedings," *Journal of World Trade,* Vol. 25, No. 6 (1991), pp. 5–42.

Wade, Robert, "Managing Trade: Taiwan and South Korea as Challengers to Economics and Political Science," *Comparative Politics,* Vol. 25, No. 2 (1993), pp. 147–67.

Waelbroeck, Jean, "Exports of Manufactures from Developing Countries to the European Community," in Colin I. Bradford, Jr., and William H. Branson (eds.), *Trade and Structural Change in Pacific Asia* (Chicago: University of Chicago Press, 1987), pp. 61–92.

Waer, Paul, and Edwin Vermulst, "EC Anti-Dumping Law and Practice after the Uruguay Round," *Journal of World Trade,* Vol. 28, No. 2 (1994), pp. 5–21.

———, "EC Anti-Subsidy Law and Practice after the Uruguay Round: A Wolf in Sheep's Clothing," *Journal of World Trade,* Vol. 33, No. 3 (1999), pp. 19–43.

———, "European Community Rules of Origin as Commercial Policy Instruments," *Journal of World Trade,* Vol. 24, No. 3 (1990), pp. 55–99.

Waterbury, John, "The Long Gestation and Brief Triumph of Import-Substituting Industrialization," *World Development,* Vol. 27, No. 2 (1999), pp. 323–41.

Weiss, John, "Trade Policy Reform and Performance in Manufacturing: Mexico 1975–88," *Journal of Development Studies,* Vol. 29, No. 1 (1992), pp. 1–23.

Westhoff, Frank H., Beth V. Yarbrough, and Robert M. Yarbrough, "Preferential Trade Agreements and the GATT: Can Bilateralism and Multilateralism Coexist," *Kyklos,* Vol. 47, No. 4 (1994), pp. 179–95.

White, John J., "A Test of Consistency in the Administration of U.S. Antidumping Law," *Journal of World Trade,* Vol. 31, No. 4 (1997), pp. 117–28.

Wignaraja, Ganeshan, *Trade Liberalization in Sri Lanka: Exports, Technology and Industrial Policy* (London: Macmillan, 1998).

Wijkman, Per Magnus, "The Existing Bloc Expanded? The European Community, EFTA, and Eastern Europe," in C. Fred Bergsten and Marcus Noland (eds.), *Pacific Dynamism and the International Economic System* (Washington, D.C.: Institute for International Economics, 1993), pp. 135–58.

Wink, Kenneth A., C. Don Livingston, and James C. Garand, "Dispositions, Constituencies, and Cross-Pressures: Modeling Roll-Call Voting on the North American Free Trade Agreement in the U.S. House," *Political Research Quarterly,* Vol. 49, No. 4 (1996), pp. 749–70.

Winters, L. Alan, "The European Community: A Case of Successful Integration," in Jaime de Melo and Arvind Panagariya (eds.), *New Dimensions in Regional Integration* (Cambridge: Cambridge University Press, 1993), pp. 202–28.

———, "Expanding EC Membership and Association Accords: Recent Experience and Future Prospects," in Kym Anderson and Richard Blackhurst (eds.), *Regional Integration and the Global Trading System* (New York: St. Martin's, 1993), pp. 104–25.

Wolf, Martin, "Cooperation or Conflict? The European Union in a Liberal Global Economy," *International Affairs* (London), Vol. 71, No. 2 (1995), 325–37.

———, "How To Cut the Textile Knot: Alternative Paths to Liberalization of the MFA," in Carl B. Hamilton (ed.), *Textiles Trade and the Developing Countries: Eliminating the Multi-Fibre Arrangement in the 1990s* (Washington, D.C.: World Bank, 1990), pp. 215–37.

Womack, James P., and Daniel T. Jones, "European Automotive Policy: Past, Present, and Future," in Glennon J. Harrison (ed.), *Europe and the United States: Competition and Cooperation in the 1990s,* A Study Submitted to the Subcommittee on International Economic Policy and Trade and the Subcommittee on Europe and the Middle East of the Committee on Foreign Affairs, U.S. House of Representatives (Armonk, NY: M. E. Sharpe, 1994), pp. 193–213.

Wonnacott, Ronald J. "Free Trade Agreements: For Better or Worse," *American Economic Review,* Vol. 86, No. 2 (1996), pp. 62–66.

Woo, Jung-en, *Race to the Swift: State and Finance in Korean Industrialization* (New York: Columbia University Press, 1991).

Woolcock, Stephen, "The International Politics of Trade and Protection in the Steel Industry," in John Pinder (ed.), *National Industrial Strategies and the World Economy* (Totowa, NJ: Allanheld Osmun, 1982), pp. 53–84.

———, "Iron and Steel," in Susan Strange and Roger Tooze (eds.), *The International Politics of Surplus Capacity* (London: Allen and Unwin, 1981, pp. 69–79.

———, "Iron and Steel," in Louis Turner and Neil McMullen (eds.), *The Newly Industrializing Countries: Trade and Adjustment* (London: Allen and Unwin, 1982), pp. 94–117.

World Bank, *World Development Report* (Oxford: Oxford University Press, various years).

———, *World Tables, 1976* (Baltimore: Johns Hopkins University Press, 1976).

———, *World Tables, 1995* (Baltimore: Johns Hopkins University Press, 1995).

Wright, Donald J., "Permanent versus Temporary Infant Industry Assistance," *Manchester School of Economic and Social Studies,* Vol. 63, No. 4 (1995), pp. 426–34.

Xie, Xin, "Contagion through Interactive Production and Dynamic Effects of Trade," *International Economic Review,* Vol. 40, No. 1 (1999), pp. 165–86.

Yamamura, Kozo, "Caveat Emptor: The Industrial Policy of Japan," in Paul R. Krugman (ed.), *Strategic Trade Policy and the New International Economics* (Cambridge, MA: MIT Press, 1987), pp. 169–209.

———, "The Deliberate Emergence of a Free Trader: The Japanese Political Economy in Transition," in Craig Garby and Mary Brown Bullock (eds.) *Japan: A New Kind of Superpower* (Washington, D.C.: Woodrow Wilson Center Press, 1994), pp. 35–52.

Yamazawa, Ippei, "Japan and Her Asian Neighbours in a Dynamic Perspective," in Colin I. Bradford, Jr., and William H. Branson (eds.), *Trade and Structural Change in Pacific Asia* (Chicago: University of Chicago Press, 1987), pp. 93–119.

Yang, Shu-Chin, "Open Industrialization in East Asia and the Quest for Regional Cooperation: An Overview," in Shu-Chin Yang (ed.), *Manufactured Exports of East Asian Industrializing Economies: Possible Regional Cooperation* (Armonk, NY: M. E. Sharpe, 1994), pp. 3–34.

Yang, Yongzheng, "The Impact of the MFA Phasing Out on World Clothing and Textile Markets," *Journal of Development Studies,* Vol. 30, No. 4 (1994), pp. 892–915.

Yannopoulos, George N., "The Effects of Tariff Preferences on Export Expansion, Export Diversification and Investment Diversification: A Comparative Analysis of the Iberian and Other Mediterranean Economies," in George N. Yannopoulos (ed.), *European Integration and the Iberian Economies* (New York: St. Martin's, 1989), pp. 66–86.

———, "The European Community's Common External Commercial Policy: Internal Contradictions and Institutional Weaknesses," *Journal of World Trade Law,* Vol. 19, No. 5 (1985), pp. 451–65.

Yarbrough, Beth V., and Robert M. Yarbrough, "Cooperation in the Liberalization of International Trade: After Hegemony, What?" *International Organization,* Vol. 41, No. 1 (1987), pp. 1–26.

Yeats, A. J., "Effective Tariff Protection in the United States, the European Economic Community, and Japan," *Quarterly Review of Economics and Business,* Vol. 14, No. 2 (1974), pp. 41–50.

Yenturk-Coban, Nurhan, "Industrialization Strategies, Foreign Trade Regimes and Structural Change in Turkey 1980–8," in Jean-Marc Fontaine (ed.), *Foreign Trade Reforms and Development Strategy* (London: Routledge, 1992), pp. 274–89.

Yoffie, David B., "The Newly Industrializing Countries and the Political Economy of Protectionism," *International Studies Quarterly,* Vol. 25, No. 4 (1981), pp. 569–99.

———, *Power and Protectionism: Strategies of the Newly Industrializing Countries* (New York: Columbia University Press, 1983).

Zysman, John, *Political Strategies for Industrial Order: State, Market, and Industry in France* (Berkeley: University of California Press, 1977).

Index